boyopolis

boyopolis

SEX AND
POLITICS
IN GAY
EASTERN
EUROPE

STAN PERSKY

THE OVERLOOK PRESS
WOODSTOCK • NEW YORK

First published in the United States in 1996 by
The Overlook Press
Lewis Hollow Road
Woodstock, New York 12498

Library of Congress Cataloging-in-Publication Data

Persky, Stan
[Then we take Berlin]
Boyopolis : essays from gay Eastern Europe / Stan Persky.
p. cm.
Originally published in 1995 by Alfred A. Knopf Canada
I. Persky, Stan 2. Gay men—Germany—Berlin—Biography.
3. Gay men—Germany—Berlin—Social conditions.
4. Gay men—Europe, Eastern History.
5. Gay men—Europe, Eastern—Social conditions.
I. Title. HQ75.8.P47A3 1996
305.38'9664'092—dc20
96-21522 CIP

ISBN: 0-87951-690-7
Manufactured in the United States of America

First American Edition

for Tom Sandborn

in memory of my father,
Morris Persky

Neither was it as it first seemed
Nor as you now make it into a story.

— Czeslaw Milosz

Contents

The Iron Curtain

ONE DAY in early June 1991, I was riding the S-Bahn from west to east Berlin. A young man named Manuel was with me; we were going to a museum or to some office on a bureaucratic errand. The elevated train passed over the old boundary where the Berlin Wall had been but a year and a half before. Now all that was left was the rubble and bare ground of a sort of no man's land below the tracks. Beyond the ruins, a twist of the Spree River lay ahead. The train would cross over the water just before it pulled into Friedrichstrasse station, which had previously been a border checkpoint. The year before, visiting what was then still East Berlin rather than simply east Berlin, I had been herded through its cattle-pen of holding areas, passport-stamping guards, and clanging doors.

Gazing absently out the window at the place that had divided two worlds for some three decades, I looked up to find myself exchanging a glance with a woman seated across the aisle. We were approximately the same age—old enough to have lived most of our lives within that fixation of history whose remains were now scattered beneath us.

Imperceptibly, as though we were in danger of being watched, we looked into each other's eyes, glanced away for an instant at the barren landscape below, and then locked eyes again. I had the unmistakable and unsettling intuition that she and I were thinking almost precisely the same thoughts. The entire exchange lasted two or three seconds at most. We didn't know each other, most likely we didn't speak the same language, yet there passed between us—I'm fairly certain it wasn't merely a "projection" of my feelings—an intimate recognition of the shared and forbidding world that once had been. The train slowed into Friedrichstrasse station, the S-Bahn doors opened onto the busy platform of commuters, and we both, going our separate ways, disappeared into the moving crowd. In no more than the blink of an eye I crossed from the shore of memory to the presence of Manuel, the blond-haired youth who was with me that day.

In 1946, Winston Churchill gave a speech at Fulton, Missouri—the home state of the then American president, Harry Truman—in which for the first time he used the image of the Iron Curtain to describe the new division of the world. I was five years old then, and wouldn't learn of the former British prime minister's speech until years later. In fact, by the time I discovered the oratorical origins of Churchill's catchphrase, it was already a fact of life for me and everybody I knew.

The Iron Curtain represented a division as compelling as that of the sixteenth century, in which the Pope divided the world between the Spanish and the Portuguese. On one side of the modern divide were the Communists, on the other ourselves, the Free World. But what intrigued me was the image itself. Indeed, I didn't understand it as a metaphor at all, but imagined it with a certain literalness. For whatever reason, I didn't conceive of it as a "curtain"—like the drapes in our apartment—but as a steel wall the thickness of a bank-door vault.

In a sense, the Iron Curtain was my initial encounter with history—the idea, however crude, that there was a flow of events *out there* that affected our lives *here*. With that image I acquired a notion of both the existence of the world—that is, a world larger than the working-class Chicago neighbourhood of Jewish and Irish boys who played baseball on factory sandlots and "war" in the milk-weed-infested empty yard adjacent to our apartment building—and the even more abstract concept of time.

Through the window of our kitchen, I could see past the empty lot, across the street, and beyond the baseball field provided by the Calumet Baking Powder Company, to the train viaduct, a raised concrete structure that cut through the neighbourhood.

Most days the tracks carried long strings of freight and tanker cars, but one afternoon I saw a khaki-brown passenger train, its windows filled with men in uniform, troops returning from the war in Europe or the Pacific. With Johnny Tallone, the boy who lived in the basement apartment below, I stuffed the lead soldiers his father had made for us (from scraps in the fabricating plant where he worked) into the windows of my Lionel model train, attempting to replicate the troop train.

There were men in uniform in the family—my cousin

Herbie, and Herb Alpert, at whose grocery store and meat market my father worked. It was the stuff of out-of-the-mouths-of-babes precociousness that one Friday night when we were at dinner at Aunt Dora's and Uncle Docky's—actually, since they were my mother's aunt and uncle, they were my great-aunt Dora and great-uncle Nathan Kane, M.D.—the doorbell unexpectedly rang. Since the late-arriving men—my father and Cousin Harry, who was married to Dora's daughter, Marge—had already come from their respective store and insurance office, who could it be? "It's Herbie," I declared (at age five or six), or heard it repeatedly told at subsequent family gatherings that I had declared. It was.

I remember—or better yet, I can *see*—my aunt Dora taking off her glasses and wiping her eyes with the hem of her apron as she came from the kitchen through the dining room to the glass-paned door that separated that part of their flat from the entrance hallway, to greet her son home from the war. For a moment I completely forget what I'm writing—post-Communist stories, pre-Utopian essays—to see the folds of skin, the pouches beneath her eyes, with tears of joy trembling in them; I forget my "subject" to see a world that's gone.

I first heard of Communists, or Reds, at the Friday night dinners at Aunt Dora's, where furious political arguments sometimes broke out. It was usually after we listened to the evening news on the radio, which always began with the sonorous basso of newscaster H.V. Kaltenborn intoning, "There's good news tonight," or alternatively, in the event of crisis, "There's ba-ad news tonight." The verbal brawl was focused on my Uncle Docky. He was a lean, stern, rather forbidding figure who had delivered me into the world, and I knew he was fond of me (perhaps a reflection of his fondness for my mother), so I wasn't frightened by his austere manner. In the waiting room of his office was a reproduction of a painting by Winslow Homer, the seascape artist. In it, an old man and a boy were on a beach. The boy was in knickers, or perhaps rolled up pants—anyway, he was bare-calved, barefooted. The old man, a sort of ancient mariner, was sitting on a log and excitedly pointing out to sea, as if urging the boy to adventure.

The arguments were about Russia, and perhaps—since the establishment of Israel was in the offing—about Zionism as well. These people—the older ones on my mother's side of the family—were originally Russian Jews. My father's people, also Jews, came from Vilnius, in Lithuania. Voices were raised. I didn't understand it at all, of course. Nor can I remember who was Uncle Docky's antagonist.

Certainly not my father, who wouldn't have held such views and, anyway, was far too courteous to indulge in such unseemly displays. Perhaps it was Harry, who worked at Prudential Life. But no, he was too much of a "milquetoast" (to use a word from that era). It must have been Herbie, who had a fearsome temper. And who else but a son would end up shouting at his father? All I remember is the punch-line, followed by someone stalking out of the living room, leaving behind a host of simmering emotions. The punch-line was "Well, if you like the Communists so much, go back to Russia, then!"

Seldom, though, was the family drama of such high political order. After dinner, the men would retire to the living room to drink coffee and listen to the radio while the women washed up. Then everyone would return to the dining room for a friendly game of cards.

There was a recurrent bit of by-play from those card games. Aunt Dora would refrain, for reasons—as near as I can recall—of frugality, from enjoying a cigarette during the game. Everyone was aware of what they regarded as her spurious reluctance. Was it because of her memory of the necessary economies practised during the Depression?

"Mom, have one of mine," Marge insisted. To which Aunt Dora, shrugging and holding up her hands as if to fend off something, would reply, "No, I don't feel like smoking." (She pronounced it "schmoking", with a Yiddish-Germanic accent that the others sometimes mocked.) Finally she'd be persuaded to accept one of Marge's Pall Malls, which were longer than Aunt Dora's own Luckies. The climax of the routine—which so touches me at this remove, which reawakens my love for her—came when Aunt Dora cut the long cigarette in half (with scissors?), declaring against a chorus of protests that the unsmoked half would be "saved for later".

In the midst of the family tumult—cards slapped down, general kibbitzing, impatient cries of "Play, play already!"— I crawled between the chairs, under the table, and, amid its claw-shaped legs, calmly drifted off to sleep. Later I would half waken for a moment as my father lifted me into the back seat of the car for the ride home.

It was my father, Morrie, who taught me to read at an early age, before I went to school. His method was quite simple.

He bought a blackboard on an easel, which had inscribed across the top of it the letters of the alphabet. I would ask him to draw something for me—a cowboy, say—and along with the drawing he would write the word, pointing out how it was derived from the alphabet at the top of the board. Soon he was recommending books for me to read. Since I trusted him completely, I was an eager student.

My father was then in his forties, vigorous, bald, resembling a photo—taken by one of my father's brothers, Lew— that I'd seen of his father, Jacob, now dead. (That gruff grandfather, according to family lore, had taken me as a child of two or three for long walks in Garfield Park, where he uncharacteristically indulged me with ice-cream cones. I was credited with Grandfather Jacob's autumnal mellowing.) My father wore a white T-shirt and, on the side of his bicep, bore a blue tattoo of a five-pointed, three-dimensional star, which he could move by wiggling the muscle—a magical feat of will since he didn't clench his fist or otherwise move his hand to flex that muscle.

A great many of the books he gave me were about the sea—Jack London's *Sea Wolf*, Jules Verne's *20,000 Leagues under the Sea*, Richard Henry Dana's *Two Years before the Mast*, and novels by Melville. I liked *Omoo* and *Typee* better than *Moby Dick*, which at first I found rather too formidable.

There was apparently a goal to my father's pedagogy. It was near the end of the "course", when I was about nine or ten. I could now go off to the library and choose my own reading, or select volumes from the Book-of-the-Month Club—say, Martin Russ' *The Last Parallel: A Marine's War Journal* . . . the Korean War was on then. One day, my father said, "I've been saving this for you until you got a little older." He handed me Jack London's *The Iron Heel,* a socialist novel set in the future, in which, to my delight, there were scenes of civil war in the streets of Chicago—the very streets in which I now ventured.

The Iron Heel, I came to understand, was a book connected with my father's sense of politics. As was Upton Sinclair's *The Jungle,* a proletarian novel set in the stockyards and slaughterhouses of Chicago, whose odours we could sometimes smell wafting across the city on hot summer nights. I was impressed by the notion that it was possible to set both imaginary and historical events in a landscape that I actually knew, that the present was not the full extent of our reality. Further, these books reflected the political sympathies of people in my life—my father's first vote in a presidential election had been cast, he told me, for the socialist candidate, Eugene Debs, who at the time of the election had been jailed for sedition. Later, during the Depression, my father had ridden the rails and been a hobo. The railways may have been owned by the great corporations, but the yards and hobo jungles were informally controlled, for a time, by the International Workers of the World. The railway of the hobos was known as the Silver Dollar Line, because for a dollar you were issued a red card that secured your entrée to boxcars across America. Gradually I acquired the repertoire of my father's stories.

By then, I was following the front-page map of the Korean War in the *Chicago Sun-Times,* with its abstract scrimmage line that oscillated wildly from Pusan in the south, where G.I.s were in danger of being driven into the sea, to the Yalu River in the north, which they dared not cross for fear of plunging the U.S. into war with China and, ultimately, the Soviet Union. Now Communists were portrayed in the pages of the bulky morning tabloid as "gooks", the Chinese and the Koreans undistinguishable.

General Douglas MacArthur wanted to take his troops across the Yalu River, but President Truman forbade it. A great public debate ensued. Truman fired MacArthur, and white plaster busts of the rebellious hawk-nosed general went on sale for $1.49 at Walgreen's drugstores. (The nose on mine quickly chipped.) I watched MacArthur, relieved of his command, on television, testifying before some governmental body. "Old soldiers never die, they simply fade away," he said, announcing his retirement.

For me that was the beginning of a brief, passionate interest in politics, a time when I monitored congressional activities with the same avidity with which my mother listened to the soap operas on the radio. The first of those marathon hearings was Senator Estes Kefauver's investigation into organized crime. I got into the habit of dashing home from school and watching the hearings on television each afternoon, as alleged leaders of the Mafia were brought to the witness table, where they mumblingly invoked the Fifth Amendment, refusing to answer questions that might incriminate them.

But it was a subsequent congressional spectacle—the hearings of Senator Joseph McCarthy—that first moved me to go beyond being a mere spectator of public affairs. Day after day on television, the puffy-faced, jowl-shaking senator from Wisconsin pursued his hunt for Communists throughout America, demanding from hapless witnesses, "Are you now, or have you ever been, a member of the Communist Party?"

In addition to Communists, the senator was also seeking to expose homosexuals, who were somehow linked to the dangerous Reds. At the time I'm not sure I had any idea of what homosexuals were, though my own fantasy life, played out in masturbation in the privacy of the bathtub (I was now twelve or thirteen), was focused on a group of schoolmates. I imagined those boys—pale, blond Henderson, a kid named Stein, and a cute redhead called Dombrowski whom I knew from baseball—ranged around the white porcelain tub, in the warm bathwater, jacking off as I was. The particular fillip of pleasure in those imaginings was that we could see each other doing it; we had agreed to subject ourselves to the delicious humiliation of mutually exposing our deepest secrets, thus achieving intimacy through acts that were the precise opposite of the poses of emerging manhood we strutted around the sandlot.

Yet it went beyond mere fantasy. The site of that space between imagination and actual touch was the train viaduct, which also served as the "stadium wall" for the softball games played after work by the older boys. It stayed light on summer evenings till nearly ten; if I try, I can almost conjure up a shiver of the darkness falling, when the game ran late and the ball faded to bare visibility. The local ground rule was that it was a home run if someone—most likely a muscular blond boy, about eighteen, named Archie, whom I idolized—hit it "on the tracks". Then one of the younger kids would have to dash into the street—Keeler Avenue—

that dipped beneath the viaduct, and illegally climb the Cyclone fence and go up the grassy slope on the other side to retrieve the ball from the tracks, tossing it down into the outfield, while Archie trotted around the bases.

On occasions when we were playing baseball—my own friends, that is, not the older teenagers—we would sometimes seize one of the boys, the red-headed Dombrowski, for example, and drag him around to the grassy slope on the backside of the viaduct, where we would "pants" him. From the street below, passing motorists could only glimpse a gaggle of teenagers roughhousing in the tall grasses of the slope. But deep in the soft grass, Dombrowski's jeans would be jerked down to his knees, and then his white jockey underpants would follow, revealing a reddish little cock nestled in a patch of vermilion-gold pubic hair.

Dombrowski, having been "initiated"—but into what? manhood? camaraderie?—would be released to cover his nakedness, and then...? Did we return to the sandlot, to our interrupted game?

Not until at least a year later, in the first year of high school—when I fell in love with the grey-eyed Mel Weisberg—did I recognize that such desires were "homosexual", and thus forbidden. And even then I made no connection between those pleasures on the grassy slopes or in the gymnasium locker room, and the lives of witnesses destroyed by Senator McCarthy's suggestions, often unsubstantiated, that they were homosexual.

How ironic to learn only years afterward that McCarthy's closest associate—the feral Roy Cohn, who was the committee's chief counsel and often conducted the preliminary questioning—was an undisclosed homosexual, and may have been having an affair with a special assistant to the committee, a private in the army. And that McCarthy was himself not above such suspicions. (Decades later, Cohn—closeted to the end—died of AIDS.)

The highlight of the hearings was the abrasive dialogues between McCarthy, perched on the senatorial dais, and Joseph Welsh, a shrewd elderly lawyer from Boston and counsel to the U.S. Army, seated at the witness table below, next to a beribboned general. "I have a list," rasped McCarthy, brandishing a fistful of documents allegedly containing the names of Communists. "Sir, have you no decency, have you no decency at all?" asked the elegant Welsh.

It was this daily encounter between two protagonists battling for the soul of the country that inspired me to join the chorus of public commentators. The tide was already turning against McCarthy; the notion of government offices rife with Communist agents was being exposed as merely his paranoid delusion; he would soon be censured by the U.S. Senate, and shortly thereafter would die in an alcoholic haze.

The vehicle I chose for my political and literary debut was the *Chicago Sun-Times*, whose tabloid format I no doubt thought more modish than the sombre broadsheet of the *Chicago Tribune*, the city's paper of record. As far as I can recall, it was entirely my own inspiration to write a letter to the editor. I think my father had developed, inexplicably, a somewhat grudging admiration for McCarthy, but I don't recall that affecting my own ideas. Apparently, all by myself, I invented liberalism.

In my letter, I urged that the public not jump to conclusions about the dispute, but rather view the matter with impartiality and fairness. To make matters worse, I was not above calculated disingenuousness. Among other things, I had figured out how to improve my prospects for publication. Appended to my signature were the words "8th grade", designed to catch the eye of editors and readers, dazzling them with the author's precociousness. The letter was printed.

Despite the doting admiration of my family upon seeing my first published work, there were those who saw through my ambitions and shaky convictions. One day, walking home from school, I met one of the older teenagers in the neighbourhood, a heavyset, non-athletic intellectual named Ben Rubin. "Did you write that letter?" he asked. "Yes," I proudly acknowledged, awaiting plaudits. Instead, he coolly gazed at me, nodded, and passed on without a word. I barely understood, though I surely felt the chill of contempt; I had been exposed as a vain opportunist.

A few years later, at the end of the 1950s, I joined the U.S. Navy and went to sea. Although this occasioned something of a familial scandal (the children of the aspiring classes were intended for the University of Chicago, not common seamanship), my father resolutely defended my right to freedom, adventure, and desire. Jack London, Melville, Winslow Homer's painting in Uncle Docky's office, won out over middle-class respectability.

One night when I had midnight watch, or perhaps galley duty, I walked out onto the fantail for a smoke. The North

Atlantic heaved like a sighing sleeper, its great blocks of purple marble shifting, rising, falling under the moon's light. The sea, I knew then (I was eighteen), was not *of* the world, with its affairs of men, its division into east and west, Free World and Communist. And yet it bound me to language and art, fulfilling as it did the promise of wonder that had begun in Homer's "wine-dark sea", and in all those other books my father had given me.

Like my father, I acquired a blue tattoo—not of a five-pointed star but of an unfouled anchor which I had admired on the forearm of a boy named Ferinde who slept in a nearby bunk.

Politics was mostly replaced by art and love, though I read, with admiration, Senator Jack Kennedy's patriotic *Profiles in Courage*. I was of so unsuspecting a temperament that it never occurred to me that the book might have been ghost-written, or that its purposes were political. I favoured Kennedy for the presidency over Dwight Eisenhower's vice-president, Richard Nixon, though I was too young to vote. And when I was stationed at a naval air base outside Naples, I was a member—however unwittingly—of the NATO forces in the European theatre, defending the Free World against the powers lodged behind the Iron Curtain. Indeed, it was when I was nearing the end of my tour of duty, in August 1961, that the Communist government in East Germany gave concrete visibility to that image by building the Berlin Wall, cutting off the enclave of West Berlin. Did I think about any of it? Or was my attention entirely devoted to an honourable discharge, shipping out, the journey homeward?

My father picked me up at the airport when I returned from Europe. He paused a moment before we got out of the car and went into the house to greet my mother. "I suppose by now you've experienced pretty much everything in the way of sex," he said. "Yes," I acknowledged. "Both with girls and—?" he asked. "Yes," I said, having mostly been in love with other sailors for more than three years, and having slept with boys my own age in Paris.

He delicately enquired—I can't remember the precise words—if my desires were by now firmly determined. Nor can I exactly remember my reply; it may have been slightly ambiguous. What was apparent was the non-judgemental nature of his questions. It was also perfectly clear that he too—while riding the rails and in those hobo jungles—had had similar experiences.

"Well, old salt," he said rather jovially, and heaved my duffel bag onto his shoulder, leading me home as he had led me into the world.

In all that followed over the next three decades—I became a writer, moved to Vancouver, and eventually became a philosophy teacher at a college—I lived in a world permanently divided by the Iron Curtain. Long after I'd acquired a more nuanced understanding of the politics it represented, I nonetheless continued—as did we all—to live in a binary political configuration.

My friend Michael Morris, who had grown up during the bombing blitz of London, once remarked to me, "We're shaped by it"—he refrained from using the word "world", intending something more complex—"even before we're able to come to terms with any of it." He was explaining why, as a middle-aged man, he still occasionally slept with a pillow pressed over his head.

Even our imaginations had been frozen by the Cold War. We could not conceive of a world in which the Iron Curtain didn't demarcate its unalterable boundaries. Numerous spy novels, the rhetoric of countless political campaigns, movies that reproduced the chilling night-time lights at Checkpoint Charlie, fuelled our imagination of the unknown world behind it.

Even today, though the rampart is but recently gone, there are those who cannot imagine that a wall was once built around half a city, not by its inhabitants, to protect it, but by its adversaries, to prevent their own citizens from the allures of the city thus enclosed. In a time when memory, history, and imagination are degraded, whose task is it to remind us of those ideas and events that offer human and earthly continuity? And yet, here I am writing an autobiographical vignette that would do so, only to pause over the recognition that *eros*, *logos*, and *polis* are so intertwined.

On television one night in November 1989, long after my beloved father was gone, I saw the breaching of the Berlin Wall—that embodiment of the Iron Curtain whose history was part of my biography. German youths partied atop its graffiti-covered façade, crowds poured through the Brandenburg Gate, the world changed. It was, as Michael Morris told me in Berlin some months later—he had been there, in the streets—the *Stunde Null*, zero hour, the moment of beginning again.

Oddly enough, the decisive instant appeared to me not in that celebrated moment but several months earlier, in May of that year. In Poland—where I had been several years earlier—they were about to elect a non-Communist government. The Hungarians would do likewise. Gentle rumblings emanated from Czechoslovakia. Even the young people of China had gathered in Beijing's Tiananmen Square, only to face a brutal, bloody response. "Openness" and "restructuring" marked the Soviet Union of Mikhail Gorbachev, who would refrain from committing Soviet troops to the forcible maintenance of Eastern and Central European regimes, instead permitting the nations of the Warsaw Pact to discover their own fates.

Thousands of East German citizens were attempting to flee their country by a circuitous route. They were legally permitted to visit Czechoslovakia and Hungary, but from there they faced the insurmountable problem of crossing the heavily guarded Hungarian border into Austria; should they manage that, they would have passage to West Germany.

On the six o'clock TV news one evening that May, it was announced that the Hungarian government, in violation of the Warsaw Pact provisions, was dismantling its border with Austria. Within months the East Germans would be permitted to cross into the West. And on the screen, most unspectacularly—simply to provide visuals for the voice-over —there was incidental footage of Hungarian soldiers snipping strands of the barbed wire that separated their nation from Austria.

It was at that moment that I realized, even as the barbed wire was being cut—snip, snip, with ordinary metal-cutting shears—that after all those years of picturing it in my mind, I was at last looking at the Iron Curtain, its bank-vault steel thickness reduced to strands of rusted wire punctuated with snags.

The Translators' Tale

I N THE SPRING and summer of 1991, I was in Berlin, thinking about the fall of Communism (it was more than a year since the opening of the Berlin Wall), reading a little philosophy (that was the subject I taught at a college in Vancouver), and pursuing the amorous adventures that leisurely evenings in bars and cafés sometimes yielded.

I was often to be found in the Café Einstein in the late afternoon, engrossed in a book or newspaper, like many of the other patrons. Though it was something of a reading-list staple when I went to school, somehow I had never gotten around to Joseph Conrad's *Heart of Darkness* until then. Or perhaps I had, and had merely read it carelessly as a student—since, when I took it up now, it seemed both fresh and yet strangely familiar to me.

As I began (or began again) the tale of a journey to what had once seemed like the end of the earth, it called up the ideas I had about Albania, a preoccupation that had been inspired by a brief newspaper article about two translators.

It had been reported that the two men, translators in Tirana, Albania, had shared "a tiny, Spartan office" in the

state publishing house for most of the past twenty-two
years. For some reason, that touching detail particularly fascinated me. "Behind battered typewriters," the article said,
perhaps a bit melodramatically, "they have battled to keep
fragments of literature alive in the darkness of Stalinist or-
thodoxy."[1]

The story had been published a few months before, in
April 1991. Reading the brief account of the two now middle-aged men, one wondered the simplest things. How had
they spent their time? What did they talk about? Keep necessarily silent about? What loyalties had caused them to per-
severe? How had they maintained their sanity?—for it
seemed an ultimate test of sanity. It was something like those
stories one occasionally ran into ages ago, in which a pair of
Japanese soldiers emerged from a jungle in Burma or Java
twenty years after the war, never having heard that it had
ended.

In the case of Mr. Simoni and Mr. Qesku—those were
their names—the cause was rather more recognizable to us.
The convulsions that swept away regimes across Europe,
from Warsaw to Bucharest, in the late 1980s, had at last, in
the early nineties, reached the hills of what was once ancient
Illyria. And blinking into the uncertain sunlight—for it was
hardly clear that our vaunted free markets would provide a
panacea for their woes—there appeared the translators of
Tirana, having, you could say, kept the faith. It was a faith
that transcended the generations-long remoteness which
shrouded their land. Albania was not a Burmese jungle or an
island in the Indies, but a southern European nation wedged
between Greece and what was then Yugoslavia, a mere

eighty kilometres across the Adriatic from Bari or Brindisi in Italy; yet for all that it might have been as distant as the moon, so successfully and for so long had its Glorious Leader sealed it off as the last and purest bastion of Communism.

I never really admitted to my friends in Berlin that I intended to go to Albania. At most, I'd say something casual and indirect like "I wonder if it's possible to fly to Tirana from here?" Perhaps I didn't even want to admit it to myself, fearing that a glimpse of its foolishness might put me off. Nonetheless, however desultorily, I made the necessary phone calls, enquired at a travel agency, checked the airline office. One day, I got my friend Manuel (he was also my current amorous adventure) to accompany me to the Albanian consulate in east Berlin, only to find the dilapidated building locked and to be informed by a caretaker that I needed to contact the office in Bonn.

My *method*—to use a word that appears prominently in Conrad's tale—was circuitous at best. Indeed, it was a sort of game that I called "following the story", in which one set certain events in motion, or created the possibility of setting them in motion, by some ordinary but deliberate act—reading a book, walking a certain route, going to a particular place (say, the bar where I met Manuel). And if something happened as a consequence, the challenge then—the whole point of the game, really—was to attend to the ensuing possibilities in such a way that the pattern of meanings we call a story resulted.

Reading the opening pages of Conrad's story, I found it easy to identify with its narrator, Marlow, the veteran sailor who was making his way about Brussels to secure a posting on a Congo riverboat of the Belgian trading company that, for all practical purposes, ruled that distant African land. I too had been to sea. As I read—while at the same time arranging my own curious journey—Albania seemed as distant as Marlow's destination, and Comrade Enver Hoxha, who had ruled it, was a figure as forbidding as Kurtż, the god-man who dominated the Polish writer's tale.

Of course, I was aware of the cliché of reading Conrad in that way. The "heart of darkness" was everybody's metaphor; whoever travelled to what might be regarded as an obscure corner of the earth invoked it. But there was nothing I could do about it. If you're a reader, sooner or later you read Conrad, and by happenstance, I was reading *Heart of Darkness* at exactly that moment.

In the end (the end of the beginning, that is), I found myself filling out a visa application while seated at a table in the Café Einstein. I was in the high-ceilinged room of the villa that overlooked the café garden, which was more than half empty that afternoon, leaving the tame sparrows who hopped up on the tables almost no one from whom to filch a stray crumb of *Apfelkuchen*. Wettest, coldest June in memory, the German tabloids blared, along with the requisite references to "global warming" and other climatic disturbances. And still chilly, even into July. The black-jacketed waiters moved among the bundled-up patrons at a glacial pace, carrying hot drinks on sterling trays.

When I asked my friends, in that studiedly casual voice I'd adopted for the purpose, "I wonder if it's possible to fly to Tirana from here?", they invariably replied, with barely restrained politeness, "But why would you want to go there?" Or else they would fail to hear me correctly, and make me repeat the name of the Albanian capital, and then they, who had been almost everywhere, would quizzically repeat it themselves—"Tirana?"—in the slightly astonished tones reserved for impossibly distant places or vanished cities of the past.

Sometimes they would attempt to dissuade me by pointing out the difficulties of acquiring a visa. "I phoned," I'd report. "To Bonn, of course," one of them assumed. "To Tirana," I said. "You can phone Tirana?" they warily asked. "Easier than east Berlin," I replied, drawing a wan smile from my friends for all the times we'd tried to make an appointment across the once-divided city.

The attaché in Bonn suggested that I needed an invitation from someone in Tirana in order to complete my visa application. When I asked him if he happened to have the number of the state publishing house there, he supplied it, and soon after I attempted to phone Simoni, one of the men mentioned in the newspaper story. After bursts of static on the line and a babble of languages (Albanian, English, German, Italian), then a long pause (he had been walking down a flight of stairs), I was speaking with the man himself. Simoni promised to send a note of invitation. And thus I "followed the story", even as I was following other stories (the blond-haired Manuel, for example, with whom I was in the midst, or perhaps at the end, of something, had abruptly— but only temporarily, I hoped—decamped). Well, if the invitation from Tirana arrives, if mail service from Tirana even exists, I told myself, then I guess I'll get some snapshots from the machine at the train station to stick onto the application form. And indeed, one by one, each of the items appeared, until at last I signed my name in the Café Einstein and sent the papers off.

A few nights later, while I was in the bath, the phone rang. Annoyed, and dripping down the hallway, I picked up the phone to be told by the Albanian attaché in Bonn—unusual that he should be working on a Saturday evening, I marvelled—that my visa had been approved.

In the post, along with the papers, he sent me a picture postcard signed with his best wishes. I didn't know what to make of such an unbureaucratic gesture. It was a picture of an ancient boy's head, marble, from Apollonia, one of the places down the Adriatic coast that the Greeks had set up in the fifth century or so B.C. "Best wishes," the postcard said.

I was on the Berlin-Zurich-Tirana flight, with a date to meet the two translators at seven p.m. at the base of the Skanderbeg statue in the town square. I hastily acquired the necessary background from *Eastern Europe on a Shoestring*. Skanderbeg, the potted history tersely informed me: fifteenth century warlord; castle in the hills at a place called Krujë, a bit north of Tirana; fought the Turks twenty times, never beaten. National hero. Of course, once Skanderbeg was out of the way, it was the Ottoman Turks for the next five hundred years. Succeeded by King Zog, then the Fascists, and finally by the Glorious Leader, Comrade Hoxha.

I don't know what I was after. Oh, to find Simoni and Qesku, certainly. And to find out how a country in the middle of Europe could more or less disappear from the face of the earth for half a century. But I think I also wanted to know what was there. As if to make up for an oversight on our part. Sure, Albania had been sealed off for god knows how long, but was that sufficient excuse for our failure to consider it? Of course, if we had, would anyone have bothered to pay attention? Marlow's celebrated utterance (I'd tossed my copy of *Heart of Darkness* into my bag) echoed in my mind—"And this, also, has been one of the dark places of the earth."

So I had a rendezvous. But first there were the "pilgrims", to use Conrad's term for them. I mean, if I could think of it, then surely the business pilgrims would already be figuring out how to turn a dollar. He was a Swiss engineer, named Weber. Boarded at Zurich. The Texans were seated in front of us. As soon as we were up, the engineer had a powerful thirst. Scotch doubles, and beer to wash them down. By the descent, he had persuaded the flight attendant to sell him some cans of beer in a paper bag. But he knew the country, I had to give him that.

When Weber wasn't courting the woman in the window seat, I asked him the usual traveller's questions. I'd heard of the Hotel Tirana. No, the Dajti, he firmly recommended. Reservations? No problem, he'd fix it up if it came to that. And was there a bus into town from the airport? *Kein Problem*, I could ride in with him. Hail fellow, well met. Well lubricated too, by the time we were on the ground.

The airport was a patch of cement in the countryside. Thirty degrees centigrade on the ground at four p.m. By the time I was walking down the double row of palm trees into the terminal, I was poached in my own juices. Lads in green with machine-guns. The usual madhouse—babies, relatives, heaps of baggage. "Fixers" everywhere. I'd heard the term back home during the Gulf War six months earlier, at the beginning of 1991.

Weber had several thousand dollars in trading goods, by my estimate. Cigarette lighters, Swiss Army knives, textiles, camcorders, the whole store; vast amounts of personal belongings, bottles of Johnnie Walker, cigars, suitcases for an expedition. We showed our papers, then lugged the whole caboodle past the boys with guns, and we were in the courtyard of the terminal. I'd barely a moment to get my bearings. Sheer confusion, it was. Crush of relatives, officials, much weeping and kissing on the cheek, the yard crammed with cabs, children begging for coins, the swelter. A whole family to greet the engineer, with hugs, kisses on both cheeks, bouquets of flowers already wilted in the heat; of course, I must be introduced, our party divided into two cabs, the engineer's trading goods stuffed in the trunk—he was already passing out cigarette lighters. And then we were off.

It was the moment of pure exultation in a strange place, whether there's anything to be had or not. Soon enough there would be the practicalities, interviews, putting together bits and pieces of history. But for now, we were barrelling down a country road, honking at peasants on horsecarts, bicycles, sheep in the road, men without shirts, in a field, squinting through the sun at us—just an instant to glimpse their bodies.

The countryside was dotted with concrete mushroom caps, overgrown now—apparently defence outposts, gun emplacements, and the like. The Glorious Leader was ready to fight the Turks, the imperialists, Titoists, Russian revisionists, the Chinese renegades after Mao—everyone he'd broken with in the name of Marxism-Leninism, in the name of Comrade Stalin, of the truth. I had the unnerving sense—for the briefest moment—of peering into Hoxha's besieged mind.

At the fork halfway between Durres on the Adriatic and the capital inland, we took the turn for Tirana. And all the time the engineer, sitting in back between a pale girl in a white blouse and her father, lectured the lot of us. I missed most of it, I confess. Words lost in the wind, while the driver was running peasants on bicycles off the road with his terrible honking. Of course, the pilgrim had a plan to set the country right, something about playing Beethoven on the radio, and the phrase "They're really children, you know"—how often had I heard that one before?

Finally we came upon the city. All the main roads of Tirana converged on Skanderbeg Square. It was a huge open space. I marked the equestrian statue as we passed; that was where my rendezvous was. Around the edges of the big traffic circle in the square, various official buildings, "people's palaces", windows bashed in and boarded up after the recent rioting. I was informed right off that the towering statue of the Glorious Leader, set in the middle of the traffic circle, had been pulled down by the people three months ago.

We dropped off the girl and her father, and some of the engineer's booty. He genially ordered them about, drank his beer, handed out gifts; he was a lean, nervous pilgrim, but no fool. Then back to the square, this time south, past yellow and red stucco buildings—government ministries, Weber said—and down Martyrs' Boulevard a block or so to the Dajti. A four-storey job done by the Italians before the Second World War, big Mediterranean pines all around shading it, and facing a spacious public park. Crowds of fixers, drivers, cadging children, and arriving pilgrims in the driveway. Naturally, no available rooms. But the engineer was jovial, extra bed in his suite, no problem for the night, fix you up in the morning, he'd enjoy a bit of company—more like an audience for his unpacking. I barely had time to splash a few drops of water on the dusty wraith I'd become, and the engineer was off, for business in Durres, I think it was.

An hour later, at the onset of dusk, I made my way over to the square. I sat beneath the fearsome Skanderbeg, perched on his mount. Presently two men arrived, as ordained. The younger one, Pavli Qesku, struck me as rather elegant—mid-forties, lean, prematurely grey hair, tinted glasses. The other older, one good ear so he had to position himself on your left to catch the conversation. That was Zef Simoni.

I'd brought books for them—I suppose it could be said that I was a pilgrim in my way, too—but rather than examine them at once, they suggested we take a stroll down Martyrs' Boulevard. They pointed out where the statues of Lenin and Stalin had flanked the thoroughfare; now only pediments remained. Everything had come down in the last six months, more than a year after the wave that swept the rest of Central Europe, more than five years after Hoxha's death. The party had attempted to make the transition; had assumed that everything would continue for ever—simply parade the image of the old Glorious Leader, gradually add that of the new one, a man named Ramiz Alia. They figured they would carry on into eternity. But now everything was breaking up. Statues toppled, street names altered.

I'd noticed on a map that the continuation of the boulevard north of Skanderbeg Square had been named for Stalin. I wondered if it still was.

"Oh, we never called it that anyway," Zef said, dismissing the issue in an understated, slightly ironic way I would quickly get used to.

"But this is still the Boulevard of National Martyrs?" I enquired, just to check.

"Well, after all, this is true," Pavli said. "We are still a nation and, indeed, there have been martyrs."

"So there is no need to change it," Zef added. They had been in each other's company for so many years that they had acquired the habit of completing each other's sentences, as old couples do.

I was impatient to get to the heart of it, to the only question I really had for them, namely, how had they survived? As we passed the Hotel Dajti on the left, and the twilight came down on the big park facing it, they represented themselves as timid men, unheroic, cautious creatures, never members of the party though they had worked in the state publishing house translating the Glorious Leader's works and speeches all those years, Zef into German, Pavli into English. Another translator, Jussef Vrioni, had put Hoxha into French. I'd seen Vrioni's name—about a month before, in an article in an American magazine, where he'd been cited as the French translator of the great Albanian novelist Ismail Kadare, who was now living in Paris. I'd even glanced at *The General of the Dead Army*, one of Kadare's novels.

But the immediate answer to my question was relatively simple. They had translated literature—Dickens, Conrad, Lawrence, Orwell even—I knew that already from the newspaper piece. But there was a new bit. They made dictionaries. It was an obvious thing for translators to do, now that they mentioned it, but it hadn't occurred to me. "So," I said, "in a sense, words saved you."

We crossed a little trickle of water just beyond the hotel, the Lana River. It flowed in a ditch below us, beneath the boulevard overpass—grass slopes, a bit of paving-stone embankment; to the right, from the west, the last of the light hit it.

"Working with words saved us from the situation in which we lived, sort of," Pavli replied. Then he added, almost more to himself than me, "Yes, to a certain extent, it is true."

"A justification," Zef explained. "In our work as translators, we used words to express other people's thoughts—and we were not in agreement with those thoughts. So we wanted to use the same words to express, not *our* thoughts, but something neutral at least." It was put with perfect modesty. My curiosity was at once satisfied. Strange how quickly it went. Now we were simply evening strollers, casually conversing.

The boulevard, a broad four-lane thoroughfare, ended abruptly at the university, which was set at the base of a hill. The students had demonstrated here the previous December, and then again in February. That, apparently, was what had started it. We took the footpath that wound around and up the wooded rise. St. Procopius hill, Zef informed me.

Somehow we got onto the subject of China. I don't remember what led to it. Perhaps something about Zef's bad ear. He had been to China during Hoxha's alliance with Mao, and the Chinese had restored some of his hearing. Even now he had only one good ear, supplemented by a bit of lip-reading. Anyway, it got me thinking about my time in China, in '77, just after Mao's death, around the time of the breakup of Albania's "firm and eternal friendship", as the formula went, with Beijing. I found myself recounting an odd little conversation I'd had with my minder. We were speaking of sexual practices, and I'd asked, a bit mischievously, if there was homosexuality in China. My guide affected to be shocked. No, none at all, he firmly assured me. None whatsoever. So I asked him if the Chinese masturbated. Oh no, he said, and then, curiosity getting the better of him, he asked me, And you, in the West, do you masturbate? Why, yes, I replied, all the time.

Zef and Pavli burst into laughter, got it right away. "So there was even a correct line on sex," Pavli chuckled. I was about to rattle on when Zef interrupted to point out some buildings to our right. "The barracks of the National Guard," he said, making it clear by his tone that the institution wasn't exactly loved. The path switched back up St. Procopius, but an unpaved road forked off towards the barracks. It was dark now, and all you could see were some lighted windows and boys in uniforms inside.

At the top of the hill we came out of the pines onto an

outdoor café, which was our destination. It was well attended, mostly by couples and some guardsmen in pairs. A table was found for us, and the waiter brought us drinks.

"Raki," Pavli ordered. "Perhaps you won't like it," he remarked to me.

It was acrid stuff, perfectly drinkable, of course. And there was bread, soup, and some roasted chicken. My hosts half apologized for the poor quality of everything, but in fact it was fine. A perfectly delightful café on a summer evening, and a bit cooler up here on the hill. After the food, more raki, and we smoked cigarettes.

One of the young guardsmen broke away from his friend and came over to our table to ask for a light. I held the flame to his hand-rolled smoke.

"You've just lit the cigarette of a National Guard," Zef said.

"Of a boy," I insisted.

"Who might masturbate in the barracks," Zef quickly added, accepting my distinction. We all laughed at that.

Oddly enough, we didn't talk about politics at all that evening. Zef mentioned that he had learned to read Greek, and had read Plato's *Phaedo* in the original. It was a work I was familiar with; I often taught it at school. Indeed, I had opinions about the death of Socrates.

I confess I did most of the talking. As I said, I had views. The part about Socrates' last day in jail, his weeping friends, the hemlock he drank, all that was true in my opinion. But the part about the immortality of the soul, I insisted to Zef and Pavli, that was added by Plato himself. I don't think Socrates believed any of that. Socrates simply thought you died and consciousness ceased or—well, it doesn't matter about my views. But it was all so wonderfully odd. I'd come all this way, to the moon, to the last outpost, to enquire about the fall of Communism, and instead we were talking about Plato, just as civilized people anywhere might have done. Of course, I had to acknowledge that the places where civilized people could talk of such things were much diminished in our time, even in my own part of the world.

It had grown late, the café had emptied, the guardsmen were back in their barracks. Zef and Pavli walked me down the hill, back into the heat of the town, now in darkness. Behind the hotel there was a sleek building that bore the only electric sign I'd seen. It alternately flashed the temperature and the time, lighting up the night. The Institute of Strategic Studies, Pavli informed me. They came into the Dajti with me for a minute so I could give them the box of books I'd brought, and arrangements were made to collect me in the morning.

The engineer soon returned from Durres. He produced a bottle of Johnnie Walker and we sat on the balcony outside the room, overlooking Martyrs' Boulevard —little traffic at that hour, only the gear-grinding of the occasional truck, a late-night bus.

In the morning, the engineer and I took breakfast together. The other pilgrims were there, impatient with the service, anxious to get on with business, to make the world go. Weber was soon off, the brooding Swiss of last night—he too read some philosophy—giving way to the nervous energy of deal-making.

Across the corridor from the breakfast room was the bar. The engineer left me there with one of the fixers he knew, in case I needed anything. I escaped onto the cement front veranda of the Dajti. Even though the flashing digital sign—forever reminding us of time and heat—reported nearly thirty degrees before nine o'clock, a nice breeze came in from the park across the boulevard. Below me, in the driveway, taxi operators were taking the pilgrims off. There were all sorts of kids hanging around. Small ones, and teenage boys too.

One boy in particular attracted me. He was in his mid to late teens, blue-eyed, with pale sandy hair and a quick smile. He was with a couple of his friends, and at first all I noticed was the boys' friendliness among themselves, the way they leaned against each other, casually draping an arm over the other's shoulders. Then the blue-eyed boy and I exchanged glances and there was a brief, wordless encounter, the sort of meeting I might have forgotten if nothing else had happened. Our eyes met again, he offered a smile. It was nothing, really. But as he passed behind me on the veranda, he touched me. He ran a feathery hand across my shoulders, just as he did with the other boys he was with. And as quickly as he'd appeared, he was gone.

Just then, Zef and Pavli turned up to show me around. I tried to make apologies for chattering on about the *Phaedo*.

"No doubt you like the part about the soul," I said to Zef. He had told me he was a Catholic. But apparently there was no harm done.

"It was very good conversation," Zef assured me.

"Yes, nice to talk," Pavli seconded.

We crossed the square and were soon in a maze of side-streets and then back lanes. There were some market stalls set up on the walks. Little potatoes, green onions, dark fresh figs, all in small quantities. Housewives spent hours gathering the day's provisions.

"Looking for things that don't exist," Pavli said.

We came to a five-storey building, made of bricks, oddly spaced, a hand-done job it seemed. "Zef's flat is on the top. He built it himself," Pavli told me. Looking up, you could see from the fresher colour of the brick that the top floor had been added recently. One could imagine the difficulties of a man in his fifties hauling the bricks up those stairs, mixing the cement, mortaring them in himself.

By the time we climbed to the top, my shirt was soaked through. Zef's wife met us and while we settled in she brought us bottled water, raki, some Turkish delight, and then coffee. I reminded myself that I was in one of those southern European cultures where they give you everything they have, however little it may be.

There were shelves of books along the back wall. With a very slight ceremonial gesture, Zef presented me with a copy of the German-Albanian dictionary he had compiled, which had been published the year before. He quoted Milton on justifying God's ways to man. "I had to justify myself to myself," he said. "To do something useful."

About noon, we went down and made the short walk over to the publishing house where they worked. First there had to be a formal meeting with the director in his suite of offices. Pavli translated. I had been through this sort of thing before. Formalities to be observed, cups of bitter coffee served. I intimated that I had some access to paper supplies, something the director —who, of course, was a party member—could note in his report if necessary. Even though it was all breaking up, and the party was in the midst of a chameleon-like effort to appear in more acceptable colours, much of the organizational infrastructure was still in place. And all the old habits. Although the director was the only party member I would actually meet, I was little inclined to question him about his view of the recent political changes. I knew I'd only get the current official line, and in any case the shade of "the last Communist", Hoxha himself, still lurked everywhere. On the stairway, going up to their office, Zef said, "Very good," appraising my performance, and the three of us laughed about it.

Then we were in the "tiny, Spartan office" that I'd read about in the newspaper piece. Well, a small professional quibble here, a detail. It was Spartan in the sense of equipment, the absence of books, of course. But not tiny. Larger than the cubbyholes most journalists and instructors had in the newsrooms and college offices I was familiar with back home. Spacious enough for facing desks, walls a bright, pale green, and there was a big window, with a breeze coming in, and a view from the second floor looking west to the hills, in the direction of Durres on the coast.

We talked about making dictionaries; there was a large, old one on a revolving stand on Pavli's desk. I'd never thought about them before, not in this way.

"Where do you start?" I wanted to know.

"You begin from anything you like," Pavli said. "Just collecting words, finding phrases, putting them on cards, keeping files. But that is only preparatory work. The real work begins when you touch a typewriter and put a white sheet in, and write 'A'. What shall we write about 'A'?" he asked.

I'd wanted to know how they had survived all those years, and here was a clue under my nose. You know how you're so familiar with an object that you barely notice it? You're looking for a big answer—something about the spirit or history—but the answer is right in front of you in a simple, material thing. In the German-Albanian dictionary Zef had given me, in the old dictionaries in their Spartan but not tiny office. It's a matter of seeing it, of resisting your own familiarity.

Zef had said, "We wanted to use the same words to express, not our thoughts, but something neutral at least." Harmless things. Words. And in the pages of his dictionary were thousands of words—*tree, sky, beach, sea*—each one an expression of thought uncontaminated by the regime.

"Something neutral," Pavli repeated, adding, "despite the fact that sometimes other people, outside us, put in words that expressed the reality that existed at that time. As they did with Zef's dictionary. They put in expressions like 'the dictatorship of the proletariat', and 'scientific socialism', and so on."

"Not very scientific," Zef commented wryly.

"But also the definitions," Pavli said. "Here, look." He turned to the word *liberal*. "'One who makes concessions towards shortcomings and mistakes,'" Pavli read, "'who is not exacting towards others; who allows irregularities which harm the work of society.' This dictionary is full of such stupidities."

Over the years, they had slowly compiled words at night, while at work they duly translated documents, position papers, the works of Comrade Hoxha. On the far wall, facing the open window that looked out towards Durres, there was a bookcase containing the books of the Glorious Leader. Zef went to it and pulled out a couple of paperback volumes to give me. He made a show of banging them against the side of the case to shake the dust from these translated but never-read memoirs. On the cover of one called *With Stalin* was a photograph of the two men, shot from below, standing on a rampart. Later, in the hotel, I skimmed its hagiographic, childishly humble accounts of Hoxha's reception in Moscow by "Comrade Stalin".

Pavli walked me back through the mid-afternoon heat to the Dajti, and we arranged to meet again in the evening. The desk clerk had a room for me. Weber was still out when I moved my things to the new room. It was small but sufficient—a bed, a writing table, lace curtains, a shower, a little balcony, and a roll-down metal shade to keep out the heat. The room faced east, looking directly onto the blinking electric sign with the time and temperature. By the time I came up from the bar, bringing back a litre of mineral water, I was soaked from my exertions. I showered, made my notes, replenished myself with liquids, read a page or two of Conrad, and then napped.

Pavli came to get me in the early evening and took me to his apartment, where Zef was already waiting for us. Pavli's wife brought us raki and then went into the kitchen while we watched television. There was an interview with a visiting

Albanian political leader from Kosovo—the southernmost, so-called autonomous province of Yugoslavia, but actually under the thumb of the Serbians. Two million Albanians lived there, and now, with the disturbances in Yugoslavia, the old dream of Greater Albania was in the air again. I happened to learn a little about it only subsequently, when I read a translation of a novella by Kadare set in Pristina—the Kosovan capital—about a failed uprising a decade or more ago. Zef and Pavli watched the interview intently; such discussion was still something of a novelty on Albanian television.

Then Pavli's wife brought in food and they switched channels to an Italian game show. It was announced as a "light supper", but in fact it was a full plate, carefully laid out. Mussels, olives, tomatoes, onions, hard-boiled eggs, and a fruit compote for dessert. All the time we were watching the politician from Kosovo, Pavli's wife had been working in the kitchen. The women evidently did all the domestic work; the arrangements were quite traditional, as we say (giving much more dignity to the word "traditional" than it deserves). I thought of a feminist friend of mine back home, and knew exactly what she would make of it.

After Mrs. Qesku cleared the table, I turned on the tape recorder for our formal interview. Now I was at work, as I had been a hundred times before, in many places. And later, no doubt far away from where this encounter had occurred, I might hear those voices again, or they would be transcribed into a sheaf of notes which would find a place in a manila folder or in the depths of the maroon-coloured gym bag I lugged around with me, a homely object I sometimes described in jest as "my office".

Zef Simoni was born in 1933 in the northern town of Shkoder, to a well-to-do Catholic family. As in neighbouring Yugoslavia and Greece, the ending of the Second World War inaugurated civil war in Albania. While Greece was allotted to the Allies, in both Yugoslavia and Albania the partisan triumph was not impeded.

"Immediately when the partisans came into Shkoder," he recalled, "they started shooting people in batches. Behind the town graveyard. And after having a batch of people shot, they put up a proclamation with the names and the crimes they were supposed to have committed." Zef was eleven.

"So they came in 1944?" I calculated.

"Yes. And they were my first exercises in literacy." I was momentarily puzzled.

"To read the names," Pavli supplied.

"It was just reading matter for me," Zef said. I had a glimpse, no more, of a boy peering up at a freshly pasted sheet on a brick wall, absorbing the litany of the newly dead with a chilling innocence. Outside, in the night, we could hear the shouts of children at play.

Pavli's wife offered us brandy. "It is a very fine brandy made at home," Pavli recommended. "Wild cherry." We each accepted a small glass.

"They were people of a conservative mind," Zef said, recalling his family. "Right-wing, I would say now. My father was first an import-export merchant, then he had a printing shop, then a magazine, and he made some translations. He was the first Esperantist in Albania."

"He translated *Pinocchio*," Pavli added.

"Into Esperanto?" I wondered, slightly amused. But no, he had put the tale into Albanian.

"He translated the biography of Skanderbeg into Esperanto," Zef said.

"So you're a second-generation translator," I observed.

"Second-generation," Zef nodded, laughing.

Once again it was a matter of words. Words for civilization, words in self-defence. But wasn't the party's concern also the use of language?

"Propaganda is made of words, of course," Pavli agreed.

"But everything is distorted," Zef pointed out. "You are told you have freedom, which others, you are told, have not. And you have not freedom. You are told you have free speech—it is written in the constitution—and you land in jail for saying the wrong things. You are told you are free to move about, and you must have documents to move from one city to another. Everything is told it exists, and it doesn't exist, or exists its counterpart." Zef spoke rapidly, forgoing the niceties of English grammar in his excitement.

"My own family," Pavli said, "was a little more exposed to such propaganda. My father was a partisan, then a Communist, and fought in the brigades of the national liberation army. After the war, he began to realize that there was something amiss. But he couldn't grasp what it was. He was a tailor. In a small town in central Albania. Slowly but surely he began to realize that the cause of the situation was the party itself, and he began to dislike it, until in 1949, after five years in the party, he refused to be a member." Pavli had been five then. "But in my family there are still some people who believe that the party is good, just that something went wrong somewhere. There are some people who are still Utopians, who have the hope that socialism is something good for humankind."

I was curious to know how they had become friends. "We worked together," Pavli said. "They just put us in the same room," Zef added, "and they said, work together." The two of them laughed at the simple absurdity of it.

"And this has gone on for over twenty years," I said, laughing also.

"Yes, twenty-two years," Pavli confirmed, "except for a period of three years when I was in Peshpatia, a small town in the mountains."

They had escaped the terror of executions and jailings, but not entirely. They had spent the years together carefully. "Very careful," Pavli reiterated. "What we said in the streets, what we said in the café."

"We expressed our more delicate thoughts in English, just in case," said Zef. "We were very careful about where we talked, how we talked."

"Or we had code names for things."

The way their voices alternated reminded me of the strophe and antistrophe of a Greek chorus. "Code names?" I repeated.

"For the government, the party, the leaders, our party secretary." Like a children's game, I suggested. "It was very childish," Zef said, "and very horrible."

"But it was not Newspeak," Pavli added.

Yet their caution did not protect them completely. Pavli was shipped off for three years in 1975 to a sort of internal exile.

"The reason they gave Pavli for sending him to Peshpatia," Zef began, "—well, the true reason was that he didn't accept to become a member of the party—the specious reason they gave him was that you keep too much Zef's company. They kept me in Tirana."

"But Zef was frightened then."

"Because in their sick mind, I was infected, hopelessly. There was some hope for saving Pavli."

So Pavli was shipped off to work as a schoolteacher in a mountain village. "Did you think you would ever return?" I asked.

"It was a closed chapter," Pavli replied. "I just took my bag, my typewriter, and my books."

"Were you married?" I asked.

"Yes, but happily we had no children then. My wife could go on working here. The government needed her work because she was chief engineer of the porcelain factory. She kept working in Tirana, and I went to Peshpatia."

"Chinese style," Zef said.

Pavli's wife was sitting in an armchair, away from the table the three of us were gathered around. For all her fulfilment of the traditional duties, she was an educated woman, skilled, and able to follow our conversation in English, occasionally supplying a correction to their account. I saw her then as if for the first time. I had only a moment to imagine their three years of separation, caused by an ideological whim, which they treated, in retrospect, as a minor inconvenience. Compared to so many others, I suppose it was.

Pavli had gone on speaking of Peshpatia. ". . . the headmaster of the school was a very nice chap, very understanding.

He gave me a whole room to myself, a bare room of course, but it was a room. There was a round stove which the schoolboys were careful to supply with firewood. It is fifteen or twenty degrees below zero in winter there. I was all by myself. The dictionaries were there, and whenever those people, security, came from time to time, unannounced, to search my room, they saw that they were harmless books. I never gave them cause to suspect."

"And in the place of Pavli," Zef said, picking up the other end of the story, "into the office stepped a chap who had been Pavli's schoolmate. He had some connections with the Minister of Internal Affairs, and I am sure he informed on me, but he informed only on the good side." Zef laughed at this small irony, then added, "I was very careful, of course."

"My former schoolmate didn't do anything while he was there," Pavli noted. "He was supposed to be a translator, but he couldn't do the job. When Zef was away, he just sat there doing nothing."

Sitting there, comforted by cherry brandy, I had to remind myself that I was listening to an account of political terror. Not executions, torture, jailings—though there was that, of course—but quiet terror, everyday terror.

"When we translated that book which I gave you, *With Stalin*," Zef began again, "we worked night and day."

"Three months of hard work in the midst of summer," Pavli said.

"Then they gave us four or five days to recover," Zef continued. "On one of these days, the chief of the enterprise came to me and said, You are invited to the Tirana branch of the Ministry of Internal Affairs. I don't know what they want from you, but you must go. I went there. Certainly, I was very afraid. But I tried to keep control of myself. I told myself maybe they had some translations for me to do. I was ushered into a room and there were two armchairs, and they smelled of sweat, a heavy stink of sweat. Because the people who went there sweated profusely under interrogation."

They asked Zef about various people he knew, and he offered bland replies. The fencing went on for some time. Then the interrogators asked about a certain person. "I said, yes, I know him. I couldn't say I didn't. And what are his opinions? they asked. I said, the generally current opinions. And what are his literary tastes? I mentioned the most conventional tastes I knew of. Then they told me, he has been slandering the party, and you must know. I know nothing, I have not seen him for six months. After that, they gave me a cigarette. They did not make direct threats to me. They told me, look, we are going to arrest this man. If you warn him, first, it will be useless, and second, you will be arrested too. So I went home. On my way home, I wanted to have a double portion of cognac just to steady my spirits." He laughed in recollection of his fear. "Then I thought that I might be followed. If they saw me drinking, they might think I had something to fear. So instead I went straight home, and lay in my bed for about half an hour. Only then did I come out and go to the café, where I had my double portion of cognac. In about six months' time, Pavli, who knew nothing about these things—"

"Zef didn't whisper a word," Pavli interjected.

"Had I told Pavli, he would think, first, that I was a hero, and second, that I must have blurted out something. So I said nothing. And six months later, it was Pavli who mentioned to me that So-and-so had been arrested. And still I said nothing."

"You didn't tell Pavli about the interrogation?" I asked Zef.

"I learned of it only last year," Pavli said.

"When did this incident happen?" I asked.

"In 1980," Zef said.

"You only told him ten years later?" I said in astonishment.

"Ten years," Zef said, and we all broke out laughing, but perhaps for different reasons. They laughed at the mixture of absurdity and horror, and because now it was possible to laugh at it, and because it was a small thing compared to what others had endured. And I laughed nervously, almost embarrassed to be made a party to this terrible intimacy.

"After six months, Pavli told me, you know this chap So-and-so has been arrested," Zef repeated. I turned off the recorder, stuffed the tapes into my gym bag.

It was a story no different from those we had heard countless times in recent years. But that was the point of it: there was nothing "Albanian" about the anecdote. The insidious method was ubiquitous: anyone, even the most intimate of your friends, might inform. A remark you'd made in the sanctity of your home, thoughtlessly parroted by your child at school, might bring the authorities to your door. No letters unread by the censors, no movement without approved documents, and of course no passports. Your fate decided in rooms, committees, none of which you had access to, but in whose anterooms you waited. And though the digital clock recorded the passing minutes, the Glorious Leader had made time stand still.

Yet from the outside, to a visitor, the place must appear but a small, dusty, inconsequential town of barely a quarter-million inhabitants, baking in the sun—poor, but with people going about their business. There was little visible sign of the oppression, or the methods that made it possible. It was as if I had travelled the length of a river—like the river in Conrad's story—to reach, as Marlow did, the kingdom of a madman.

The parallels were eerie. Like Kurtz, Hoxha had not always been mad. He had begun with the intention of improving the lot of humankind, the great dream of our time. And those of us on the left had even grudgingly admired him, as the ruler of a tiny, mostly agricultural country who had rather heroically broken with first the Soviets, for deviating from Stalinism, and then even the Chinese, for abandoning Maoism. But in his obsessive effort to perfect human beings, to create, like a god, "the new man, the new woman", he had gradually turned the inhabitants into slaves.

"You translated Conrad," I said to Zef.

"And perhaps you think you are a bit like Marlow?" Zef joked, intuiting my pretension.

But there was no Kurtz at the heart of this darkness, no self-critical last cry of horror to ponder. All that remained was the rubble of Hoxha's rule. And the inhabitants, of course. We had thought of them almost as savages, just as Conrad had recorded that men of the imperium thought of distant peoples of a different colour a century ago. Yet I had discovered, as had Conrad, that they were the same as us.

I didn't think all that at the moment; only later, when the voices recorded in my little machine had become words on pages. But there was something more, something that did occur to me as we spoke, though I didn't mention it to Zef and Pavli. I had yet to free myself from the human dream that had given way to the dictator's inhuman methods. Does Marlow murmur, quoting a forgotten poet, "Spirit of the night, teach us to bear despair"?

It had gotten well on into the evening. There was more to ask, of course, but they had arranged for me to do interviews with some other people beginning early the next morning, a Saturday, and the following day we would hire a driver and go to Durres, so there would be time to talk then. However, I couldn't resist asking about the present, now that the nightmare was over, or almost over.

"The change can be seen if you follow a couple of people walking in the streets," Pavli said. "They have stopped turning their heads back to see if we're following them. We no longer turn our heads back."

Zef walked me back to the Dajti through the silent streets of Tirana. From the balcony of my room, I faced the electric sign flashing in the night. It was almost midnight. Just under thirty degrees. The sign blinked on and off, flooding my room with pale light and then plunging it into darkness. In bed, I turned away from the wall where light flared every few seconds.

Six hours later, I woke up. Beyond the Institute for

Strategic Studies, beyond where the town ended, there were pale brown mountains, with Mt. Dajti to the east. A haze lay between it and the edge of town. I stood on the balcony drinking coffee. Directly below me, three floors down, was the raggedy, semi-abandoned garden of the hotel. Palm trees, an empty fountain, untended bushes. A skinny yellow cat prowled through the brush.

The opposition Democratic Party was headquartered in a sort of villa, set back from a busy street, with a wide gate at the front to admit vehicles. Inside, even at eight a.m., clusters of men were gathered in the driveway-courtyard, petitioners perhaps, or local functionaries. An outside staircase led up to a warren of offices. We were ushered into a large room with a long rectangular table. At the head of it, talking on the telephone, was a stocky young man in his late twenties, with unkempt curly black hair. There was a window behind him, covered with shutters through which slivers of sunshine filtered, playing upon the gauze curtains that hung before it.

When he put the phone down, we were introduced. His name was Azem Haidari, he was a graduate student at the university and had come from a small mountain village, Treppoja, in the north; married, two children.

"If you want," Haidari said, via Zef's translation, "I will tell you about the democratic movement in Albania, the Democratic Party, the political life, and the Parliament." As a result of the elections in the spring, he now sat as a member of that body. We had about an hour's interview, variously interrupted by the urgency of the telephone and by people poking their heads through the double doors with

brief messages for the young politician. It was a standard interview; he spoke as a man with responsibilities. But I saw
that both Zef and Pavli rather admired him. They liked his
vigour and, apparently, the colourful mountain villager's
way of speaking—he didn't mince words. When he was on
the phone, I could get a hint of a more animated, indige-
nous style that no doubt had popular appeal. But with me he
was diplomatic, without irony.

As much as anyone, here was the person who had loos-
ened the grip of Hoxha's successors. "The dictatorship was
so savage there was no possibility of even thinking of estab-
lishing another form of government, because the mere
thought of it put your life in jeopardy," Haidari said. But the
explosions in Eastern Europe had had their echoes even in
Albania. "Mr. Alia, recalling the fate of Ceausescu, saw that
he had to do something for democratization.

"But his speeches, his manoeuvres, were only intended
for export," Haidari said dismissively. "They were intended
to give the impression that something was being done,
whereas nothing was being done." It was that impasse that
led Haidari to take political action, organizing the students.
The way he put it was very innocent—it was the language
of the nineteenth century's "springtime of nations"—and
yet it had the self-deprecating awareness of a man standing
before a mirror, giving an account that would later be read
as history. "When I was a student, I always recalled President Kennedy's words, Ask not what your country can do
for you, ask what you can do for your country. So I decided
to give my all to Albania, even my life. At first, the possibility of emerging alive from the first demonstrations after

forty years of Communist rule was very slim indeed. Nevertheless, against all these odds, we succeeded in carrying out our peaceful demonstrations. The moment came to do something for Albania and I am very happy this offer of sacrifice was accepted." That was all it took, if not to topple the regime, at least to shake its foundations.

Later, towards the end of the hour, the mountain man declared, "I love life, but I have the opinion that life should be loved only for as long as it lasts, and we should not think to prolong it more than its course. You can't escape your fate." It was not the first time I'd heard young men fearlessly proclaim such things, and I've seldom doubted them. Yet it was always eerie to hear someone say it. I couldn't imagine dying for my country.

Just at that moment, the phone rang. Haidari picked up the receiver and soon was speaking most animatedly. I saw alarm in Zef's and Pavli's eyes.

"There's been a shoot-out," Pavli said, following the progress of the conversation. "One of his cousins, a young cousin of his, has been shot."

"Where?" I asked.

"In Treppoja."

"How did it happen?"

"The situation is stable," Pavli said, ignoring my question.

"But who was shooting?" I wondered. Haidari's voice subsided.

"He made a speech in Parliament about Kosovo," Pavli explained. I put it together in bits and pieces—the arrival of the visiting politician from Kosovo we'd seen on television had heated the political atmosphere—then there was Haidari's speech on the suppression of the Kosovan Albanians by the Serbs—no mincing of words, apparently—and somehow the news of the speech—was it heard as a call to arms?—was connected to the flare-up in his home village, not far from the border.

On the outside staircase going down, Zef said, "In six months he could be dead." Meaning young Haidari, courting fate as he was. Then we were back in the streets, in the unforgiving heat. Mid-thirty degrees before noon. As we walked, Pavli recalled that the former student leader had accurately predicted that the newly elected government would be forced to form a coalition with the opposition "by the time the cherries were ripe".

"And when do they ripen?" I asked.

"In May and June," Pavli said. "And it happened. Now he says the present government will fall by the time the watermelons are ripe at the end of the summer. By the time the watermelons ripen." Pavli seemed taken with Haidari's agricultural turn of phrase.

Our next interview was with a writer named Trebeshina. It was held at the apartment of a young friend of his, also a writer. Trebeshina was in his mid-sixties, but you could see he had been badly used. He spoke in a hoarse whisper through yellowed and broken teeth. His was a tale of jailings and neglect. He had been imprisoned twice by the Fascists, against whom he had fought in the Second World War, and three times by the Communists. The first time, in the fifties, was a literary jailing. "I was always against the socialist realism," he said. "I was of the opinion that if there is realism, there is no need for socialist- or Fascist- or so on." He wrote an open letter to Hoxha and got three years for it.

I didn't quite catch the reason for the next incarceration, but the third one, in 1980, came about when he publicly declared his refusal to vote. For that he got a long stretch. He'd only been released in 1988. And though he'd written much after the open letter, none of it had been published. He had been ignored, neglected, always at odds with the Writers' League. He didn't share the conventional estimate of the great Kadare. "A collaborator," Trebeshina rasped. When I asked him about hearing of Hoxha's death while he was in prison, he replied, "He's not dead." At the end of his fragmented recital, Trebeshina said, "I always wanted to ring the bell for the others, but I did not. During all my life, I was a Don Quixote."

Pavli walked me back to the hotel. We went along the Lana River, where a peasant sat on the grassy embankment, tethered to a couple of grazing sheep. The electric sign now registered thirty-six degrees. Pavli left me in the driveway of the Dajti. He and Zef had arranged a meeting with Kadare's translator, Vrioni, for the evening.

I had worn my lightest shortsleeved shirt, but I was soaked through, and slightly dazed, grateful to get to the shade of my little room, clutching the bottles of water I'd acquired in the bar on the way up. Before I showered and napped, I made my notes, the paper practically melting under my hand. It was as if all substance had dissolved into a primordial ooze—the water I drank greedily, the perspiration pouring out of me, smearing the ink, dampening the pages. The interviews with Haidari and Trebeshina had been ordinary enough, the sort of tales of courage and suffering in a heretofore almost unknown place which are then inadequately condensed into the columns of the dailies. But this time I had been affected. I could feel the ends of my nerves. Perhaps I too, like Trebeshina, was a Don Quixote. It seemed to me that your entire life as a writer leads to the one street you are walking down, to the miserable little pile of dark figs you are looking at, to the rasping, bitter voice you are listening to. Everything has led to this moment. And yet you do not know the story, except as it unfolds before you. You do not know the story, I repeated to myself.

I went down to the veranda of the hotel early. The boy was there, the one I had seen before. Perhaps I'd gone down early because I'd gathered from Zef's tone that our meeting with Vrioni would be a rare prize and I didn't wish to be late. Or perhaps because I hoped to see that boy again. I had thought about him, several times in fact. He had made an impression.

We greeted each other like old friends. We shook hands, and he touched me on the shoulder. Blue eyes, nut-brown tanned skin, radiant smile. His name was Ilir. Ilir as in ancient Illyria. It was impossible not to think of the head of the boy in the postcard that the consul in Bonn had sent me, to see something in it more than mere well-wishing.

Ilir was with a friend his own age, to whom he introduced me. They both had a little English, though I had some difficulty following the anecdote they were trying to tell me. His friend was a music student, as was Ilir, or perhaps a dancer, I couldn't quite get it.

They knew all about current music. "Michael Jackson," Ilir said, "he is a great man. And M.C. Hammer, very beautiful." I was rather amazed by their knowledge, though also appalled that, of all things, this was what had penetrated the ideological defences of their shrouded land. "But how do you know all this?" I asked Ilir. They had seen it on television from Belgrade, which apparently transmitted the European version of the American music channel MTV. So, score one for the Global Village. I was too charmed by Ilir to be contemptuous of the pap the world wanted to feed him. Indeed, it seemed remarkable that in this remoteness he was a thorough contemporary of lads his age anywhere in the world. If I had to choose between Hoxha and MTV, well, why not?

There was a complicated story about a man named Hussein—"not Saddam Hussein of Iraq," Ilir laughed. This Hussein had promised them some papers, but I couldn't make it out. For what purpose? "Rap," Ilir said, "for the rap." There was something about videotapes, but I got it mixed up.

Then Zef and Pavli turned up for the evening at Vrioni's. I shook hands with Ilir's friend, but the farewell with the boy was more elaborate, kisses on both cheeks, hand-holding, assurances that we must get together again. I was quite dazzled, infatuated of course. I don't think it was entirely sexual . . . well, but who knows? Or if I did know the extent of my desire, I preferred to keep my understanding of it inarticulate even to myself. It was just that it was so astonishing to come upon someone like him here, in this place.

Walking to Vrioni's, I must have babbled, telling Zef and Pavli about the boy. They seemed amused I was so taken, the way you are when a visitor comes to your home town and enthuses about something there that you've never thought of, but that nonetheless leaves you pleased for both your visitor and yourself.

On the way, they reminded me that Vrioni had for a time worked in the publishing house as a translator. In fact, at the time of Pavli's exile, Vrioni's name had also appeared on the list of those to be sent off to get "closer to the people".

"He was sent too?" I asked.

"He was meant to be sent," Pavli said, "but on special instructions from His Highness—"

"—who knew some French," Zef interjected,

"—who read His own books in French," Pavli continued, "and liked the way they had been rendered in French—"

"—because Vrioni had translated His own works," Zef put in.

"There was no one who could translate His works as well as Vrioni did," Pavli added.

"So He was not going to saw off the branch He was sitting on," Zef concluded.

Vrioni lived in a detached two-storey house with a small front garden. His wife greeted us at the door and led us into the living room, where Vrioni was waiting for us. He was a tall, elegant man. I was told later that he was seventy-eight years old, but I never would have guessed it from his looks or his manner. He was the son of a wealthy landowner, and had been raised and educated in France before the war.

When he returned to Albania after the partisan triumph, Hoxha had him jailed for thirteen years. Then he became a translator, of Hoxha's books as well as those of Kadare.

His wife brought in a bottle of Johnnie Walker, with glasses on a tray, and, after placing them on the low, glass-topped table before us, retired upstairs, explaining that she was feeling poorly. Our conversation was in French. Vrioni could speak English, but he made it clear that to discuss certain concepts only French was adequate. Zef and Pavli filled in for my deficiencies.

We hit it off right away. I mentioned that I liked jazz and uttered the name of the legendary French jazz guitarist Django Reinhardt. Immediately Vrioni lit up. He rummaged about beneath the sound equipment at the side of the room until he produced a cassette. The room filled with the instantly recognizable arpeggios of the three-fingered jazz guitarist, joined by a violinist. It was Reinhardt's version of the "Marseillaise", accompanied by Stefane Grapelli, recorded just after the Allied victory in 1945, Vrioni told us. For a few minutes we simply listened with pleasure and sipped our whisky.

Vrioni was most dubious about Albanian prospects. He began to tick off on his aristocratic fingers the reasons for his doubts in that precise manner of French intellectuals. First, the level of Albanian culture was abysmally backward. I interjected that I had met a sixteen- or seventeen-year-old boy in Tirana who was extraordinarily well versed in contemporary music, having watched television from Yugoslavia. My host was unimpressed. He continued his dissection of the country's gloomy future.

I mentioned that I had seen Vrioni's name in the American magazine article about Kadare. It was clear that he had more than a proprietary interest in the Albanian writer. His translations into French had made Kadare's reputation. Without the translations which had so pleased the French public, the great novelist might be unknown today. There was a hint even that something more than translation was involved. It was almost as if he regarded himself as Kadare's co-author. And he had also translated the Glorious Leader. Vrioni went to the bookshelves on the far wall and returned with a couple of volumes, opening one to the title page. On it was Hoxha's inscription, in his own hand, to his "Comrade" for his "tireless work" in rendering the leader's writings into "perfect" French. Vrioni translated Hoxha's praise of himself with considerable drollery, assuming our appreciation of the implicit ironies.

I noticed that, on the low table before us, there was also a copy of the French translation of Milan Kundera's latest novel, which I had recently read myself. That led to Vrioni's enquiring about a Mexican novelist he had only heard of on his last trip to Paris. Did I know of Carlos Fuentes? I remarked to him that this conversation might take place in any capital of Europe. Yes, people were always surprised to encounter a cultivated Albanian, Vrioni said. "Of course, you know Montesquieu's *Persian Letters*?" he asked.

In that eighteenth-century work, the imaginary Persian through whom Montesquieu provides his portrait of the ills of France appears in a Paris salon and is asked, with near-disbelief, How is it possible for a Persian to be in Paris?

"I, too," Vrioni said, "have been at a salon in Paris, and

upon identifying myself as an Albanian I was asked, by a man who knew his Montesquieu, But how is it possible for an Albanian to be in Paris?"

For all his civility, even the charm of his vanity, there was something unsettling about Vrioni. I remembered the rasping voice of the broken Trebeshina, the Don Quixote; at the name of Kadare he had spat the words "A collaborator." To be able to write, and to use his fame as a platform from which to criticize the regime, however indirectly, had he not also lent that renown to a justification of the regime? Had Kadare not faced the moral dilemma of the person who sustains the culture, which he imagines as belonging to posterity, but only at the cost of semi-collaboration with the totalitarian power, which he must persuade himself is merely temporary? Was that not also true, albeit to a lesser degree, in the case of Vrioni? Here we were in this comfortable home, with whisky on the table, the latest novels, a modern sound system, and amid all these elements necessary to the maintenance of a civilization was the very hand of the Glorious Leader, the madman, thanking his "tireless Comrade".

Vrioni's ailing wife appeared at our departure. It was already night as Zef and Pavli walked me back towards the hotel. Martyrs' Boulevard was jammed with people on that Saturday night, walking in family groups, sitting on the low wall along the park, milling about in conversation in the hot darkness. I was overwhelmed by the sheer physicality. When the ideological shroud is pulled away, what you're left with is warm, human sweat.

We wanted to arrange for a car for the following day. Ilir was with some friends in the congested driveway beneath the veranda of the Dajti. He dashed off into the shadows to secure a driver, soon reappearing with a man who appeared trustworthy enough. We agreed to meet in the morning, and Zef and Pavli melted into the throng of strollers on the boulevard.

I told Ilir that we were going to Durres the next day. "I also," he said. "For the swimming." But perhaps we could meet later in the afternoon for a soft drink. "Yes, yes," he said enthusiastically. His voice was like the chirring of birds. We would meet at five. The boy had a way of being almost constantly in physical touch, with hand-holdings, an arm wrapped around you, a caress. Upon parting, an embrace, a kiss on both cheeks, the smoothness of his skin.

In my room, I admitted that I had been conquered—I had let something into my heart. But what was the nature of such feelings? And what was the relation between them, and the more casual feelings I had for the blond boy in Berlin? I recalled in Plato's works a conversation about profane and exalted loves. There were things I almost didn't want to know, moments when my desire seemed an abyss of the self. Yet desire too, I knew, belonged to the story.

In the morning, as the sun came in through the chinks of the half-pulled metal shade, I could hear the birds below in the otherwise empty garden. The driver proved to be quite reliable, and we were promptly on the road for our little holiday. As we passed buses jammed with like-minded weekenders heading for the sea, I found myself involuntarily glancing up at the windows of the packed vehicles on the unlikely chance that I might catch a glimpse of the boy on his way to the beach.

At Durres we inspected the ancient Roman amphitheatre, first century I think it was. It had been but semi-excavated, located as it was right in the middle of a residential neighbourhood. The heat was stunning. It was a relief to duck into the shaded galleries and interior stairways. A Byzantine church had been installed into its midst in the Middle Ages; the whole place was a rockpile jumble of two millennia. At last we emerged into a portal overlooking the whole of the site. I can't recall if they had dug all the way down to the great half-circle stage of the theatre, but it was easy enough to imagine. When we finally clambered off the heap, I was grateful to our thoughtful driver, who had found a watertap which he ran for his parched inspectors of antiquities.

Then there was the local museum to see. It was across the street from a narrow beach at the sea's edge. I only had half an eye for the ancient statuary, for now I was longing for the Adriatic, which I could smell from there. "Where I come from," I said to Zef and Pavli, "it's considered good luck to dip your hand in the sea, if you're a visitor." I've no idea if that's true, but my hosts apparently felt we had fulfilled our duties as tourists, and obligingly led me across the road. It was a scruffy beach, pebbles and shells mostly, but the Adriatic stretched out before us in a long, low succession of thin layers of wave. I reached into it and wet my hand, scooping up some water to my face, while the sea ran over my foot.

I displayed sufficient enthusiasm for this natural wonder that Zef and Pavli decided to show me the beaches at the south end of town. It was a five-minute drive. Down the wide stretch of sand was an area of resorts and hotels, where the workers and their families went for holidays and where the country's few tourists had been permitted during the old regime, to provide a source of foreign exchange. We stopped at one of the hotels to get a cool drink. We sat in a large, cavernous hall that gave out onto the crowded beach below and the Adriatic rolling in, and sipped an orange-flavoured concoction. Afterwards the three of us strolled through the mob of bathers, families, groups of boys playing football in the sand, bodies everywhere. Absurdly, I hoped to spy Ilir in this multitude, though I knew I wouldn't. But what struck me was that when the ideological fog lifted, what you had were the people—not the abstracted version, as in "the people", but the physical fact of them—and these people, the Albanians, were not so different from the rest of humanity, not dissimilar to the Italians or Greeks, who were on their own beaches that Sunday afternoon.

In the car again—now we were travelling inland and north, to Krujë—the image of that human flesh shimmering in the sun remained with me for some while. I turned to Zef and Pavli, sitting in back.

"Communism never talked about the body," I declared.

"It never talked about the spirit either," Zef countered.

"But it had an equivalent to the spirit," I replied. "It had the notion of revolutionary consciousness. At least that was a mental thing. But they claimed to be materialists, and yet they didn't speak—except mechanically—about the body." To be fair, in the world I came from the body was relentlessly displayed, but for all its commodification it was rendered almost equally meaningless.

Of course, the return of the body is not the same thing as

the birth of a citizenry, I admitted. The madman had broken many bodies here, but when the kingdom fell apart—for a variety of reasons, including the simple fact that it didn't work—the body of, say, old Trebeshina was, in a sense, replaced by that of the boy I was enamoured of.

Yet bodies, left to themselves, form only the relationships of a society—at best the wisdom of the elders, at worst the gangs of the cities. Whereas the dictionaries Zef and Pavli made belonged to a culture, even a universal culture, out of which citizens might emerge. I had no more idea of how it might turn out here than anyone else. But wasn't that true of so much of that new entity that we referred to by the old name of Europe? For the moment, it was simply bodies that impressed themselves upon me. Bodies that, as Pavli had said, no longer had to turn their heads to see if someone was following. Perhaps I had a touch of sun, I don't know.

At Krujë, in the mountains, there was a reconstruction of Skanderbeg's castle and a sweeping view of the valley below. We dutifully toured the site of the warlord's redoubt. Nearby there was a little outdoor restaurant, and we sat in the walled garden by a fountain, and feasted. Below us, at a table placed near the edge of a precipice, commanding a view of the valley, was a party of Italians. They were very jolly, yodelling out into the mountains, hoping to produce an echo. The waiter told us, however, that, far from being the frivolous tourists we might imagine, they had taken in some young Albanian men who had fled to Brindisi—I remembered the footage of overloaded boats I'd seen on TV the previous spring—and now they had come to visit the parents, to bring them news of their sons.

Sheep wandered about the garden, eating bread from our hands, nudging up against our knees, while we dug our fingers into their white, oily curls. But even as we feasted, dipping our bread into the dish of oil in which the olives soaked—Zef said matter-of-factly, "I haven't tasted olive oil in two years"—and as the Italians hulloed and yodelled, our talk strayed from the bucolic surroundings.

"What did you think the day Hoxha died?" I asked rather suddenly.

"It isn't very Christian," Zef answered, "but it was perhaps the finest day of my life."

"How did you hear about it?"

"We were not together at the time," Pavli said.

"First, there was only classical music on the radio," Zef remembered. "And we thought something had happened. And of course the only thing that could have happened was that He died. So we waited for the official announcement, which was at the twelve o'clock news."

"I was travelling that day, to my home town," Pavli recalled. "I took my little daughter with me. I went to see my father, who was sick. On my way to the train station, I met an old journalist. He approached me with sort of—I can't explain what his face was like when he saw me—but he desperately wanted to tell me something. He approached me with half a smile and said, He is dead and gone. I got it immediately. When I reached home, I told my father, I gave him the news. He just rejoiced. 'I saw him go before me. I don't mind if I die now.' Those were his words."

Pavli fell silent. We listened to the water falling in the fountain.

Zef said, "We hoped that his death would be the end, but the regime lingered on for another six years."

"The true end of the dictator," Pavli continued, "was on that famous day when his ten-metre-high statue was brought down. My wife was walking with her bicycle in the square and she saw people gathering, rushing about, and the police throwing tear-gas bombs. Nobody cared about their lives, they just rushed towards the statue and managed to bring it down. Afterwards, a tractor pulled it to the campus, where the students were on a hunger strike. They cut off his head, which was sent to the students. And then the body—"

"—it was dragged along," Zef interjected, "like a dead crocodile."

"Without its head," Pavli added.

In the mid-afternoon we came down from Krujë, back towards Tirana. I would be leaving the next day, so, though there would be a farewell, this was in a sense the last of our conversation. And at the end, as we had begun, we spoke of dictionaries. It was as if they hadn't made themselves clear enough, hadn't got it right, and it was somehow important to them that I understand.

"If we had been hot-headed, and just burst in a fit of passion and told them everything we had in our minds, we would have been content for a while, but our work would not have been done," Pavli said. "Dictionaries are not *our* work. It is something which belongs to the whole people, and people who make dictionaries are only a few idiotic, I would say, hard-working asses who take upon themselves the work of a lifetime."

"Eccentrics," Zef said, chuckling. "But it was some sort of justification."

"Or a revenge on our own selves," Pavli offered, alternatively. "After having humiliated ourselves, serving Him so devotedly, we wanted to do something to atone for what we had done."

Zef disagreed. "I, for my part, didn't think of it as atonement. I considered it only as a reply to people who, after liberation—I was always hoping for liberation—to people who would ask me, And during these years, what have you done? It was meant as a reply."

"So that you could say?"

"I did something useful," Zef concluded. The car pulled into the driveway of the Dajti.

I went down to the hotel veranda at five. Ilir was there, in a white T-shirt and jeans. When we went into the bar to get mineral water and soft drinks, he wouldn't let me pay; instead, he made some arrangement so that I was his guest. Upstairs, in my room, we sat on the little balcony facing the electric sign. I coaxed him into shedding his T-shirt, what with the heat. A fresh, glowing patina of tan that had been acquired on the beach at Durres that day burnished his torso.

He was a dancer. His father wanted him to study law, I think it was, but he wanted to dance. There was some difficulty with language; we used Zef's dictionary to get through the rough spots—I would think of a word we needed in English and translate it into German, and look it up and show Ilir the corresponding word in Albanian, and then say the English for it. Cumbersome, but a bit like a game. He was in one of those folk-dance ensembles approved by the regime.

But the boy's passion was for ballet. Classical and modern ballet, although he called the latter "abstract". "Ballet abstract," he said. He told me the story of a ballet he was in at school—*The Silver Birds*—written by his teacher, his "choreograph". And then I finally got it about "the rap". What he was interested in was rap dancing. He'd seen this fellow, Hammer, an American, who was a performer of rap dancing, on Yugoslavian television. And the famous Michael Jackson, of course. I hadn't paid much attention to any of that, but one absorbs it, since it's in the air, so I knew what he was talking about. The sound of rap was like the staccato of a firing squad, I'd thought. But Ilir's idea was this. He too wanted to be a choreographer. And the ballet he wanted to create would be a combination of classical ballet and rap dancing. Well, why not?

We sat on the balcony and chatted away for a couple of hours. There were other stories. Something about his sister, or sister-in-law, wanting to flee Albania for the Italian refugee camps, how he'd pleaded with her not to go. And once he'd been to Turkey for two or three weeks—I didn't quite get why—he'd stayed with a family and they'd been very nice to him, but he'd gotten homesick.

It was all quite marvellous. I'd gone all the way to this benighted place, and I'd found what I'd been seeking, I suppose, in more ways than I'd expected. Ilir was outgoing, unselfconscious, his voice was a little breathless. Perhaps all the pidgin English, pidgin Albanian, made it seem much simpler than it was. I didn't think he represented the "spirit of Albania" or some such nonsense. There was a temptation to make that of him, of course, he was so full of his own light. But that's a dangerous sentimentality, too. He was simply himself. But he was of the place also, he would have to live here when Vrioni and Don Quixote and the translators had gone on. He might even make a ballet, if the place wasn't overtaken by chaos, if it didn't revert to hill banditry and blood feuds, if, against the odds, the musical body of this boy and the "deliberate belief" (as Conrad calls it) of the dictionary-makers could forge a citizenry. Ilir wanted to see me again the next day, before I left. He would bring me a *regalo*, a gift. He'd come at nine the next morning.

That evening I took dinner in the hotel, in a large hall at the end of the long corridor, beyond the bar and breakfast room which flanked its length. Through the dining-room windows you could see the boulevard, filled with people passing up and down in the middle of the huge avenue. The pilgrims, myself included, were at their cutlets. The Texans were at a table on one side of me; I gathered they were off to Cairo the next day. Apparently they'd done a deal for oil rights down at Flora—to the south, below Apollonia, the old Greek town—in return for which they would provide computer equipment (probably obsolete) from head office in Houston or Dallas. And at the table on my other side there was another businessman, with a woman, earnestly lecturing a local fellow, who seemed quite deferential before the pilgrim's sermon on efficiency and whatnot.

I took the air for a bit, among the strolling crowds, before retiring to my room. Before I nodded off, I saw the end of it, of the story I was following here. When you're vouchsafed—in advance—a glimpse of the tale in its entirety, you simply shudder with gratefulness to the god for whom the Greeks named that town of Apollonia.

Ilir arrived promptly at nine. The haze was just lifting from Mt. Dajti. He had a plastic sack filled with *regalos*: a bottle of Albanian raki, another of wine, some candies, and a collection of video and cassette tapes—Beethoven, and a local singer, and M.C. Hammer, which he'd taken off the radio, TV footage of the visit of the American secretary of state to Tirana—even a snapshot of himself. He emptied his treasury upon me. Would I send him a video of Hammer or Michael Jackson? "Yes, of course," I promised, "but there's one more *regalo* I'd like." He was puzzled. What more could there be?

"I'd like to see you dance," I said.

"But where?" he asked.

"Here," I said. At first he made the faintest show of resistance, but he was an artist, and accustomed to performing. Beethoven is not really for dancing, he pointed out, even as he snapped the tape into my little interview recorder with the familiar dexterity of teenagers everywhere.

He placed himself in front of the gauze curtain before the window. It was embroidered with birds, and the faintest breeze moved the cloth. I pressed the button and symphonic strains emerged. At first, I didn't think it would come off. There was barely sufficient room to move between the bed and the doorway to the bathroom, three or four paces at most. I don't know what I expected—that it would be quite provincial or crudely amateurish, perhaps.

I needn't have worried. He struck a pose, this boy in T-shirt, jeans, and sneakers, and quickly found space to soar and plunge and turn. I don't know how to describe it. You could say, I suppose, that his terrible innocence took wing—if it was innocence, if it was terrible. What does Rilke say? "Every angel is terrifying"?

When the Beethoven ran out, he immediately found the woman pop singer on the tape, and danced a mixture of Turkish and folkloric movements. For the finale there was a performance of rap dancing to Hammer chanting the refrain "Can't touch this," repeated again and again. It was one of those boasting songs from the American ghetto, full of aggressive sexual double-entendres and self-acclaim for the performer's artistry. Although I'd only paid annoyed attention to it when I'd seen it in passing on television, it now struck me as quite beautiful; I saw the art of it. Ilir simply viewed it as another form of modern dancing. For him, the elements of the culture had no gaping spaces. For his needs, Beethoven and Hammer were contemporaries. And the tiny room was as adequate as the stage in the amphitheatre at Durres.

At the end, he collapsed into the chair at my desk, heaving for breath. He was covered in a light sweat—it gathered in the trough above his lip, and in the hollow at the base of his throat. I could smell him, breathe him in. He glowed. I offered him a can of cola. It was soon time for him to go; he had a test at school that day. An embrace, kisses, a hug in which for a moment I held that dancing body against my own. "Can't touch this," I said. "Can't touch this," he repeated with a grin.

The rubber tires of the plane squeaked down onto the tarmac at Tegel airport in Berlin as I turned the last pages of

Conrad's story. I was left at the end with Marlow, Conrad's yarn-spinner, his interminable voice having ceased, his face as impassive as that of a meditating Buddha.

I got up, reaching into the overhead baggage rack for my maroon-coloured gym bag. Coincidentally enough—and this was one of those thousand things you couldn't possibly make up—my seat companion was a riverboat captain, just returning from someplace in Africa where he worked for a German resource company. We wished each other well at the end of our respective journeys.

That evening I had a drink at the Café Einstein, and when I said to a friend I'd run into there that I was just back from Tirana, he made me repeat the name and then tried it out himself, as if uttering the name of some place on the moon. I extracted Zef's dictionary from my bag as evidence that I wasn't making it up. "But why did you want to go there?" he asked, tolerantly amused.

I soon took my leave, making my way in the cool, damp night across Nollendorfplatz, beneath the soot-stained nude statues embedded in the upper façade of the Metropol Theatre, into the web of narrow streets to the west, where the bar I frequented was located. It was late, and the blond boy wasn't there.

In his place was a rangy young man in his early twenties, tall, rather dark, athletic, not exactly my type. How quickly the sublime was replaced by the vulgar, I thought, slightly bemused, yet noticing that I wasn't tempted to exalt the former at the expense of the latter.

We struck up a conversation in broken German, the one language we had in common. He was from Zagreb, in

Croatia, an economics student; his family had sent him off to Berlin for safety in the midst of the Yugoslavian shooting. By chance, one of them, his mother or perhaps a grandparent, was Albanian, and he seized with delight upon Zef's dictionary, which I had placed upon the bar between our elbows. When we encountered a word in German that was outside his vocabulary, we repaired to Zef's translation of it into Albanian, just as I had done with Ilir. I was a bit frightened of him, but in the cab he took my hand in his much larger one, reassuring and exciting me by circling his finger in my palm. At home, I satisfied him as best I could.

Borkowicz's Death

I F THERE WERE a graduating class photo of the dissidents who brought down the Communist regimes of Eastern and Central Europe, at the end of the 1980s, Jan Lytinski would be found among its ranks. Did someone say that to me, or did the thought simply arise on its own? Indeed, there was such a photo, or something very like it, illustrating an article by the Polish writer Adam Michnik in the *New York Times Magazine*, which my friend Tom Sandborn was reading as the transatlantic flight took us towards Europe at the beginning of the first springtime of the 1990s.[1]

The photo recorded a meeting of about two dozen Czech and Polish political activists, held at the border between their countries in the summer of 1988. They were posed in a wooded area before a small sign warning in Polish, "State border, crossing forbidden"—an order they had lightly disregarded in the same way they had ignored or defied so many other dictates of the authorities over the years, with consequences that were in many cases not at all light.

I recognized a few of the figures. Michnik was there, of course; he was holding his fingers aloft in a V-sign. The curly-haired Czech playwright Vaclav Havel was crouched in front of him, glancing off to the side, away from the face of History that his Polish colleague had recognized. Jacek Kuron, who had been among the first of the Polish intellectuals openly to challenge the Communist power there (and had abundantly paid for it in prison time), was sprawled in the grass at the bottom of the photo, a brimmed cap atop his bulldog face, his hand slightly blurred as he waved at the camera. In the middle, standing next to Michnik, was a slight, greying man, hands delicately clutched together, wearing a sort of ski sweater embroidered with stylized reindeer. That was Lytinski, to whom I had acquired a tenuous note of introduction from an acquaintance at home. If it was a graduating class photo, how many of them—now sitting in newly constituted parliaments and editorial offices— could have anticipated the world they would be graduating into just a year or so later?

That, in fact, was what Michnik was attempting to come to terms with in the essay Tom was reading as we sailed above the clouds. "The final days of 1989 brought with them the end of the Communist era," his article bluntly began. "The system that had proclaimed itself the future of the world was buried in the ashes of burning Romanian towns. No doubt there will still be police and military relapses. . . . But the idea has died. For Communism, it is the end. At last."

I too had been struck by the image of those burning towns three or four months before. One day the previous December, I'd seen an item on television about an insurrection against the heretofore impregnable Romanian regime, in the city of Timisoara, near the Hungarian border. Already that year, in swift succession, the Solidarity movement in Poland (in which Michnik, Kuron, and Lytinski were prominent) had defeated the Communist Party in elections; the Berlin Wall had buckled, then come down; the Czechs —led by their philosophical playwright, Havel—had begun a "velvet revolution" in Prague's Wenceslas Square; and now something was happening even in distant Romania.

It was so remote that there wasn't even video footage immediately available, merely a voice crackling on a line from Budapest, reporting apparently extensive shooting. A few days later the regime had collapsed, and now there was abundant and gruesome television footage, pictures of the hasty execution of the elderly Communist dictator, Nicolae Ceausescu, and his wife. For all the finality of those images, it was difficult to discern the character of events there. Was a "popular revolution" in progress (there were night-time crowds on the screen, tanks, flags, the sound of gunfire), or was Romania experiencing an internal Communist Party coup (a prominent party leader had emerged at the head of the newly cobbled-together provisional government)? It was thus in a murky interrogative mood that I plotted my itinerary.

Or rather, *our* itinerary, since I immediately fastened on Tom as my ideal fellow traveller. Ours was the sort of friendship in which I could call up one day out of a clear blue sky announce, "We have to go to Eastern Europe." Shouldn't those of us who had lived in a world divided by the so-called Iron Curtain attempt to comprehend its epochal fall? Or, as I later read in a book that put it more succinctly, "You might just decide that the most important thing in your life this year was to find out the truth about something." Tom immediately agreed to arrange tickets and contacts for a whirlwind journey that would take us to a half-dozen Eastern European capitals.

The somewhat strident opening of Michnik's piece (for I thought of him as a writer especially sensitive to nuances of history and language) was succeeded by some reminiscences of people he considered particularly important to the stirring events of recent years—the Russian physicist-turned-human-rights-activist Andrei Sakharov (whose graveside Michnik had attended only months before), and such others as his old friend Havel, who had lately become the president of Czechoslovakia, as well as Hungary's Janos Kis, a philosopher who shortly would be standing for office in the election there.

"Today, I can't help wondering," Michnik mused, "what gave those people the strength? What made it possible for Sakharov, Kis, Havel, to live for years the way they did live? Why did they abandon academic careers and sacrifice freedom, calm, and personal security for a hopeless battle against the Communist leviathan? Not one of them ever declared himself to be a man of religious calling or a politician. And yet, embroiling themselves in politics, they bore moral witness. And they prevailed over the political professionals of police dictatorships. How was that possible?"

But for modesty, Michnik could have added his own name to that distinguished roster. There had been a famous occasion several years before, when an angry mob in a small town near Warsaw surrounded the local police station and seized two or three thoroughly frightened policemen. The men's lives hung on the thread of the crowd's mood. The authorities had branded the opponents of the regime "antisocialist elements", and with characteristic Polish humour the slander had been turned into something of a joke; teenagers wore T-shirts that mockingly said, "Antisocialist element". From that crowd threatening to become a lynch mob, Michnik leapt onto the roof of an automobile or bus and announced himself to the enraged masses. "You know me," he said, "I'm an antisocialist element." The crowd laughed, and the lives of the policemen were spared. (Only months later, Michnik was back in jail.)

The more pressing question, however, was what sort of Europe would emerge from the cataclysm. "The European spirit," Michnik observed, "is struggling with the narrowly nationalist one. . . . This European mosaic of nationalities could be swept by a conflagration of border conflicts. These are unhappy nations, nations that have lived for years in bondage and humiliation. Complexes and resentments can easily explode. Hatred breeds hatred, force breeds force. And that way lies the path of the Balkanization of our 'native Europe'," he warned.

"For now two roads lie open before my country and to our newly freed neighbours. One road leads to border wars, the other to minimizing borders, reducing them to little more than road signs; one road leads to new barbed-wire fences, the other to a new order based on pluralism and tolerance; one road leads to nationalism and isolation, the other to a return to our 'native Europe'."

But what did that idea of "a return to Europe" mean? "A

commitment to certain attributes of European culture," Michnik explained. "It means replacing the totalitarian dogmas with an attitude that presupposes a critical distance towards oneself, and it means respecting tolerance in public life and skepticism in intellectual matters."

I had been to Warsaw before. I'd spent a week there in 1981, at the end of a lengthy visit to Gdansk to record the stories of the workers at the Lenin Shipyard. Led by the irrepressible Lech Walesa, they had gone on strike in August 1980 in order to secure recognition for Solidarity, the first independent workers' organization in the so-called "workers' states" of Eastern and Central Europe.

Now, nearly ten years later, Tom and I stood at the entrance of a dog-leg, dead-end lane lined with four-storey apartment buildings, tucked into a maze of narrow streets just a few blocks off Marshalkowska Boulevard, the main thoroughfare of downtown Warsaw. A crabapple tree, burst into full pink blossom, was at the corner of the tiny street. While waiting at the doorway of a building about two-thirds of the way down the lane, where we had secured a sublet, we could hear, floating from a nearby open balcony, the sound of someone playing Chopin on a piano.

Peter Borkowicz had arranged the apartment. It belonged to the Titkovs, who had been longtime friends of Peter's recently deceased father, old Leonard Borkowicz, and who were on holiday in Israel for the month. Peter was friends with the Titkovs' daughter, an actress named Olga, who would be looking after us. So already there were a couple of generations whose connections we would have to sort out—brothers, husbands, an aunt of Peter's whom we had promised to visit, in-laws, ghosts, the lot.

For that matter, there were our own ties to Peter. I had met him years before, at a talk I was giving on Polish politics. Since political circles are famously internecine, Tom too had in due course gotten to know him. In fact, Tom had been friends with the woman Peter married and with whom he'd recently had a child. So it was only natural that Tom would contact Peter to put his connections to use. And eventually, we'd all—around a dinner table—report back to Peter.

The apartment was on the top floor. The living room, which also contained a couple of beds, gave out onto a balcony overlooking the storybook lane below. It joined a dining room (I immediately claimed the table as my workspace) that had a view into a tangled courtyard out back, dominated by a large chestnut tree, its candle-shaped heaps of white blossoms in full bloom. On the far side of the small kitchen, adjacent to the dining room and just off the entrance corridor, was a tiny child's room, with a narrow bed. It looked like a monk's cell, and I decided to sleep there, while Tom staked out the front room as his quarters.

"You must be Olga," I said, when she appeared at the door. She was a beautiful woman of about forty, and her long dark hair had a mahogany glow. "Peter sends his greetings."

"How are you?" she asked as we shook hands, smiling in recognition at the mention of Peter. "Was the train ride tiring?"

"No, it was all right," I said, and then, out of nowhere, I added, "But I've been thinking a lot about death."

While waiting for her, I'd found a copy, on her parents' bookshelves in the front room, of Tadeusz Konwicki's *A Minor Apocalypse* (I happened to have brought along an English edition of it). It was a novel written the year before Solidarity, in which the narrator, Konwicki himself, was visited by two old comrades from the opposition who proposed that he set himself on fire in front of the Communist Party headquarters that evening. "Here comes the end of the world," it opens.

Perhaps it was my thumbing through the Titkovs' copy that had produced the odd mood that led me to announce my brooding thoughts. Olga took it in stride.

She replied—even before offering the usual visitors' orientation about which key worked for which door, and what our duties might be (they consisted of nothing more elaborate than remembering to water the geraniums on the outside landing)—with a prefatory remembrance of how she had gotten to know Peter. He had arrived in Poland to work in a theatre company, and since she was in theatre, they had inevitably met . . . which led to something of an explanation of the relationship between Peter and old Borkowicz, whose first wife had emigrated to Canada long ago, taking Peter with her, so that it was only as an adult, really, that he met his father, Leonard.

Somewhere in that description of the family tree, which included the interlinked roots of the Titkovs, Olga remarked in passing, "You know about Borkowicz's death, of course." Though I didn't, I merely grunted, sensing that there was something hush-hush about it which one should know, but which one couldn't really admit to not knowing.

Perhaps it would come out over the next days. She went on
to describe some details of Borkowicz's funeral the previous
autumn, which Peter had come to Warsaw to attend.

After providing the household instructions, Olga had to
dash—she had a rehearsal that evening. We would have dinner with her in a day or two, she promised, at which we
could meet her brother, Andrzej. Unfortunately, her husband was in New York trying to sell a musical. Yes, she
could make contacts for us with some of the people we
wanted to talk to. I gave her—rather impetuously—a copy
of a book I'd written about homoerotic desire; she knew a
gay rock singer I might be interested in meeting. And then
she was off to recite lines—by Chekhov, I think.

Perhaps it is not enough (or is even slightly deceptive) to say
I had been in Warsaw before, and leave it at that. The truth
is, I had fallen in love—a brief, chaste love; or because of its
brevity, possibly I should call it an infatuation—with the
lead singer of a rock band called, appropriately enough for
the times, Crisis. His name was Mirek. Though it had been
a long time ago—and what significance could one claim for
such an encounter?—nonetheless, when you return to a city
where you've been in love, it's almost as though the love is
still there.

Indeed, as soon as Tom and I arrived in the city—we
were walking through the underpass beneath the intersection
of Marshalkowska Boulevard and Jerozolimskie Avenue, the
main crossroads in Warsaw—the familiar dank odour of the
tunnels below the city traffic brought with it a whiff of romantic nostalgia. I had often walked with Mirek through that

underpass, on our way from the Forum Hotel on one side of the Marshalkowska, where we ate late-night desserts, to the Metropol on the other side, where I had a room, and at whose lobby entrance he said good-night to me.

The first time we met was in Gdansk in 1981, the springtime of Solidarity. It was in the midst of a vast crowd. I had arrived on a Thursday night, the eve of May Day, put up at the hotel across the street from the train station (from the window I could see the dinosaur-like cranes of the shipyard looming in the shadows of streetlamps), and quickly struck up an acquaintance with Christine, a French journalist. She promised to take me out to the union's headquarters on Monday, right after the weekend holiday.

Whatever conceptions or illusions I had about the great workers' holiday were immediately dashed. No Red Square parades (images stored in my mind from a repertoire of TV clips) in this coastal city, where the workers had rebelled against the workers' state the summer before. Instead, that first day, I found myself on a bus that drove out to Gdynia, the next shipyard town up the coast, where I was a half-comprehending witness to a flower-laying ceremony marking the deaths of workers a decade earlier, in one of the last proto-rebellions before Solidarity.

I had the weekend to wander around. The real holiday, it turned out, was on Sunday, which commemorated, unexpectedly, the Constitution of 1791. That scrap of parchment was Poland's bid to make common cause with the quasi-democratic Enlightenment, an ill-fated venture resulting in a partition of the country that removed Poland from the maps of Europe until the end of the First World War. In any case,

I stumbled onto a crowd (maybe 25,000 people) and followed it across the square named for King Jan Sobieski, as it moved towards the capacious St. Brigid's Catholic Church at the far end.

In that jostling but sombre crowd, I found myself alongside a young couple. He was twenty-three or twenty-four, frail in a waiflike way, with short blond hair chopped in a semi-punk style. He wore jeans and a black sports jacket. Both Mirek and his girlfriend, Barbara, had enough English to explain what was going on as we were pressed together in the emotional crush of people—it was the first time the Communist regime had been forced to legally permit Constitution Day ceremonies; the year before, people had been arrested.

We latched onto each other for the day. A crammed eleven a.m. mass in the church, speeches in the plaza, red and white wreaths of carnations draping the equestrian statue of the king, late lunch at the hotel restaurant, and by evening we were sauntering through the now-deserted Sobieski Square, the carnations shimmering with dew at the foot of the bronze mount. It was at that moment, perhaps, that I knew Communism was over. Not that I had any prescient insight that it would end (the division of the Iron Curtain still seemed permanent), but simply that I had incontrovertible, firsthand evidence that people didn't believe in it, notwithstanding whatever unrealistic hopes I might have, as a leftist, that some genuine reformer would rescue the botched dream of socialism.

I was attracted by Mirek's seeming helplessness, his pallor and mild irony, the way he entered the crowd of history.

But I didn't fall in love with him then. In fact, I can't even recall if we saw each other over the next few weeks. I was preoccupied with recording the chronicles of the shipyard workers and intellectuals who had organized the Solidarity movement.

But when I got to Warsaw—I'd had enough of interviewing—I spotted a poster announcing a rock concert in which Mirek's group, Crisis, was fronting for a better-known band called Perfect. At the end of Mirek's set, I went up to him. He seemed surprised and delighted that I had gone to the trouble of finding him, and immediately detached himself from the inevitable gaggle of adoring teenagers. We went for coffee at the Forum, talking about everything from Poland itself (he was slightly cynical—the cynicism of a people whose hopes had been dashed throughout history) to the lead singer of Perfect (we agreed that he was a terrible narcissist). By the time Mirek left me at the door of my hotel across the street, I was infatuated.

After that, we saw each other every day until I left. We took walks, ate at the hotels, and strolled through the tunnels of the underpass. Sometimes we went to the apartment of one of the musicians in the group, which was just a couple of blocks up Jerozolimskie. His name was Zbigniew and he was the leader, manager, and boss of the band. He had a tape of the concert, which he played on a primitive reel-to-reel recorder that had to be rewound by hand. "Just look at this," he said disgustedly, sneering at the tape deck as if it represented the entire mess of Poland. Then he'd bawl Mirek out for singing off key, or not practising enough. While my friend endured these harsh criticisms docilely, I, slightly embarrassed for him, gazed out the window at the gothic-Stalinist Palace of Culture—an unwelcome fraternal gift from the Soviet Union—that dominated the city as much as the Russians did Poland.

One evening, Mirek took me there to see a movie. It was by the Russian director Tarkowski, and had been banned for some years but was now, in the thaw, suddenly available. Before the movie began, we went to the washroom in the basement. It was an opulent, marble-sheathed affair, a strangely beautiful room, its grandeur out of proportion to the alimentary functions for which it was intended.

We stood side by side at the urinals.

"I think," I said haltingly to Mirek, "that I've sort of, well, fallen in love with you," and rushing on—if I didn't get it out now, I never would—added, "I'd like to sleep with you."

It was hardly the most romantic setting for blurting out my confession, but having done so, I was at once relieved, excited, and as embarrassed as I'd ever felt as a teenager.

Mirek betrayed no anxiety or revulsion, but was momentarily nonplussed by the euphemism. He looked down at his cock, which I peeked at also—uncut, pale as his face— and casually enquired, "Does sleeping together mean having sex?"

"I'd like that," I said.

"Well, I'll have to think about it," he replied, not at all perfunctorily, his blue eyes meeting my gaze. I breathed again. We zipped up, and went upstairs to watch the film. Its story took place in the late Middle Ages—the soundtrack was in Russian and there were Polish subtitles—and what remained in my memory was a sort of canvas balloon or dirigible on which the movie's protagonist, clinging to its surface, careered over his peasant village.

Although Mirek never spoke of it, he decided not to make love with me. But when we walked through the passageway under Marshalkowska Boulevard that night, he slipped his arm beneath mine, not discouraging my affections, which he received quite tenderly. When I sat on my bed in the room in the Metropol, looking out onto the now quiet late-night traffic circle below, my fantasies were strangely chaste. Though I thought of Mirek naked, I never imagined us as other than simply cuddling. And though he had decided not to make love, when we sat at a linen-covered table in the Forum, eating a dessert, I had the pleasure of wondering whether his thoughts occasionally turned to my desire for him.

Inevitably, one night, having journeyed beneath the intersection a last time, he said a final goodbye to me at the hotel entrance and went to rejoin his friends. I went up to my room and stood at the window, trying to pick out, among the figures walking on the far side of the boulevard, his slim form dissolving into the shadows.

Anna S. lived in a tiny apartment in an indistinguishable row of concrete blocks of flats on the far side of Warsaw. In the early evening, the taxi driver had to slowly cruise up and down several rows of those identical blocks before we were able to pick out the dimly lit number we were seeking. I had her name from the same person who had provided the note of introduction to Jan Lytinski.

She was a woman in her late thirties, married with two

children, who worked as a translator. Her husband, an academic of some sort, was in Dubrovnik, Yugoslavia, at a conference, earning some much-needed foreign currency. She settled us in a cramped, book-lined study. The older boy, Milosz, about ten, presently wandered off to another part of the flat, while the younger son, Karol, a six-year-old, crawled over her, demanding attention. Anna's hair was drawn back in a bun; she rested her chin on the palm of one hand, her fingers nervously stroking the side of her nose beneath the rims of her glasses. She looked tired, as if she was drawing on depleted reserves of energy to see us.

She wanted to know, reasonably enough, who we were, what we were going to do with the material we were gathering, whether we were connected with a newspaper. "And are you going to use my name?" Anna asked.

"It would be up to you," Tom said soothingly. He had the same habit as Anna, I noticed, of absently stroking the side of his nose.

"Well, I don't know," she said. "My opinions and my views about the situation in Poland are not very popular, and are very pessimistic on the whole."

"Fair enough," I assured her.

"We'll see," she said. "We'll see what happens, and what I'll say," and then she briefly laughed, as if amused by the thought that what she might say was unpredictable. I nodded in agreement. "So, I'll make you coffee," she said, rising. "Do you take sugar?"

"You said that some of your opinions are unpopular," Tom reminded her, after she returned from the kitchen and had shunted off the younger boy to join his brother.

"Yes, well, all criticism against the present government is unpopular," Anna replied. "If I talk to people and I say, I think there is something wrong with the situation of books, for example—there are so many taxes on them. Because what the government did, they stopped all the subsidies; culture is treated like factories, everybody must earn for himself, so books have suddenly become very expensive. But if I say that in some cases this policy is no good, everybody says, But how should it be? I don't know how it should be"—she shrugged—"because I am not an economist. I only see how this situation is very hard for people."

She and her husband, she emphasized, were better off than most people, because they had access to foreign earnings, but still, "we eat all the money we have, because food is so expensive; we buy fewer books than before. Definitely fewer."

Anna's complaints were not at all ideological; they were literal, emanating directly from her experience—almost, one could say, from her body, which sagged with a touch of exhaustion and anxiety, even as her younger child came back into the cramped study and clung to it.

"Today I went to the bookshop that has all the interesting books," she said, "the ones that either haven't been published before, or were published in the underground. I wanted to buy a book or two, but the price is 16,000 zlotys, or 18,000 even, for a thin book. Well, it's too much."

"And the price before?" I asked.

"Six months ago, it was less than half, 3,000 or 4,000 zlotys. And of course all the wages are blocked; they are raised very, very slightly each three months. I agree that maybe it's the way of starting a new economic system, a new political system, but I'm very pessimistic about the results, because now we have 'world prices', it's called." And the "world prices" didn't go very far on an average wage of 500,000 zlotys (about $50 U.S.).

"Now they are planning to put the prices of the apartments up," Anna added. What was the current rent? "For this flat here, we pay—let me think, it changes almost every two months, it goes up—but now it's about 60,000 zlotys. If the plan is realized, I think it will be 300,000."

"But if the rent goes to 300,000 and a person is making 500,000, how can they. . . ?" I wondered.

"Well, exactly," she said. "What they say—I heard it on the radio the other day—is that people will stop paying rent, like they do in Brazil. In fact, it's becoming more and more the general opinion that we are going into not the kind of capitalism in the U.S.A., Canada, or Western Europe, but the kind in Brazil."

I noticed I was of two minds about what she was saying. I liked the precision with which Anna presented the concrete details of her own daily life. The actual prices of things, the calculation of those prices against the monthly wage, the ominous anticipation of the next phases of the "economic shock therapy", as the free-market plan, now only a few months old, was described. Yet, at the same time, even though it was illogical on my part, I was resistant to her criticism. I had scant loyalty to the capitalist panacea of the marketplace, yet I found myself cheering for the success of this plan, which was dreamed up by an American professor and the Solidarity economists. I didn't want to hear Anna's apprehensions; I put some of them down to the class snobbery of intellectuals, dismissing others as the inevitable temporary glitches of a vast transformation. Still, as she spoke, I gradually built up a picture of this intelligent, worried woman, more or less housebound with her children, listening to serious radio and television programs as she did household chores, developing her own opinions.

Anna was also dubious about the capacity of Polish workers. "It's always been one of the characteristics of the Polish people," she insisted, "this not wanting to work, trying to get as much money from nothing as possible."

"But all of my Polish friends here work very hard," I objected.

"Well, yes, but you move in certain circles," she replied.

"*Touché.*"

"The most popular theory," Anna continued, "is that it started in the years when Poland was divided between Russia, Prussia, and Austria, that not working for the occupiers was all right. There were only about twenty years in between. Then came the German occupation, then it was the Communist system. Nobody works for himself. The people in the shops, they got paid, no matter whether they sold anything or not; so why bother?" She straightened up into a shrug, and spread her hands in a gesture of hopelessness.

Nor was that the worst of it. "There is something very frightening that is now coming up . . . always hate for people that are different. There are many more slogans on the wall against, for example, Jewish people"—her eyes widened to emphasize the absurdity of it—"and there are basically no Jews in Poland. A few hundred." She supplied the example of people with AIDS trying to establish a hospice in Warsaw. "They found this place, five people with the virus, and they started to live there, and they were almost burned and killed by the neighbours. I think the majority of people in this country are very stupid, and very intolerant. Even the doctors don't want to take care of such people. If the doctors have such attitudes, then ordinary people are absolutely sure that breathing the same air and drinking water from the same well gives you AIDS. I don't know, I'm not very happy about my children growing up in this country," she added, suddenly subsiding, sinking into her chair.

But when I asked her further questions, she pulled herself up from her weariness to produce an additional litany of worries: crime, drugs, poverty, nationalism, the Catholic Church's backward views on abortion. "I'm afraid of the atmosphere of this country that my sons will be growing up in," she reiterated.

"People in North America," I lamely suggested, "are also making complaints, about crime, and drugs, and homelessness."

"Well then, these are about the only things in which we are nearer to the West," she quipped.

At the end, as we were gathering our things to leave, Anna's mood lifted in a sudden moment of reminiscence. "The best time was the last part of 1980, and 1981, when Solidarity started, because then—well, I was ten years younger." Tom and I laughed with her, acknowledging that so were we. "It seemed so wonderful," she said, "everything was wonderful, and it didn't matter that there was nothing in the shops, that you couldn't buy anything. I remember once

I was talking with my best friend—we were pregnant at the same time, she with her second child and I with my first—and we were sitting and talking. There was some strike going on, and we were saying, What happens if the Russians come?, and her husband said, You shouldn't worry, any Russian tank will take you to the hospital for half a litre of vodka." She remembered when they had made jokes, but quickly added, "Then came martial law."

I too remembered it that way. When I had been in Poland before—only months before the military coup ordered by the new party boss, General Wojciech Jaruzelski—it had been a time of dreaming, of tales of heroic deeds in the shipyards, of gentle blond boys who sang punk rock. Upon leaving Gdansk, I'd hosted a farewell dinner for the friends I'd acquired during the weeks of interviewing. We ate at the Grand Hotel on the beach at Sopot. That evening someone spoke of the legendary wild white boars who were reputed to wander the dune grasses at night. We had walked out onto the long wooden jetty that looked across the Baltic to Sweden, and for a moment it felt as if we had left the century, as if, amid the beaches, the imaginary beasts, the grandeur of the old hotel, we had returned to an earlier time, from which we would be able to chart a course that might avert the horrors ahead.

Immediately upon seeing Slawek Starosta—the gay rock singer Olga had suggested I meet—I recognized him as an updated, post-Communist version of Mirek. Starosta poked his head into the cubbyhole at the University of Warsaw where we were waiting for him, to assure us he'd be along in a few minutes. I got a glimpse of a young man, mid-twenties, with a blond brushcut—one lock of hair artfully falling onto his forehead—fashionable gold wire-rimmed glasses, the high collar of an embroidered white Russian peasant shirt.

Until that moment, I had harboured the absurd fantasy that I might run into Mirek again. Instead, the new era was providing a contemporary counterpart in his place. Mirek belonged to another time, a time that was gone and, I dimly intuited, whose passing had somehow taken him with it. I also immediately registered that I would not become infatuated with Slawek, but that I was nonetheless curious about who he might turn out to be.

The manager of Slawek's two-person group, which was called Balkan Electric, brought us coffee as we waited in the high-ceilinged, narrow room that was one of the warren of offices in the student building. I sat next to a tall window whose long wooden shutter had been turned back, providing a view onto Novy Swiat, the busy avenue outside the university. The manager introduced himself as Jarek. He was in his late twenties, a graduate student in political science, with a closely cropped reddish beard and a dark shirt buttoned to the collar. Slawek was momentarily tied up with the arrangements for a concert that night, Jarek apologized.

Instead of waiting around, dawdling over our coffee, as I'd expected, the three of us immediately plunged into a conversation about the very thing Tom and I had often puzzled over when we joked about being "leftists—whatever that means". It began as the usual dissection—at least, usual when you're talking to Polish intellectuals—of complex elements of Polish society and their effect, in turn, upon the equally complex current situation.

Jarek's starting-point was the modern formation of the working class and the rapid movement of the peasantry to the cities after the Second World War. I remembered Anna's unhappy remarks about workers, though she had qualified her criticisms with a historical explanation of their resistance to working for the enemy. "During a very short period," Jarek said, "they became workers in states in which the working class had a special status. They heard from everywhere that this special class should rule the country, should rule the world."

Oddly, it was the success of the Communists in instilling working-class consciousness—even as the workers saw that it was the party and not themselves who were doing the ruling—that had given rise to Solidarity. "In 1980, Solidarity as a workers' movement was acting against what they rightly saw was not the workers' party, but a bureaucracy." And the same was true in the past year, when the party fell. "But this year," Jarek continued, "we can say that what is happening is really against the working class."

When I looked up from my coffee cup, a bit puzzled, he elaborated. "Nobody is going to say, 'You should have a social service because you are a worker.' Nowadays, it's 'We should handle our own business ... and we should help ourselves.' And it really means that egalitarianism, which was very popular in 1980 and which created the movement against bureaucracy, is not valued any more. It's a real break, a big change in society." Was that his personal feeling too? He began by demurring—"I have no opinion"—but then added, "It is not possible within a few months to come out of real, bureaucratic socialism into very poor and very aggressive liberalism, which means you can die in the street if you aren't able to work."

I noticed that Tom and I had suddenly perked up. What had begun as polite conversation to pass the time was unexpectedly revealing itself as fully engaging in its own right. The habit of interviewing often produced pleasant surprises. The Polish word for "interview"—*wywiad* (pronounced "vivyat")—seemed to hint at such intellectual pleasures; its sound suggested the English word "vivid". The interview was a relationship in which a kind of vividness might be achieved by virtue of the unspoken permission to say things that strangers wouldn't normally say to each other. While it courted the danger of superficiality (of course we wouldn't come to know each other in an hour or two), it harboured—like a sudden sexual encounter—the possibility of unexpected vivacity. Identities shifted into focus—the rock band manager became an astute grad student, the foreign visitors were not merely journalists but also participants, and apparently familiar with the references, the vocabulary.

"I was not a Communist," Jarek began again. "I was working here in a student organization which was socialist." We didn't interrupt to determine the distinction between Communists, socialists, and whatever other shadings might exist. "Many people who were non-socialists were members," Jarek went on. "But I was a leftist—and what really happened in our country in the sixties and seventies is that leftists were destroyed."

It was the first time I'd heard someone in Eastern Europe use the word "leftist" in its familiar sense. A decade ago, when I'd asked about the meanings of "left" and "right", my Polish friends had taken great pleasure in sending up those terms. "Okay, let's begin with the Communist Party," they began. "Now that's"—there was a significant pause, as if they were trying to locate it—"the far right," and then everyone broke up in laughter.

"To be a *leftist*"—in some official or practical sense, we understood Jarek to be saying—"meant to be a Marxist-Leninist. Anything which was not linked with the official ideology of the party should be stamped out and persecuted as illegal activity against the state." With the entire space for leftism occupied by the party, there had been no room for alternative versions of a non-capitalist politics, and leftism in general had withered.

"At the same time, the Communists knew that social support for the regime was dropping. So they began to negotiate with the Polish Catholic Church, which really meant that Communists killed leftists in our country, and gave special benefits to the rightists," Jarek argued.

But wasn't the present government—the Solidarity regime of people like Michnik, Lytinski, Kuron, even the weary present prime minister, Tadeusz Mazowiecki—"leftist"? "Yes," Jarek was prompt to concede, "it's a good centre-left government at the moment, but then you have to take into account the currents and tendencies within Solidarity. You see, the Solidarity 'court' in Gdansk is dominated by rightists, who also want the Church to have power."

"Court?" I repeated, to make sure he had used that word in the royalist sense.

"Yes, the entourage around Walesa," Jarek said.

So even if Michnik, Kuron, and Lytinski were what might be called leftists, while Prime Minister Mazowiecki represented the tradition of intellectual Catholicism, both the circumstances of the country and the pressures within Solidarity meant that they found themselves as advocates—more than advocates . . . administrators, even legislators—of a "fast track" transition to the free market. In the long litany of ironies that make up Polish political history, the workers' movement that had ousted the "workers' party" was now issuing the lay-off slips to the workers. Just as Jarek was about to go on, Slawek arrived.

There was an abrupt shift of mood and subject. Jarek and Slawek briefly talked business—that night's concert, no doubt—and then Slawek turned to us, ready to fulfil the combined obligations of rising young rock star and gay activist.

"Can you come to the gig tonight?" he asked.

"Sure," I said, picking up a nod of agreement from Tom. "But first I'd like to know something about the gay movement in Poland."

Slawek sighed, tossing back his head, allowing the one long blond lock at the front of his brushcut to bob up and flop onto his forehead.

"Does everyone from the West ask you that?" Tom chuckled, half apologizing for our obviousness.

Slawek laughed, took a breath, and said, "So, from the beginning . . . ," and since even the two or three years to be recounted seemed like an eternity to someone his age, he sighed again. "The beginning. . . ."

That afternoon, I was on the telephone to Olga from her parents' apartment. "We saw Slawek this morning," I reported.

"Oh, good. How did it go?"

"Fine. Tom and I found him very charming. Ambitious, but charming." Tom had remarked, when we'd finished the interview with Slawek and Jarek and were on our way to our next appointment, "Well, he's full of himself, but they all are at that age." I had laughed, as much at the avuncular heights from which we viewed the young these days as at the accuracy of his observation. "Though not offensive," I amended. "Not offensive," Tom nodded.

It turned out that both Olga and I had a few minutes to chat—our dinner wasn't for an hour, her crowded schedule also happened to have a gap in it; it was one of those rare stretches of timelessness in which two over-busy people discover that they are free to luxuriate.

"We're seeing them for an early dinner tonight, and then we're going to Balkan Electric's concert."

"Did you meet the other singer?"

"Violeta?" I said, recalling the name of the curly-haired young Bulgarian woman—hence the "Balkan" part of the group's name—who was Slawek's stage partner. "Just for a minute. And we had a talk with the manager."

"Slawek's boyfriend," Olga said. Until then, it hadn't occurred to me that they might be lovers.

"Oh, and we saw Peter's aunt afterward," I suddenly

remembered, even as I did a quick double-take to reconfigure Slawek and Jarek's relationship in my mind.

"Yes, Maryla. How was it?"

"A comedy of errors," I said. "She had a message for Peter in Polish which we recorded on the tape, and that was fine."

"That's for the papers Peter has to sign. He should've done it when he came for his father's funeral, but it was all such a hurry, you know." Olga knew all about it—the details of familial property settlements.

"But I had gotten the idea, from Peter I think, that Aunt Maryla was in favour of the party, still, so all my questions were designed to get her to explain why she believed in Communism."

Olga burst out laughing.

"It was a disaster, of course," I admitted. "At one point, after I asked a bunch of questions about Marx, she said, 'I suspect you're leftists.'"

Olga thought that was very funny—the bumbling truth-seekers and the wise old aunt. I can't remember how we got onto the next thing. Perhaps we were talking about the time Peter first returned to Poland to get to know his father, Leonard (and I may have mixed some of this up with things that Peter told Tom and me later), but she said, referring to old Borkowicz, ". . . and he had just been retired from his job."

Olga was about to go on to another thought when I interrupted. "What do you mean, he'd just been retired?"

"Well, in 1967, when the Arab–Israeli War broke out," Olga began. "Just a second, I have to turn the kettle off," she said. "After that war, in 1968," Olga continued, returning to the phone a couple of minutes later with a cup of coffee (I happened to have one at my end, too), "there was a very big wave of anti-Semitism in Poland, and all of the intelligentsia, and most of the Jews who had any kind of post in the party or government, were immediately relieved of their positions. You know, they were accused of being Zionists and . . . well, any kind of Jewish background."

I suddenly recalled that Olga's parents, whose apartment I was in at that moment, were on holiday in Israel. "So, your father too?"

"Oh yes, of course. I mean, Peter's father, Leonard, wasn't a practising Jew or anything like that, but he had a Jewish background, and for anti-Semites, you know, it doesn't really matter."

"So old Borkowicz was basically a party figure."

"And a very distinguished one," Olga said, launching into a précis of Leonard Borkowicz's career. As early as his teenage years, Borkowicz had been imprisoned for being a Communist activist. Before the Second World War, he had already spent perhaps a total of seven years in jail. When the war broke out, Leonard ended up in the Red Army that was being formed in Poland—he, his brother, and his sister.

"You mean Aunt Maryla?"

"Yes," Olga confirmed. Leonard and Maryla's brother died at the battle of Lenino; meanwhile Borkowicz worked his way up the ranks to a fairly high officer's position, colonel or major-colonel. After the war, the party appointed him governor of the district of Szczecin, a sizeable province along the Baltic that had been part of Germany but was now allocated to Poland as a portion of the war settlement. It was a complicated situation, involving both the resettlement of Germans and extensive reconstruction, and Borkowicz had apparently made a success of it. There was a book on the subject, and even a documentary film.

Afterwards, Borkowicz became the Polish ambassador to Czechoslovakia and was stationed in Prague for a couple of years. But the happiest part of his life was after Prague, when he was appointed head of the Polish film industry, a job he evidently enjoyed thoroughly. Peter had told me how, even after his dismissal, his father had maintained his contacts with artists, so that when Peter went to Poland as a teenager to meet Leonard, the renowned director Andrzej Wajda turned up for dinner one night.

The end of Borkowicz's career had been abrupt. The 1967 Arab–Israeli War coincided with one of the periodic convulsions within the party and the country. The Israeli connection provided an excuse to make officials of Jewish origin—they had a long history in the party and were irra-tionally resented, both inside and outside of its ranks—the scapegoats for the crisis of the moment.

"They retired him instantly, just like that," Olga said. "And he was still a young man, you know. He would have been . . . well, he was seventy-seven when he died in 1989, so he would have been—"

"Mid-fifties," I supplied. "And was your father also thrown out?"

"That's right. My father was the minister of health. He and Leonard had been friends since the war. Actually, my mother was in the Red Army with Leonard. But the whole thing was much harder on Leonard. You know, my father was a doctor, so when he was thrown out he was able to go into private practice. But with somebody like Leonard, who was a professional bureaucrat . . . well, it was very hard. In Poland in those days, everybody had a job, and that was one of the ways the state used to punish people. So basically he was left with unemployment, with nothing."

I couldn't recall if I had seen photographs of Leonard Borkowicz at Peter's house, or if Tom had once told me about a dinner at Peter's when the elder Borkowicz was visiting from Poland. In any case, I had the image in my mind of a lean, fit man with a rakish moustache, resembling Peter and similarly animated. Talking to Olga now, I had to take into account that beneath the present surface—rock musicians, Anna's thoughtful worries, the entrepreneurial spirit—there were also long, tangled histories like those of her and Peter's fathers, lives of a generation now coming to an end. The dream, as well as the nightmare of the dream, whose responsibility they had accepted, had ended. They had woken to its emptiness, or had turned to other faiths (did that explain the Titkovs' holiday in Israel?)

"Look, I have afternoon rehearsals this week and I'm due there now," Olga said, "but why don't you and Tom come for dinner tomorrow night? My brother Andrzej will come to get you around six. Is that okay?"

Slawek and Jarek picked us up at the Titkovs' and—all of us crammed into their tiny Polski Fiat—we drove to a Vietnamese restaurant they liked. Slawek was wearing an outlandish, multi-coloured, bright pastel costume, a sort of jumpsuit made of flimsy polyester material. The shirt part had only one lapel-wing on the collar; the other half was in the style of Russian peasant smocks. I figured it was something he'd be wearing on stage that night.

"Yes, but it's also part of Balkan Electric's clothing line," the rock singer explained. He stood up at the table in order to turn around and show us what I took to be a large, garish designer label, in Polish, on the back.

"It says," Jarek translated, "'. . . and it's cheap, too.' You know, like, you can afford it."

"Well, Balcerowicz would approve of your industriousness," I teased. An economic scheme to encourage exactly such entrepreneurial ventures, known as the "Balcerowicz Plan", had been named for the then-current finance minister.

They ignored my irony and went on to describe their idea of setting up a bed-and-breakfast arrangement for gay tourists in Poland. And then there was talk of record contracts, foreign tours, making the hit charts. They were, in that way, just like young, ambitious music producers in Paris or London or New York. They were not at all like my lost Mirek, who sang, not into any horizon of success (no such horizon existed then), but simply to say something about how things were at that moment.

Yet, even as Slawek was enthusiastically embracing the free market, he also wanted to enjoy a rebellious image. He mentioned in passing someone who had been a member of "the late Communist Party", and then, thinking we might view that as a criticism, quickly added, "which I have nothing against. Well, I do have something against it," he amended, "but now I'm more on the Communist side than on the Solidarity side, because I always want to be in the opposition." He laughed, by way of intimating that he was only half serious.

We had consumed the spring rolls and won-ton soup, and while waiting for the pork brochettes we naturally went on to discuss the presidential ambitions of Lech Walesa—it was what everybody talked about at the moment. Anna had declared her disapproval to us. So had Peter's Aunt Maryla. "He's not the right person," she had said. "He should be the leader of the trade unions, not the president."

For a moment I tuned out of the chatter about the charismatic Walesa. Instead, having thought of Maryla, I suddenly remembered what she had said earlier in the day, at the end of our conversation. It had almost slipped my mind.

An image of her tiny apartment—coffee cups and sugar-crusted cookies on a clear glass plate laid out carefully on a tiny table—reappeared before me, as well as the sense she conveyed of her own dignity. When I asked her if she had ever expected the end of Communism, she said, "I never thought I would live to see this."

"Do you feel a great disappointment in terms of your own life?" I asked. All those years in the party, the anti-Semitic dismissals, a tiny, nearly worthless pension at the end. Again, it was one of those "rude" questions you would only think of asking in an interview.

"My own?" she asked.

"Yes," I said.

"No. Goethe said that to be sorry for what you've done in your life means to betray yourself," she replied.

"Well, once Goethe has been cited . . . ," I said, trying to turn her remark into a what-more-can-be-said pleasantry to conclude our chat. But it hadn't been a mere pleasantry.

"Walesa says he doesn't want to run to become president," Jarek was saying, "he's running only because he wants to make the changes faster." Walesa, safe in his Gdansk redoubt but without office, had been coy too. "This is not true. He wants to be a president," Jarek insisted.

I'd met Walesa once, during those weeks in Gdansk a decade ago. I'd tried to apologize to Elena and Kasia, two of the young translators who had accompanied me to the string of interviews with shipyard workers. "No doubt you've heard their stories many times before," I said, by way of thanking them for their extraordinary patience in helping me obtain the precise details about what had happened during the strike that had so shaken the regime. "No we haven't, not at all," Elena replied. For a moment, I was puzzled. But then it turned out that the international press corps, to whom they provided their services, were not the least bit interested in these by-gone tales; they only wanted Walesa's latest pronouncement on the affairs of the moment.

It was, ironically, my patience—which I joked was a Canadian characteristic—that they insisted be rewarded by an interview with the leader of Solidarity. I was taken down the corridor where I'd seen the trade union organizer pass on many days, eventually nodding in my direction as I became a fixture in the local landscape. At the last minute we were joined by an American journalist. Walesa immediately explained to us that he'd been up all night, walking a crying baby—he and his wife had a half-dozen children—in the wee hours.

I wanted to know what Walesa had been doing on the eve of the strike that brought him to fame. At first he impatiently declared that he couldn't remember, but when I pressed him he bluntly, but with good-humoured shrewdness, answered, "Why should I tell you, when I could write the story myself in a book someday?"

I let the American reporter take over. He wanted to know about policies, the balance of power, inherent contradictions. Walesa was suitably enigmatic, oracular. At the end, someone took a snapshot of me standing next to the Solidarity hero, but the light was at our backs, coming through a window, and the photo turned out to be dark, our faces barely discernible.

Jarek and Slawek saw Walesa as an icon of the past, restless and power-hungry, and increasingly dangerous now that he was separated from his original group of social democratic advisers and allied instead to both church and nationalist elements. The centre-leftists were putting up Mazowiecki, the prime minister, to run against the national hero. Jarek and Slawek sneered at Walesa's political ignorance, and his allegedly unintelligible use of the Polish language. "We have to wait for the English translation of his speeches to find out what he said," Slawek improbably claimed.

In the car on the way to the concert, Slawek mentioned that he'd be performing his latest song that evening. It had been occasioned by a project he'd undertaken on AIDS education.

"I decided to write a song—just a love song," he explained. "It's called 'Do Love, Don't Kill'."

"Like 'Make Love, Not War'?" I asked.

"Yeah. It's really our first song in Polish, even though the title's in English, because I wanted people to understand what we're singing about. The song, actually, is not about safe sex. It's more general, about love and . . . there's one small fragment in the text where you can find out that I'm singing this love song to a guy."

I'd wanted to know how explicit or "out" he was. "You and Jarek seem to be pretty discreet as a couple," I observed. "But are there times when you've had to make clear your sexual preference?"

"Well, *clear*," Slawek replied, drawing out that word and seemingly dwelling upon it. "I mean, I don't like to be over-homosexual. I don't like anything that is too clear. That's straight, or that's serious. So no, I never gave an interview where I said, I'm gay, or I'm homosexual. But always I make some remark, like I gave an interview and said, 'Balkan Electric loves young and handsome men.' I think it's clear enough."

I wasn't sure what I wanted, or what I was looking for. Well, I did know: I was looking for Mirek, and I wanted, for better or worse, Solidarity as it had been. Back when I had interviewed the workers at the Lenin Shipyard, they had joked about the impossibility of "privatization" and instead were groping towards a notion of industries run by a "workers' council" within the context of a socialist market. "After all," they quipped, "we can't return the shipyard to the Lenin family." But the present moment was deromanticized:

the hero had become a populist with demagogic possibilities; the gay young rock star managed his identity with an
understated, fashionably entrepreneurial touch; even parts of
the shipyard were being sold to an American industrial
heiress of Polish descent.

"You know, for me it's like I went through twenty years
of the gay liberation movement in six months," Slawek said.
"I mean, coming out to my parents, the gay-is-good thing,
militancy, the infighting of gay politics, AIDS, everything. It
was all speeded up." Perhaps everything in Poland had been
speeded up in the same way—democracy, capitalism, individual lives.

Jarek found a parking place in front of the Remont student club. Early arrivals were standing around on the sidewalk. Going down the steps into its semi-basement past a
ticket-taker, I recognized the club as the one in which I had
heard Mirek sing. Jarek and Slawek went into the hall to set
up.

There was a large foyer, with walls painted black, outside
the auditorium. Along one side was a bar where you could
get beer and soft drinks. Tom bought me a mineral water.
Most of the space was taken up by a raised lounge area filled
with tables and chairs; some kids sat on the ledge of the floor
space. A couple of televisions were showing safe-sex educa-
tional videos made in Norway; naked young men swam
across each others' bodies, a beautifully toned boy's thigh
was caressed by a male hand, a bare butt turned in a half-
light of shadow.

In the gathering crowd, I noticed—and the awareness was
sudden, as if my desire had been dormant for days—several

beautiful boys, teenagers, scattered among the couples and grad students, along with a sprinkling of the middle-aged. I fastened on two kids, maybe seventeen or eighteen, who appeared to be together, sitting up against the far wall. One was a blond in a black shirt, athletic, thick-fingered, sombre-faced with classically handsome features. His companion was lithe, animated, wearing a brightly patterned T-shirt.

As they sipped soft drinks, sitting side by side, casually absorbing the homoerotic images that flickered on the screens, I wondered what they saw. How did it appear to them? Slawek had told me that, though he had had brief affairs while travelling—there had been a Norwegian for a week, then a German—he hadn't met a gay man in Poland until he was twenty-two. When one youth in the Norwegian video ran a hand over the inside fleshy part of the other boy's thigh, did these two boys see each other in their places? How small a quantity of the erotic it required for me to become entranced by desire. A face, a movement (the way the lithe one gestured with his hand), a glimpse of the enticing mystery of them awakened me. They were two boys sitting in a basement student café, in the range of a (global) machine that was simply *on*—others in the lounge, engaged in conversation, drinking a beer, could ignore it with the casualness that television-viewing proposed—its multiple, replicating screens showing, if only you had an eye for it, the most secret gestures, body parts, and intimacies imaginable.

Inside the hall, people stood pressed together in the darkness. Slawek and Violeta, accompanied by synthesizers, tambourines, and rattles, appeared on stage, fashioning a wonderfully exotic yet recognizable set of rock songs—

lilting Bulgarian folk melodies meshed with the percussive thump upon which we'd been raised. We were swept into its rhythms. Someone released a beachball-sized balloon that bounced over the crowd, an occasional hand punching it back up into the air when it drifted down to us. The two boys stood shoulder to shoulder next to me, the butch one with crossed arms, swaying a bit to the music; his Ariel-like companion was on the verge of dancing. Later, after the concert ended, as the crowd flowed through the lounge onto the street, I watched them leave together. What do they talk about on the way home? Is there a place for them—a room, a dark corner of a park in the warm spring night? What do they do with each other? Do wisps of the TV images, of the refrains from Balkan Electric's songs, haunt their minds as a hand with delicate fingers urgently unzips the fly of the sturdy blond boy? At the end of Communism, lovers . . . still slightly furtive, uncertain.

Jan Lytinski's office was in a corner of a chunky four-storey labour ministry building in one of the sidestreets of downtown Warsaw, just behind the Forum Hotel on Marshalkowska Boulevard.

Lytinski was sitting at the far side of the room, in front of a glowing computer screen, when the secretary ushered us in. He detached himself from the machine and came over to join us. We sat on opposite sides of his desk. The ski sweater had been exchanged for an inexpensive, somewhat shabby suit, but he was recognizably the slight, greying man, worn beyond his forty-five or so years, whom we had seen in the *New York Times* photograph.

Despite his accountant-like appearance, during the 1980s—from the inception of martial law in 1981 until the resurfacing of the opposition at the end of the decade—it was people such as Lytinski who were arrested and tried, who served time in jails and internment camps, escaped, and issued declarations from the underground. They had, in Michnik's phrase, borne "moral witness". In the West, we had almost forgotten about them.

"It was a strange and interesting time," Lytinski reflected, when I asked him about it. "The struggle between the government and Solidarity was like a positional war. It was obvious that nobody was able to win. And in some sense," he added, "it was a lost period. Because under the cover of martial law, the Communists tried to make economic reform. But they failed. They destroyed the whole system, the whole economy, practically, with martial law, but they didn't build any other system."

"But wasn't it also a lost period personally for many people?"

He made a sound in his throat as he considered how to revisit the past.

"Do you remember where you were on December 13, 1981?" I asked, slightly shifting tack; this was the date that martial law had been declared.

"I'd just come back from some lectures in the south of Poland," he answered. "We were forming what were called self-management clubs. When I got to Warsaw, the telephones had been cut off. I returned to my flat and the police were already there."

There was a soft knock at the door. It was the secretary,

bringing coffee and a sheaf of papers which Lytinski thumbed through.

"These are the month's unemployment figures," he said, pushing the papers in my direction. There were columns of numbers listing the jobless by cities and regions. The total came to about a quarter of a million people. "We're trying, according to the plan, to hold the figure to about 400,000."

Though we were urged by the present—fluid, troubling, unknowable—it was the lost years of the past that drew me. What had he thought then?

"I felt from the very beginning that it was a kind of tragi-farce. In the internment camp the conditions were quite good. We had books, we could write. Some people said they were tragic conditions, but it was not true," he modestly testified. "But it was also a comedy. In the street, people were being arrested for wearing Solidarity badges."

Lytinski had gone on trial, along with Michnik and Kuron, in the fall of 1982. "We were sentenced to two and a half years." But he'd escaped the following year and melted into the Solidarity underground in Warsaw. They had been desultory years. The structures and committees they attempted to organize, the occasional demonstration they set up from the shadows, the manifestos that were issued, had a certain futility to them. "But we signed our statements with our names," Lytinski quietly insisted.

"Did you have to move around?"

"It was a very complicated system of changing flats, but we practically lived a normal life. Yet it was a very bad situation. It was normal life without normal responsibility. Very demoralizing," he said, then added, "It's much easier to be in prison and afterwards get back into normal life than it is to return from the underground."

The phone rang. While Lytinski talked to someone at the other end, Tom and I exchanged a connecting glance as we listened to the traffic outside in the sunny spring forenoon. We had developed a sort of minor telepathy while conducting interviews, a delicate sensing of which one of us ought to "lead" the questioning. I appreciated Tom's patience with my drawn-out pursuit of the details of an old story.

"That was from Gdansk, a friend," Lytinski explained, when he'd hung up. Solidarity was holding its first congress since the fall of the Communist government—actually its first congress since just before martial law was declared.

"How's it going?" I asked.

"My friend said it's very boring," he chuckled, and we, veteran meeting-goers ourselves, laughed with him.

Solidarity had outgrown its trade-union origins long ago, but now its character as a civic movement—born at a time when the notion of civil society had been repressed—was coming apart at the seams. Proto-parties were emerging from its factions. "Walesa is a real problem," Lytinski remarked. I was more interested in why, and how, Communism had fallen.

At the end—in late 1987, through 1988, into the spring of 1989—power had changed hands, almost imperceptibly to those of us outside the situation, at a series of so-called round table discussions. Lytinski had been part of the sub-table negotiations concerning the mining industry. I asked him if it had been obvious that Jaruzelski's government would have to make concessions allowing the relegalization of Solidarity.

"To me it was quite obvious, and to many of us, that we weren't paying anything," Lytinski replied, "that every agreement was to our benefit." He shrugged. "We had nothing to offer. It was obviously the beginning of the end of the system."

But surely Jaruzelski's aim had been for the party to retain power.

"They had no choice once the process started," Lytinski said. "Of course, nobody predicted it would develop so fast. And yes, they hoped that they could save the power." But the party made mistakes—technical mistakes, Lytinski called them—when they agreed to the first partial elections, which would permit Solidarity to gain parliamentary representation while the party retained its formal majority. They hadn't anticipated that the results of the election, technicalities aside, would spell the party's doom.

"Had the party abandoned all ideological beliefs by then?" I wondered.

"They had lost a sense of their existence. In the election they tried to attack us on TV, but it was ridiculous. Of course, it didn't seem so ridiculous then," he amended. "The campaign was a struggle about memory: they tried to remind people of the disorder of the last period of Solidarity, before martial law, and we tried to remind them of the first period of Solidarity, of hope."

We went downstairs and walked towards the nearby Forum Hotel for lunch, through the falling confetti of the blossoming fruit trees that lined the sidestreets. Lytinski asked how we were getting on in Warsaw.

"We were at a rock concert last night," Tom reported.

"Oh, yes. Which one?"

"A group called Balkan Electric."

"Oh, they're one of the best right now," Lytinski said. Tom and I exchanged a surprised glance.

"You listen to rock music?" Tom asked him.

It turned out that our shy labour ministry official was rather thoroughly knowledgeable. As we strolled towards the hotel, he recalled that during the days of the underground he and a co-fugitive—a man named Bujak, who was the head of the Warsaw underground—found themselves in a strange apartment, headphones in place, lost in the sounds of the Beatles' *Abbey Road*. We laughed, picturing the incongruity of a world in which the authorities scoured the streets for opponents who had disappeared, borne away on the lilting wave of romantic rock 'n' roll.

"When I was here before, in '81, there was a group called Crisis," I said. "Did you ever hear of them?"

Lytinski paused to search his memory. "Yes . . . yes, I think so."

"I was friends with their lead singer—his name was Mirek." Perhaps I hadn't abandoned my absurd hopes.

Lytinski thought again. "No, I don't know what became of them," he said.

The ground-floor lobby of the hotel was unexpectedly crowded with noisy teenagers. They appeared to be in some sort of uniform, and most of them had knapsacks. As we threaded our way through their loud chatter in various languages, I saw that it wasn't exactly uniforms, but that they were wearing similar clothing, lots of short-sleeved white shirts and blouses, and then I noticed that most of the boys were sporting yarmulkas, and that there was a scattering of blue-and-white Israeli flags. They were young Jews.

We'd been haunted by the presence of actual and remembered Jews in the last days: Anna's complaints about the absurdity of the current anti-Semitic remarks—"and there are, basically, no Jews in Poland; a few hundred"; the stories about the party purge of old Borkowicz and Titkov; Olga, her brother, Andrzej, Michnik himself. For that matter, I was one of that wandering tribe too. Still, finding them in the hotel lobby, in sudden profusion, was like encountering a herd of unicorns.

It was some sort of Israeli-sponsored youth convention in which the youngsters—according to the banners and signs that Lytinski translated for us—would be travelling to Auschwitz-Birkenau to tour the concentration camps in remembrance of the countless dead who had been slaughtered in Poland a half-century before. Their natural ebullience jarred against the grisly prospect that awaited them.

Nor were the young Jews the only mythical creatures on view. There was one last ghostly apparition. At the door of the restaurant, a man was coming out as we were going in, and we squeezed past each other.

Once seated at the linen-covered table, Lytinski remarked, "That was my secret policeman."

At first we didn't know whom he was referring to, then we tried to recall the nondescript figure we'd passed a moment before.

"Your secret policeman?" I asked, a bit puzzled by the possessive adjective.

"Yes, that's the man who was assigned to keep me under surveillance." Lytinski seemed amused that history had contrived to make them diners at the same restaurant. We glanced back at the empty doorway.

The matter of belief continued to nag at me, even as lunch was drawing to a close. Perhaps I was only wondering about my own convictions. If the party had ended up without belief, was it nonetheless not possible that the ideas in whose name they had ineptly (even brutally) ruled still meant something? "Or has Marxism become utterly meaningless?" I asked.

Lytinski didn't answer immediately. He lit a cigarette and, through exhaled smoke, finally declared, "Yes, it's the end of Marxism as an ideology." He paused. "All over the world. Not only here. I think that Marx is a very interesting thinker, but not a man whose ideas can create political movements. Now Marx finds his proper place in history as a philosopher."

"A philosopher?" I repeated.

"Yes, understood by specialists," Lytinski confirmed. "Nobody knows exactly what the 'left' is—" Once more, the puzzling definition of ourselves appeared before us.

"I think of Kuron and Michnik as the left," I interjected.

"They are described as leftists, but what does it mean today?" He shrugged, perhaps including himself in that fading definition. "Of course, there is a difference of attitudes between various groups," he granted, "but the left is no longer a reality, as it still may be in the West. Here everybody simply connects it with the former system."

"So if Marx returns to philosophy, Lenin simply returns

to history," I suggested. I recalled Konwicki's mockery in *A Minor Apocalypse*, describing how, from the ageing party building "already showing cracks at various spots" a vast white banner fluttered in a breeze, hysterically proclaiming, "We have built socialism!"

Lytinski seemed willing to let it rest there. "Lenin returns to history," he exhaled.

Woven into the fringes of interviews, histories, and the rest of our activity of "gathering material", our own lives in Warsaw—Tom's and mine—were slowly being fashioned among the days. Mine was meditative, dreamy, memory-filled. At any given moment I might drift off from the scene before me, even as it continued to register in consciousness, and fall into a half-trance that mixed past events and reverie.

The day was ordered by the practical tasks we organized under the rubric of understanding "the fall of Commmunism". Yet the incipient lives we had begun living here had a dimension apart from what we were formally doing, an in-ternality which, if pursued, might yield persons slightly different from who we imagined ourselves to be. Tom and I had been friends all of our mid-adult lives, sharing depths of feeling whose navigation required few words. Still, we were a study in contrasts.

I, who was outwardly unflappable by day, tossed and turned in my monk's cell at night, as the shades of blond boys flitted through vast chambers; Tom, admittedly noisy by day—his sneezes and bursts of laughter richocheted through rooms and streets—slept without snoring, subsid-ing into the slumber of the just. Though he was volatile, insistently Utopian, while I was measured, wary even, nonetheless practical matters fell to him. It was Tom who endured the gruelling chores of waiting in line for train tickets, obtaining transit visas, hauling the heaviest part of the baggage; I was a slacker, suddenly (slyly?) hopeless at the simplest tasks. Tom still sought—to cite that aphorism from Marx's *Theses on Feurbach* that urged action over interminable contemplation—to change the world (he sought out grouplets, networks); I had become interested (finally? despairingly?) in trying to understand it.

If I was dreamy, Tom was diligent. In the mornings he hopped into his grey jogging sweats and went off for a long run. Though I'd never seen him at it—only his going and then coming back, coated in sweat, peeling off his gear on the way to the bath—I imagined his running to be peaceful, something like the flight of birds.

Meanwhile I was left at the dining-room table, hunched over a book (Konwicki's novel), drinking coffee, wreathed in cigarette smoke. I had been up for some time, having risen from the narrow child's bed in my room (had Olga once slept there? or her brother Andrzej?). As I stumbled through my morning toilette and boiled water for coffee, the ghosts who had haunted me at dawn slowly faded.

I gradually woke up—it took me hours—into the city imagined by the Polish novelist. In fact, in each place I went to I seemed to acquire a sort of muse or guide. Konwicki's Warsaw required no less than a Virgil to lead you through its surrealistic, decaying, mouldering inferno. In the present, bucolic Warsaw in which I dreamed, outside the french doors on my left, a chestnut tree filled most of the space in the semi-courtyard, almost growing onto the wrought-iron balcony (had I ever seen such a tree before?); on the wall before me I gazed, as I had for days, upon a painting of a woman walking towards me on a white gravel path.

But in Konwicki's Warsaw, rising up in my imagination, the Palace of Culture was mildewed, lichen-covered, sweating; trams inexplicably broke down in mid-route; the careening police cars always had a headlight out; "a great cloud of virulent exhaust fumes from poorly tuned motors floated down the shallow ditch that was Novy Swiat Street." In apocalyptic Warsaw, bridges collapsed into the sewer of the Vistula River, escarpments tumbled from buildings ("Suddenly a slab of sandstone went flying off the Palace of Culture, taking a wreath of lightbulbs with it as it fell"), planes casually crashed ("something had gone wrong, some defect, and the silvery, rust-eaten machine began plunging toward the beach on the other side of the Vistula with the obvious intention of nose-diving onto the golden sands of that broad shore").[2]

Amid the foamy water from burst waterpipes, the liquefying asphalt of the streets, the senile, lumbering figures of the party congress whose antics appeared on ubiquitous television sets ("Someone had turned off the sound as people always do when programs like that are on"), "Suddenly and for no special reason," announced Konwicki, "I felt like looking at the world around me, to see nature ... which, it seems, is dying out and had been mourned for years before indifference was finally victorious.... I was looking in the direction of the Poniatowski Bridge, which had unfortunately collapsed a few hours back. It was no great catastrophe, there were other bridges. Anyway, I was looking toward the Vistula and I could see the blackened tops of the houses on the shore, I could see the poisonous mouth of the river, the beaches at Praga. . . . A crippled landscape, ugly yet at the same time beautiful, because it was all we had left, and so that dolorous sight, gale-tossed and lashed by hail every quarter of an hour, still gave me some heart." At the end, my crotchety muse simply sighed, "this city of ours, this dying microcosm in the middle of Europe."

Andrzej led us from our nest of narrow streets to a similar tangle of meandering lanes nearby, where Olga and her husband lived. Her brother was a small, delicately built man whose temperament seemed at once sweet and melancholy. He worked as a film director, making both documentaries and dramatic features.

"Olga said that perhaps you might like to see something," he shyly offered.

"Very much," Tom accepted.

"Well, there's a VCR there. We'll see." He was more interested, he warned us, in the psychology of relationships than in anything political. Tom and I liked him immediately.

Olga's apartment was comfortable, spacious, thoughtfully arranged. She was at the stove in a large, open kitchen; an island work-counter separated the cooking area from the table, which was already set. An uncorked bottle of white wine awaited us.

Yet I had to take only one look at Olga—even as we were in the midst of greetings, and she was asking, "Shall I pour you a glass. . .?"—before I interrupted, asking, "What's wrong?" The uncanny intimacy I had experienced with her, as if we had known each other for a long time, suffused our brief relation with sudden intuition.

"Last night, at the theatre," she replied without preamble, "minutes before we were to go on, the assistant director had a heart attack and died." He had been a young man—only forty-two—and they had known each other for years.

For a moment the four of us were caught in a pall of silence, Tom and I buffeted by a grief that wasn't ours, but that touched us nonetheless. But the small pleasures of the living, suddenly magnified, summoned us; we must go on. Olga invited us back from the sharp edge of mortality, lifting the beaded bottle of wine and filled our glasses. The dead man returned to her private sorrow.

After dinner, she urged Andrzej to show us some of his work. I noticed that she displayed a protectiveness towards her brother, and guessed it might have something to do with her commercial success, or her husband's; perhaps she feared that Andrzej's work would be in some way overshadowed.

In the living room, Andrzej slid a cassette into the machine. It was a documentary he'd made recently about a Gestalt therapist. Although I couldn't follow the bearded group leader's version of therapy—it was in Polish, of course, and took place in a forest—Tom, who worked as a therapist among his various other occupations, didn't have any trouble understanding what was going on.

Then Andrzej showed a second film, one that required no linguistic or therapeutic skills for comprehension. It was an intense, brief portrait (no more than ten minutes), without dialogue, of the old Jewish section of the city of Krakow, in the south of Poland. There was simply a succession of images of its present streets, eerily depopulated, with patches of cracked plaster walls, light on the narrow brick lanes, bits of colour, a doorway; interspersed with those mundane scenes were stretches of historical footage from the 1930s, in black and white, of Krakow's ghetto. From that other world, men in long dark coats, women, their children, shuffled into groups, herded towards an impending horror. I strained to catch their fleeting faces as if I were trying to spot a relative arriving in the crowd at an airport. In the space between their innocence and our knowledge of what happened, clouds reflected on a tombstone rushed across its face in a time-lapse sequence.

Later in the evening, when we had drifted back to the kitchen table and Andrzej had opened another bottle of wine, I asked Olga, "Well, what exactly happened?"

She had been at the sink, rinsing a glass, and was coming to join us, drying her hands on a dish towel.

"One morning, Leonard Borkowicz called my father and said to him, Come over at ten-thirty," she began, again in no doubt as to what I was asking about. "My father said, Why? Just come over, Leonard tells him. So my father comes over at ten-thirty, and Leonard is dead."

"No," I murmured. So this was Borkowicz's death, which Olga had alluded to that first day.

Leonard was in his bed, the poison or pills (I didn't ask which) having fulfilled his intentions. Olga paused to shade in the complications. There was a second wife—"she didn't live with him"—a girlfriend or mistress, perhaps, due to arrive at noon—"He didn't want her to find him; and there's a daughter and, well, you know. . . ."

"Families," I said.

"Families," Olga repeated. "So you know what it's like. He wanted it done that way and that's how it turned out. You know, since my father's a doctor, he would see Leonard's body, take care of it—"

"So your father found him. . . ."

"Yes, he finds him. No pulse"—she shrugged—"so he calls an ambulance. Well, you know, they take forever to come. So Uzek comes—"

"Uzek?"

"One of my father's friends. He used to be in the security service. So he says, I'll call the Minister of Security—well, actually it's the ex-minister because—" Olga made an impatient gesture with her fingers to signal the inevitable tangle of relations and assumptions that undergirded even the simplest anecdote—in this instance the whole group of retired and purged and pensioned-off former officials. "So Uzek calls the ex-minister, the ex-minister calls the present minister, and he sends over some agents to handle this, because the police and the ambulance aren't coming, you know, it's just a corpse. But for the party, it's a delicate matter, so they send these guys over. And there's a note."

"Borkowicz left a suicide note?"

"And he wanted to show them the note—"

"This is your father, now?"

"My father and Uzek. They don't, you know, want to be accused of murder or whatever. So they show one of the agents the note."

For a moment the apocalyptic comedy of my muse Konwicki began to leer. His catastrophic, crumbling Warsaw seeped into the tale—the missing ambulance, bumbling party hacks stumbling around the furniture, the stillness of the body that was once the living Borkowicz.

"So he starts reading the note out loud."

"The agent?"

"Yes. And then he comes to the last part of it, and—it's a very short note, I've seen it, and it's mostly instructions for my father to handle the burial, and so on—and the agent gets to the last part of it, the last sentence. And it says, 'Just so there's no misunderstanding: I am glad to have seen the end of Communism.'"

"That's the last line?" I gasped.

"He just put that in, I'm glad to have seen the end of Communism. Well, this guy's reading this, and he's like, Oh God!"

We laughed with Olga as the elements of the "tragifarce"—was that what Lytinski had called it?—collided once more. There were motives, consequences, intentions to sort out, and for a few minutes we awkwardly asked the usual questions. There wasn't a "reason" for Borkowicz's suicide, at least not one that was sharply delineated; he was seventy-seven, he ... well, there was whatever there was. The last line of his note, however, had a practical import. If it was the intention of the party to use his death, by means of a public funeral for an "old and honoured comrade", in the struggle over memory, Borkowicz's note had effectively forestalled it.

But underneath it all—the contested politics, the absurdities, the aspect of mortality that is always grotesque—there was Borkowicz himself, at the end, alone, writing a note which in its own way was also a testimony, a declaration of "moral witness", as Michnik had put it.

Both then, at the moment of Olga telling us of it, and much later (after we had seen Peter and gone through the story again), my breath was taken away by Borkowicz's suicide note. It was as if I had come all this way to hear a shaggy-dog story, one drawn out over days, weaving its way through other conversations, events, reflections, before delivering its punch-line. At times—after Olga had first remarked, "You know about Borkowicz's death, of course" —I had simply forgotten about it, filed it away (under the heading "If you think of it, remember to ask Olga"), consigned it to the casual details that knit together the familial web of Peter's kin.

Just so there's no misunderstanding, Borkowicz had written. But what was our understanding? You come to a place, irrespective of what you may know (having read Michnik's essay, Konwicki's novel, having loved Mirek), in a state of more or less thorough ignorance. And there's an initial insight that whatever you encounter is, more or less accurately, a *core sample*, that it constitutes a representation of all there is. Anna, Balkan Electric, Lytinski, Borkowicz's death. Just a moment of understanding before becoming ignorant again—now profoundly rather than naively ignorant—upon recognizing the complexity of what there is.

But afterwards it would remain with me, stay in my mind, seem to be one of the essential features of the idea of "the fall of Communism". It fell because a man, in the penultimate act of his life, could declare, Just so there's no misunderstanding, I am glad to have seen the end of Communism.

I stood on the crowded platform of the railway station, waiting for the Warsaw-Berlin train to begin boarding. The long line of dun-coloured passenger cars stretched down the track under the vaulted roof of the gloomy terminal. Tom and Andrzej had gone off for a minute to check our booking. Andrzej, though he was in the middle of shooting a play for television, had sweetly come along to see us off.

The woman who happened to be standing next to me—she was heavily made up, and filled out a floral-patterned silk dress—told me that her brother lived in West Berlin. "But they're trying to deport him," she said. "They treat Poles badly." On the other hand, she couldn't really blame them, because many Poles—and here she indicated the nervous crowd about to pack the train, many of them travelling to Germany to buy goods that could be resold on the Polish market—were loutish drunks, avaricious, etc. I lost a sentence or two as I lit a cigarette. ". . . and the Jews," she was heatedly saying.

The crowd surged onto the high metal stairs, mounting the train cars. Andrzej and Tom turned up and we began wrestling with our oversupply of baggage, clutching tickets, saying farewell. I was halfway down a crammed corridor, trying to locate a compartment number. Tom was at the far end of the car, where Andrzej was passing him the last of our luggage from the platform.

The rest happened both very quickly and with aqueous slow motion. I was partway into a compartment, jostled by several people behind me who were insistently shoving to secure scarce places. I attempted to heave my suitcase onto a luggage rack, at the same time half turning my head to offer verbal reassurance to the figures behind me, bulky men, a mass of bodies in an oozing scrum that surged along the narrow corridor.

As I twisted, I caught a glimpse of Tom, at the end of the car. He was bellowing, a fearsome wounded sound coming out of his throat, his face contorted with rage and pain, screaming, hoping that making as much noise as possible would somehow save us.

"They've got everything," he yelled, seeing me down the corridor. I reached for my wallet. It was gone. Tom had the passports, travellers' cheques, tickets. They were gone, too. For a second I quietly anticipated the mess of the next several days.

Outside the car, on the platform, a blur of running figures surged past Andrzej's vain efforts to stop them. I watched through a dusty window as his slight body, one arm outstretched, toppled to the ground. For the briefest moment, as though it were the sort of freeze-frame he might shoot in one of his films, I saw Andrzej's falling body caught in the not-yet-created world after the end of Communism.

Berlin/Boyopolis

Thoughts on
Representation,
Desire, Epistemology

Double Exposure

HERE'S A PHOTOGRAPH—taken by Herbert List in 1933, somewhere along the Baltic seacoast— of a masked teenage boy (or actually two masked boys, who are one and the same—the shot is a double exposure). The boy's hair is dishevelled by the sea breeze, his torso bared; there's a beach in the background. The mask is white with oval eye-cutouts, the kind you get at birthday parties. It descends about two-thirds of the way down his nose, the tip of which peeks out, touched by pale sunlight.[1]

"Every picture is a detective story," said my friend Michael Morris, a Canadian painter living in Berlin, who had given me List's photos to look at. "A story of relationships," he added.

Michael struck a match and held it beneath the kettle on the stove to light the gas. I'd just dumped my bags in the

room between the kitchen and Michael's studio, where I'd
be staying for the remainder of spring and most of that summer. My body felt as if it had momentarily separated from
the rest of me. I asked Michael distracted questions about
events since I'd passed through Berlin the previous year—a
desultory collection of topics that ranged from the effects of
German unification to whether there were any interesting
gay bars in east Berlin.

Baltic Sea, Germany, Circa 1933

But my panicky body was otherwise engaged, seeking
familiarity in mundane things. I was re-registering what
it knew: the location of the bathroom (just down the
hallway, next to the kitchen), the chestnut tree in the courtyard outside the third-floor windows, even the comforting

embrace—a few seconds before—with Michael. The photo of the masked boy was the first thing I saw. The beauty of his delicate torso put me back in touch with myself.

List, the son of a Hamburg coffee importer, had been about thirty when he shot the photograph. Flipping through the pages of the book, I'd innocently asked Michael, "And who is List?" He related the details: List had been to Latin America—to Brazil, among other places—for the family firm, but after his father died in 1931 he took over the business in the venerable trading city on the Elbe; at the same time, he also devoted increasing attention to photography.

He had taken pictures of boys before. In fact, an early one—of a young swimmer in a skimpy white bathing suit standing in thigh-high water—turns up on the cover of Stephen Spender's belatedly published gay novel, *The Temple*. There was a copy of the novel, I'd noticed, in the bookshelf alongside the narrow bed where I would sleep. Although I'd seen that cover photo in the bookstores several times, vaguely admiring it each time I passed, it was only now that I realized it was by List. Once I began reading Spender I'd discover that the photographer was also a character in the novel.

According to the biographical notes appended to List's book of photos (I pieced it out in my rudimentary German), "He roamed through Hamburg and the surrounding countryside, taking his camera with him on weekend trips to the Baltic beaches, where he staged his first surrealistic still-lifes, often with young friends, whom he incorporated into his images." This was when he began to investigate the mystery of the boys' beauty, rather than simply offering artifacts of his adoration.

So I begin with that photograph of List's. I'd expected to continue my irregular researches on the fall of Communism, get to know Berlin, improve my German, read a little philosophy (I was thinking about epistemology, the study of how and/or why we know anything)—but instead there was a photograph.

I didn't know Berlin, east or west, pre- or post-Communist. Tom and I had passed through the previous year, but we only paused long enough to "cover" the East German election in March 1990—I had the vague notion that I might write some analysis of it for one of the newspapers back home.

It had been billed in the press as the "first free election" in the German Democratic Republic (D.D.R.) As it turned out—given the unification of Germany in October 1990—it was also the last free election in the D.D.R. In fact, it wasn't even all that free, seeing as how the major West German political parties swooped in and established well-funded, slickly promoted eastern subsidiaries. The event, in retrospect, resembled a highly financed corporate takeover more than an electoral contest.

The band of intellectual dissidents and reformers—I'd seen them on television in 1989, just before the Wall came down, addressing huge rallies from a balcony overlooking a square in Leipzig—was soon relegated to the political sidelines. Though they had been instrumental in toppling the already shaky Communist government that had ruled since the end of the Second World War, the reformers were themselves swept aside (the independent party they formed received only three or four per cent of the votes).

The headline I read the morning after the election (in the *Wall Street Journal*, I think) was "Funeral in Berlin"—the funeral being that of Communism. The burial of the hopes of the dissidents and the reformers, as well as the possibility of some alternative to existing social systems, was ignored.

Even by the time of the elections, less than half a year after the opening of the Berlin Wall, the West had lost interest in the details of the outcome; it merely wanted confirmation of its beliefs, not the contemplation of ironies.

When Tom and I were waiting for our flight home from Berlin in 1990, I'd found a moment to call Michael. Had I said something as casual as "Well, maybe I'll come back next summer"? It seemed silly, or worse, to have obtained no more than a glimpse of Berlin, since the city would likely be pivotal in the development of the new societies made out of Communism's ruins. But was I expressing an intention, or merely admitting an inadequacy? And when I returned, did I intend to make a "reading" of the situation? I had met a woman—a church pastor—in a café in Alexanderplatz, on the night of the election; I'd had lunch with a Communist reformer, the deputy editor of a newspaper. Their phone numbers were still in my notebook. Or were my intentions more diffuse?

Whatever I'd intended, I began with the photographs of Herbert List. There must have been walks in between, meals, conversations—the things you do when you arrive—but all that day, into the evening, I looked at photographs.

The masked boy holds his hands out; in each of his upturned palms there appears to be a good-sized white pebble. They're hard to make out, partly from the overlapping exposures, but more because of the way his fingers shield them. Indeed, it's his fingers I see: ample, surprisingly thick for his boyish body, perhaps grains of sand clinging to the skin. The blunt fingers look as though they might come forward through the surface of the print. As soon as that thought occurred to me, I saw that the *fixity* of the photograph engendered the desire to see it move, to see a story begin. In this case, it was a simple erotic fantasy in which the cupped palm that held an egg-shaped pebble now slid forward, tidelike, between my legs, the fingers brushing the insides of my thighs, until—as easily as they cupped a stone—they held my balls.

The reading lamp on the trestle table where I worked glowed in the chill of early evening. List too may have had just such a lamp. He ordered the furniture for his studio apartment, according to Spender—I'd begun reading his novel—from a commercial outlet for the products of the Bauhaus school. It was the sort of thing, Spender claimed, that would get noticed in Hamburg in the late 1920s. The thought crossed my mind that even the illumination of rooms had a history, significance, that the light in the room where I worked had first appeared in rooms such as List's, with the lamps designed by Wagenfeld (Michael told me his name). Milky opal glass cupola, industrial chrome fittings, transparent stem, and green-tinged base of Scottish pyrex. It was a declaration of affinity with "the modern".

So were the photos, which wed the cult of the body (the adolescent boy's body of the youth movement) to motifs from surrealism (Man Ray, Max Ernst, de Chirico's *The Enigma of Arrival*), yielding a cool "decadence". Double image, then:

Herr List by day, the Hamburg coffee merchant in herring-bone tweed; but on weekends Herbert List, with a camera eye to the erotic. He's in a white shirt, sleeves rolled to the elbows, at the beach on the Baltic, breeze against his forehead, taking pictures of a masked boy in swim trunks. There's a snapshot of List at the back of his book of photographs.

Later I found another photo of List, taken by Spender during a walking trip along the Rhine in 1929. He's sitting on a bench, alone, wearing leather shorts, with bare tanned legs, his flesh more a gleaming pelt than skin; Spender speaks of his "jet-black Aztec eyes".

But I mustn't yet think of List as the isolated figure he would become. As Spender's portrait of Hamburg in the late 1920s makes clear, he was hardly alone, but rather in the midst of parties, frolics, friends. He had been instructed in the use of cameras by a young photographer named Andreas Feininger. His friends were students, young artists, attractive girls and boys, children of the mercantile bourgeoisie in the days of the Weimar Republic.

And what about Spender himself? In *The Temple*, the tall, gawky, straw-haired English youth records himself as the uncomfortable object of the desire of another young man from Hamburg, with whom he was obliged to have sex. Yet Spender didn't sleep with List. I repeat Michael's phrase, "Every picture is a detective story, a story of relationships," almost like a mantra.

In each place I enter—a room, a city, a country—there must be a way of orienting myself. And that point of orientation—in this case an experience of bodily desire upon seeing the photograph of a masked boy—is a beginning, the start of a possible story, or various stories. For not only was I reoriented to myself (my identity had disappeared in the airports, on the buses), but in looking at that photo I was, in an admittedly very odd sense, also looking at Berlin, at Germany.

The mask, with its oval eye-cutouts, gives the face of the German teenager a Japanese cast. The eyes are hidden in cut-out caves, black pools. His expressionless lips glisten waxily in the sun. The multiple upheld hands are like those I've seen on statues of buddhas. If I gently pressed the exposed tip of his nose, the way one pushes the stairwell light-button at night after cruising the bars in vain—within days I would find the bars—would the bodhisattva boy move his lips, utter a riddle of enlightenment?

I'd been in Berlin a week or so. At first the city had been a blur of public buildings, half-remembered street names, the Brandenburg Gate, but gradually a neighbourhood had emerged. Michael's apartment was at the south edge of a little district that centred around Savignyplatz, through which the elevated S-Bahn ran. Soon I sauntered along the central boulevard of west Berlin, the expensive Ku'damm, filled with shops, display cases in the middle of the sidewalks, tourist cafés I was disinclined to enter. Amid the motley architecture, I could pick out five-storey self-satisfied *Jugendstil* buildings from the turn of the century, that had either survived the bombing of Berlin, or perhaps been reconstructed. Most of the city remained in a sort of fog, punctuated by faintly glowing landmarks for me: the Café Einstein; the Martin Gropius museum, where the springtime art show "Metropolis" was on display. East Berlin was simply "over

there", "you just take the 100 bus at the Zoo Station and . . ."
(listening to the instructions, I quickly fuzzed out).

More important than the gradual horizontal unfolding of
the city, however, was its verticality, its historical stratifica-
tion. In once-divided recently reunified Berlin, you could
hardly cross a street without a reminder of its past, from the
German Romantic Enlightenment of the mid-eighteenth
century through the Second World War to the absorption of
East Germany, whose everyday tasteless objects suddenly
became kitsch post-Communist "collectibles".

To someone who lived there, a Berliner, it would mean
little, of course; but if you had packed a copy of Kant's *Critique of Pure Reason* (as I had), and then found yourself walking along Kantstrasse (it was two blocks north of Michael's
apartment), it would seem as though the streets of Berlin
were a grid recording the history of Western thought. It
would be weeks before the intersection of Kant and Leibniz
meant nothing other than the location of the nearest post
office. If I had come to Berlin to make a "reading" of the fall
of Communism, i.e., of the present situation, instead there
was a city, which is to say, an entire history to read.

And of all that history, I hadn't expected to be gripped
first by the period of Nazism. My fascination with it was almost a cliché, notwithstanding my own, however faint,
Jewish heritage. Again, it was an interest awakened by that
bucolic beach photo—taken, it turns out, in 1933, the same
year the Nazis superimposed the sign of the swastika on all
other images in Germany. How soon the adolescent body in
List's picture would be "de-eroticized" (except, perhaps, in
the photographer's homosexual gaze) and "purified", as

Hitlerjugend. In their narcissistic scorn for politics—in love with their entangled but free bodies—List and his friends missed the possibility that the youth cult might be turned to other purposes.

Outside the Wittenbergplatz subway station—past the eastern end of the Ku'damm, where it made a dogleg into an ugly little stretch of busy commercial street called the Tauentzien—a sign on a stanchion said, "So that we'll never forget those places of horror," followed by a stark listing of the concentration camps. As I was reading it from across the street, standing in front of the KaDeWe department store, a passing double-decker bus imposed itself on my line of sight, plastered with ads for a local car dealership. Then it was gone, but not before it cut through the litany so that for an instant it seemed as though "Schneider Nissan at Nollendorfplatz" was listed between "Treblinka" and "Theresienstadt".

But as the woman church pastor had said a year ago in Alexanderplatz—she seemed to me now a sort of oracle, jolting me back to the present—"Not *Nazismus*, but *Narzissmus* [not Nazism, but narcissism]." It was not just the neo-Nazis we had to fear—though they would be there, menacingly, now at the edges of the frame, now in the flames at the centre of a newspaper wire photo—but also the self-absorption of Narcissus, reflected in the plate-glass windows of the Mercedes showroom on the main boulevard.

List spent the late 1930s in self-imposed exile in Greece, but returned to Munich in 1941. At the end of the Second World War, he gazed upon the rubble of the Third Reich,

the bio notes reported, "where he photographed the destroyed city as though it were the ruins of ancient Greece."

Unlike dreams, which are drenched in possible meanings,
photographs offer a momentary neutrality from the insistence of meaning; it is up to the viewer to tease a narrative
from them.

Photography, Spender has List say, "is a skill. It's a matter
of having a good eye, as in shooting, which is what it is quite
rightly called. A good photographer . . . is like a hunter in
search of some particular animal which he happens to see
more clearly than other hunters, at some moment. But the
animal, however special to him, does not come out of his
particular soul. It is given to him by the world, on which he
is totally dependent for it."

Though I begin with those photographs of List's (something given to me by the world outside), the point is that I
begin—in Berlin, that is—in ignorance. Ignorance of location, language, of all the systems that constitute a world for
us—systems of transportation, local geography, desire.

For example, one night, as Michael and another painter
and I were walking along Mehringdamm, a divided avenue
lined with hulking buildings with double inner courtyards,
Michael remarks, "This is real *Berliner*." Just as I might say
about an otherwise unremarkable intersection in my own
city, say Hastings and Cassiar, "This is really Vancouver"—
one of those throwaway lines that can only be uttered after
half a lifetime of living there.

At the same time as I was looking around—we were on
our way to a little art show opening at the Gay Museum—to

see how this unprepossessing urban thoroughfare might add up to "real *Berliner*", I also had a sinking feeling that whatever I might come to know in the time I had (a few months), I would remain ignorant of that kind of knowledge.

But a photograph is, in a way, immediately accessible. It's a given. You can assume that it is already focused and composed, unlike ordinary life. Upon seeing it, you know something, even if that something is no more than its obvious subject matter. Despite its composition, you have an experience similar to that of watching a photo develop. It's enough to simply identify its emerging elements: that's a boy, that's a beach, etc. It doesn't yet matter whether or not you know it's a photo by List, taken along the Baltic, in the year of the Nazi triumph.

Eventually, you may or may not encounter the bits of location data that attend it: date (1933), place (Ostsee, or the Baltic, as we say), bio-notes, the resemblances to other pictures in List's posthumous book; even your own understanding of its context (historical, political). And beyond all this are the circumstances: it was a photo I was given by my friend Michael one day in Berlin . . . the possible items that constitute the circumstances stretch out indefinitely, from the room in which it was seen to one's relationship to the things in it. That is, I strike up a relationship to the *what-has-been* that the photo fixes (one of desire, awe, curiosity, etc.), and that relationship is itself a little story, a narrative. So List's photos of desirable young male bodies are my first real knowledge of Berlin. As are the boys I see in the streets, cafés, bars. At the outset, desire is the only epistemology I have.

Or is it more accurate to say that desire is the only

epistemology I have left? That is, am I so attentive to desire precisely because other ways of knowing have, along with Communism, collapsed? That would be intellectually neat—in the sense of tinging my desire with an elegiac quality—but it wouldn't be quite true. I may be more aware of desire because of being politically bereft, but desire has an independent character, is always there in relation to the confusions of first encountering a place. It is a method for finding my way.

I was fascinated by the beauty of the photographs Michael had given me, and by the stories they seemed to intimate—if only one had the patience to look at them carefully enough. The looking itself was a process—repetitive, dreamy, its rhythm reflected in the sentences I might write about what I saw there. One day I got the idea that there might be some point (I wasn't sure what) to writing descriptions of them.

What I had in mind were those experiments in careful description conducted by Alain Robbe-Grillet, the French writer, in the 1950s. Or perhaps I thought of it as roughly equivalent to the sketches Michael often made of the boys who modelled for him. As in the double exposure that first attracted me, I too proposed a sort of doubling. I imagined that the descriptions would be accompanied by the photos themselves, so that the reader would be able to compare them for himself or herself. It would be, if nothing else, a way of coming to know something.

"But why do you take photographs?" Spender persisted.

"Just to provide myself with memories of boys and other things I have seen and shot," List replied, almost offhand-edly. "What I like is the truth of how something—that struck me very much—*was*, at that instant."

Where the torsos overlap in the double exposure, a mysterious, irregular, inky shape appears, abstract yet composed of recognizable items—fragment of chest, nipple, bicep, hand. Where their heads overlap, one boy's mask is half darkened, like a harlequin's. The double exposure is itself a mask, as a mask, in a sense, is a doubling of the face through semi-concealment.

Before me on the wall are two large glassed-in frames, painted grey, together forming a square about two metres by two. Inside the frames are sixteen pieces of construction paper, cross-hatched in a grey gouache by Michael's friend Vincent Trasov, and containing in the centre of each, in stencil typography, the word *Knabe* ("boy"). On the wall behind me there's a similar "word-painting", except that the word is *garçon* ("boy"). And elsewhere in the same room, off in a corner, is a single panel with the stencilled word "Boyopolis".

Day after day, in the room I call the Boyopolis Chamber, I gaze at pictures of boys and young men, in photography books, catalogues, magazines, porn, photo albums, that Michael Morris has lavished upon me. List's book is spread open on a trestle table, lit by the opal light of the Bauhaus lamp. The word *Knabe*, repeated again and again, floats in a grey field above my head. Slowly I turn the pages. And each time I pause before the double exposure of a masked boy.

I imagine the boy taking off that mask. And if the photo is the image by which I began reading a series of stories—

desire, Berlin, Germany, the fall of Communism (stories sometimes concentrically arranged, sometimes tangled within each other)—then the removal of the mask seems like the pulling down of the Wall. The Wall, which was hiding something that everyone knew was there, in the same way that a mask doesn't really hide anything either.

Leapfrog

Two boys in black swimsuits leapfrog the bowed body of a third. It is 1933, a Baltic beach, photographed by Herbert List in multiple exposures. They spring off his bent back, late afternoon sun on their chests, legs spread-eagled, crotches clearing the submissive torso below. Behind them, in an earlier time exposure, two boys in black bathing suits, anticipatory excitement in their smiles, are poised to take a run at the boy who bends obediently forward, hands placed for support just above his knees.

All these photos of boys—to borrow a painter's term (since I am, for the moment, living among painters)—are primed with an erotic coat. Some become art, others porn, memories, ads (like the poster of a handsome boy with glistening hair that I saw the other day in the window of a beauty salon).

In the late afternoon, beneath the boys leaping in mid-air, flat sheets of the Baltic Sea slide in succession over each other, like tectonic plates leapfrogging the earth. How far I am from such physical playfulness; how intimate I have become with such obedience.

Baltic Sea, Germany, Circa 1932

Reading Ourselves

Tabasco's was at the very end of Fuggerstrasse, in the web of narrow streets just west of Nollendorfplatz. Adrian first mentioned it to me, when I asked about rent-boy bars, as the place where Attila Lukacs—a painter friend of Michael

Morris's for whom Adrian was stretching canvas—occasionally went.

Tilly (as Michael dubbed Attila) either grudgingly or with slight embarrassment (I couldn't tell which) said, "Oh, that's where I go when I don't want to be seen." He tagged a high-pitched cackle of laughter onto that admission. Attila offered a deprecating account of Tabasco's as a scene where rather scandalously young Polish boys hung out.

Indeed, that was apparently its reputation. When I later mentioned it to Frank Wagner, an art critic I knew, he asked, a bit puzzled at my interest, "But that's a pederast bar, isn't it?" And then added, as if to soften any intimation of disapproval, "The one in the very pretty building, right?"

"And they don't do anything," Attila went on, "they don't fuck, don't suck, don't get sucked. They *may* let you watch them jack off." He made it sound as though it was hardly worth the trouble.

By the time I visited Tabasco's, Berlin was becoming familiar to me. I had gradually settled into a routine—reading in the mornings, afternoon walks, and, that first week, social excursions at night with Michael, to a gallery opening or for a drink at Wanda's, a nearby bar that he occasionally frequented. And in our comings and goings, various routes were established. At first, short ones up to Kantstrasse, for groceries and the post office. Then more extended explorations east, in the direction of Nollendorfplatz.

To get to Tabasco's, I walked the length of the tourist-crowded Ku'damm boulevard—movie houses, department stores, double-decker buses weaving through steady traffic;

then cut across Wittenbergplatz, the street flowing in two streams around the temple-like subway station on a concrete island; down a sidestreet, across a divided boulevard, and through a copse of trees to the beginning of Fuggerstrasse.

I immediately felt the magic of that narrow street of apartment buildings, punctuated with bars and restaurants. Its power, which consisted of thousands of stories originating in its meeting places, was familiar to me. From the moment I set foot on Fuggerstrasse, I knew I was fated to walk up and down its length a hundred nights.

Tabasco's was, as Frank had noted, located in a pretty music-box of a building, in red brick with scalloped and colonnaded balconies upstairs. Two or three of the Polish boys and a couple of darker kids ("Turkish delight", Michael called them) were draped around the doorway.

There was a double door with small glass panels, one door of which was open a crack. I squeezed between a young Turkish man seated on a barstool next to the cigarette machine, and a pulled-back dark drape weighted with a leather hem.

It was more or less what Christopher Isherwood's accounts had led me to expect. His books—both *Goodbye to Berlin*, composed on the eve of the Nazi takeover, and *Christopher and His Kind*, the memoir revised in light of the gay movement—are not only possessed of the enduring beauty of art, but also practical.[2] I thought I had returned to Berlin to mull over the fall of Communism. Instead, the stratum of the city's history that I gravitated towards was the district to which a small band of homosexual English writers—Auden, Spender, Isherwood—had made their pilgrimage in the late 1920s, to enjoy its amorous possibilities, to write, to inscribe themselves within the place. The rooms where Isherwood had lived were only a block and a half away from Tabasco's, at the top of a five-storey building on the tree-shaded Nollendorfstrasse. When I first discovered the plaque by the building's entrance, I walked across the street and fell into a reverie, waiting for Isherwood to appear in the doorway. As always, the nature of time was unforgiving, yet I was still slightly surprised not to see him in the flesh. Later, the sign of his presence would become something of a totem to which I nodded as I passed by in the evenings. I'd come here, in part, on the strength of his stories; they were an emotional guidebook to the dawning Berlin of the 1990s.

"I can still make myself faintly feel the delicious nausea of initiation terror which Christopher felt as Wystan [Auden] pushed back the heavy leather door-curtain of a boy bar called The Cosy Corner," Isherwood wrote later, no longer constrained to conceal the motives which had brought him there. "Christopher met a youth whom I shall call Bubi (Baby). That was his nickname among his friends, because he had a pretty face, appealing blue eyes, golden blond hair and a body which was smoothskinned and almost hairless, although hard and muscular. On seeing Bubi, Christopher experienced instant infatuation. This wasn't surprising; to be infatuated was what he had come to Berlin for."

The blond boy who appeared at *my* side, about nineteen, had a medium brushcut, blue-grey eyes, and a snub nose, and was wearing a college-style windbreaker of fleece—

brick red, with green piping and a yellow block letter "C". I
was at the end of the bar in the front room; beyond me was
an archway that led into a second room with a pool table,
back bar, and video games manned by Polish adolescents.
The blond-haired kid, whose name, I soon learned, was
Manuel, was wedged into a corner, bantering with the bartender.

"Bubi had to be The German Boy, the representative of
his race. By embracing Bubi, Christopher could hold in his
arms the whole mystery-magic of foreignness, Germanness.
By means of Bubi, he could fall in love with and possess the
entire nation."

We stared at each other for a while, then he broke the ice
with some remark that possibly included me, if I chose to
take it up. He didn't speak any English, even though he'd
recently spent some time in Fort Lauderdale, Florida. I offered to buy him a drink.

The night before, after dinner at Michael's, I'd been introduced to a card game called "Swim". The way it worked
was that, when you lost, as I quickly did, you put coins into
the pool in the centre of the table and were said to be
"swimming". When you ran out of coins, you were
"drowned". Talking to Manuel had something of the confusion and amusement of playing "Swim", only for slightly
higher stakes, since its prospects, unlike those of the card
game, were unknown.

"Manuel?" I repeated, a little puzzled. "But that's not a
German name, is it?"

"Yes," he assured me. But it turned out that it was really
"Jorg e' Manuel", although he only used the last part.

"That Bubi was a blond was also very important—and not merely because blondness is a characteristic feature of The German Boy. The blond—no matter of what nationality—had been a magical figure for Christopher from his childhood. . . ." Perhaps I could make something similar from the fact of being a Jew, of my own attraction to the blond German (image from a wartime newsreel seen in childhood?) "Bubi had been, among other things, a boxer, so he must have been capable of aggression. But with Christopher he was gentle, considerate, almost too polite."

When midnight rolled around, Manuel walked me outside, which I took to be a local courtesy. I was thinking, in a self-congratulatory way, little more than "This is all very pleasant for starters." Found a bar, negotiated my way into another language, got dazzled. Not bad for a night's work. That's when I realized that Manuel was making an offer.

"How much?" I asked him.

"It's up to you," I took his reply to mean.

"A hundred marks?" Had someone told me that that was roughly the going rate?

Manuel said that he usually got somewhat more, but that if I would pay for the room, it would do.

Almost without thinking about it, I followed him up the stairs of a by-the-hour hotel. A man and a woman went up ahead of us. It was full. We tried another one in the next block; same story.

"Berlin's a sex world," Manuel said. "Morning, noon, night. It's always like that."

"How about my place?" I suggested, rather unoriginally.

"You have an apartment?"

"Yeah. Well, I'm staying with a friend in Charlottenburg. He's a painter."

"A painter?"

"Yeah. An artist. He's okay."

We crossed the wind-swept Martin Luther avenue.
Clouds scudded across the night sky. The taxi slid up the
Ku'damm. The crowds on the showcase boulevard had
thinned out by this hour, straggling along the pavement past
squat, lighted display cases, or in occasional knots clustered
around a crouching con artist running a shell game.

Michael was still up, and was about to greet me at the
door when he noticed Manuel in my shadow. A faint smell
of turpentine wafted down the long corridor of the flat.
There was a bit of what-has-the-cat-dragged-home? in his
arched eyebrow.

Behind the door in my room, the blond boy and I kissed.
I read the moment of our mouths coming together as—to
put it in the late style of Isherwood—the sign of the unpuri-
tanical European Boy, the German Youth, Berlin itself.

A minute later, when I came back from the can, Manuel
had stripped down to blue undies. Yet he was in no hurry.
He had a well-proportioned but undefined late-adolescent
body, and talked in soft, patient tones, with occasional gestures for my benefit.

At the mention of my being a writer, Manuel said he was
in a book, in an interview about his life as a hustler. In fact,
he had been in Hamburg the other day for the book launch.
When I expressed some puzzlement about it, he wrote
down all the bibliographic details in a neat hand on a slip of
notepaper: *Hustlers' Lives*. As always, I was curiously excited

to see someone I desired writing something—even if it was only a note.

He lay in the narrow bed, his sizeable uncut cock quickly hard. I was finally able to anticipate and interrupt one question in his language with the reply: "I like to do everything. *Alles.* And you?"

"The same," he laughed. "*Egal.*"

He was deep in my throat and I'd entered his body between his buns with a finger. Like swimmers, we came up for air. "Do you want to fuck?" he asked. I'd begun to acquire a sex vocabulary by studying the personal ads in German porno magazines, but I was especially excited to hear the verb *ficken*—"to fuck"—used practically for the first time. Even so, there was an instant of linguistic uncertainty. Had he said, "Do you want to fuck me?" or was it "Do you want me to fuck you?" While in some dim recess of my mind I was struggling to recall the rules for the use of personal pronouns, my body had already decided. I handed him a condom.

Then, as in the card game, I was "drowning". Our mortality was all that stood between us, at least for a moment. Then there was a soft gasp, and he carefully withdrew, showing me the condom sagging with the weight of his milky cum. Our mouths met.

Later I walked him downstairs, through the little inner courtyard where the candle-blossoms of the chestnut tree quivered in the night breeze. It was a space I traversed regularly, sometimes several times a day. Now it was romantic—indeed, since this wasn't the late 1920s but the time of postmodernism, post-Communism, it was absurdly romantic.

How romantic, we might think self-mockingly, as if reading ourselves in the light of the illusion yielded by an hour of paid-up sex. We shook hands at the shuttered newspaper kiosk, Manuel crossed the street, and the boulevard took him away in a taxi.

Michael was washing paint off his hands when I returned. "Whatever were you two talking about for so long?" he asked, beginning the debriefing, as if I were an astronaut back from outer space.

Archives

In one of the spacious rooms of the Martin Gropius museum, whose windows look out onto a field that has the appearance of an overgrown ruin, but which in fact commemorates those tortured on the site by the Nazis, Michael pauses to chat with a bearded man he's run into.

Attila and I go on into the next rooms of the "Metropolis" art show. It's one of those curatorial power bids to define the culture of the next postmodern decade. "No points for that," Attila mumbles, with the confidence of a young painter who has the world at his feet. He strolls across the gallery in a pale green bombardier jacket; his hair is cut in a skinhead style, fresh fuzz shading the top of his skull, and his eyes, slightly bulging and fringed by lashes so faint as to seem nonexistent, give him a raw, peeled appearance. I glance in blissful ignorance at the nearby pile of rubble—it appears to be a destroyed basketball court—that he's indicated and swiftly dispatched.

When Michael fails to appear after a few moments, I retrace my way back to where we left him. He's standing alone, in the same spot, his back to the windows overlooking the uneven field. A chill spring mist soaks the grass. Oddly enough, just before coming to Berlin, I had a dream in which I was by Michael's side, gazing at exactly such a landscape. "What's it called?" I'd asked. "The Field of Martyrs," Michael had said.

Now, across the distance of the room, I see in the middle-aged man the bewildered child who was an infant during the blitz. His father, a British soldier, was killed in Sardinia. At the end of the war, Michael was shipped off to western Canada, to be raised by his widowed mother.

His pear-shaped frame sags as if struck by a blow. I hasten to his side.

"What's wrong?"

"That was Kurt's lover," Michael says. "He just told me Kurt died." Michael didn't have to add "of AIDS". It's one of the things that goes unsaid these days.

"Kurt?" I repeat, unable to place the name.

"He was one of the boys I drew," Michael explains. "You know the one outside the bathroom? . . . He must've been twenty-five, twenty-six."

The long, dark hallway of Michael's flat is hung with various paintings, photos, and posters, and lined with large canvases-in-progress, their surfaces turned away to dry. Just outside the bathroom door, a stack of framed watercolours stands upright on the floor, leaning against the wall.

In the top picture of the stack, a naked boy, eighteen or nineteen, sprawls across a bed on his belly. In two or three short, curved strokes in black, Michael has deftly outlined his perfect butt; beige-coloured flesh tones complete its enticing, sweetly rounded firmness. The legs float upward, disappearing into the top of the drawing; his face, chin resting on his hands, gazes up at us with big eyes from near the bottom of the frame.

In the middle of the night, when I sleepily go for a pee and fumble for the electric switch at the bathroom door, the fluorescent tube inside flickers, buzzes, and then glows, spilling light across Kurt's body. His image lingers with me as I crawl back into the warm sheets, slide into sleep once more.

Thus I am again admitted through one of the thousand gates—on this occasion, another man's grief—into the realm of Boyopolis. Days later, apropos of nothing, but thinking of Kurt's death, Michael says, "I can't get it out of my mind"; or I ask him for a word in German—it happens to be "tactless"—and he remembers, "That was one of the last things Kurt asked me: 'Do you think I'm tactless?'" When I see Kurt in the drawing, the shadow of all the young men who have died in the plagued decade darkens my thought; but of course my desire for the beautiful youth in the watercolour is not diminished, or no more so than for, say, a boy in a Herbert List photograph whom I will never meet.

When Tom and I passed through Berlin about a year before, we were grateful recipients of Michael's kindly rescue. He embraced us on the Ku'damm as we stumbled off the airport bus, dazed by a glimpse of blinding sunlight on the Spree

River, overloaded with luggage, disordered by time zones, and took us home, chatted us up until we were sane again, found us a place to stay.

During that first conversation—mostly about the Berlin Wall, which had been breached but six months then—Michael disappeared from the kitchen for a minute, to go into the room I would later inhabit and think of as the Boy-opolis Chamber—the room containing Vincent's painting of the word *Knabe*. He returned with a photo album bound in grey imitation leather. Perhaps its display had been prompted by my asking him about his drawings and water-colours of nude young men—a huge pile of them, more than a hundred—that I'd seen in Vancouver at the apart-ment of a friend of his. Michael flipped through the plastic pages of snapshots, somewhat hastily, I thought (perhaps he was uncertain of Tom's reception of them), and though I only caught the literally barest glimpse of naked youths, hard-ons, long coltish legs, as he chatted on with giggled asides, as if a bit dismissive (or perhaps only protective) of the contents of the album, it was enough to focus my mis-placed traveller's body in desire, to make me regret not being able to linger over and savour those images.

Indeed, once I knew I would be returning to Berlin, among the dozens of anticipations (of politics, language, sex) there was a tiny pleasant thought that I might have a chance, at my leisure, to look at those pictures once again.

In between that first quick visit and the time when I was installed in the Boyopolis Chamber, I acquired one of Michael's watercolours, a drawing of a lanky young man, naked except for a T-shirt that itself bore a screened photo of another boy's face. The boy in Michael's watercolour hooks his thumb under the edge of the T-shirt, lifting and pulling it away from his flat belly; his other hand reaches down into the pubic hair above his cock; his head tilts towards his genitals. For months I'd seen that boy's picture daily, in the room where I worked, above my computer. He had, unobtrusively, become my companion from the realm of Boyopolis.

When Michael passed through Vancouver that summer—his new drawings were on exhibit at a local gay nightclub—he mentioned that the boy's name was Markus, and offered to have a few photos of him sent to me. In due course they arrived, but I found them unsatisfying, preferring the watercolour.

Now, I open the album, which I thought of as the Boyopolis Album, though there were other similar albums in the bookshelves, to be greeted by a photo of Markus, nude, crouching by the side of a low bed, momentarily looking up into the camera—I see his knees, and ringlets of reddish-gold hair. Another naked blond youth (his name is Willy) is on his knees and elbows in the bed, looking over its edge at a profusion of Michael's drawings (of the boys themselves) scattered on the floor before them.

Talking with Michael, I quickly discovered, took the form of *illustrated conversations*. A chance remark would send him into the little library-and-laundry room off the kitchen, where he rummaged through bookshelves stuffed with catalogues and picture books. That first afternoon, he reappeared with the oversized volume of Herbert List's pictures to illustrate a point—was it about modernism? or boys? or German history?—that he wanted to make. And when I showed interest in List's photo of the masked boy, Michael said, "Well, if you like that . . ." and scurried off, this time coming back with a book of Herbert Tobias's photos. Sometimes it'd just be the latest batch of snaps of local lads Michael had gotten back from the photo shop, but around those photos there'd be the particular rhythm of how he told a story, little brushstrokes of remarks or a luminous half-phrase. The illustrated conversation, apart from its considerable entertainment value, solved a problem: for Michael, as for many painters, words were ancillary to how he saw the world.

Of course, those conversations and their illustrations are only sporadically about Boyopolis; just as frequently, Michael returned from the library closet—for he was also providing me an immersion course in modern art—with re-pros of Max Beckmann's paintings, or photos of the blood-drenched performance rituals of Hermann Nitsch, which supplemented a running conversation we had as we made our way through the city, visiting exhibitions or attending gallery openings.

The artifacts of a *session* which Michael assembled from various caches, and displayed during an afternoon in which we drank coffee, smoked, watched the clouds from the kitchen window—included drawings, photos, water-colours, and gossip. And those objects, brought together, seemed to say, This is what we're left with, traces of fabled moments. Or perhaps the little treasure trove said, This is what there really is, what it refers to is merely our lives.

Items from disparate sources coalesce to become a *set*: List's photos, those of Tobias, some bits of porn (four boys and a woman), and the Boyopolis Album itself become one such bundle for me. (I reject a work called *Androgynes*; put the Bauhaus books in another pile; set aside an illustrated history of Berlin.)

There is a photo of Markus showing his body from the knees to just below his nipples, focusing on his erect cock, which he holds at the base with his long fingers. The angle of the photograph makes his hardened penis, its head half-covered in foreskin, seem huge. In another picture, he leans back in a chair, one leg pulled up against his ass—it reappears in a dark mirror behind him—the inner calf muscle flexed, while his erection rises halfway up his bared thigh. I admire the pensive calmness of his face, a curly lock of hair falling onto his forehead. And finally he is sprawled on his back in a bed, jacking off; his right hand covers the top of his dick in a slight blur of movement, he lifts his head from the pale blue and white bedcover to look down his tanned frame, mouth gaspingly open, as his other hand presses the place just below his scrotum.

Seen in succession, the photos tell a story, something like those books of cartoon drawings we had as kids that you flipped with your thumb to make a moving picture. Or rather, I begin to have a relationship with the people in the pictures. In the porn booklet about the four teenage boys having sex with a young blonde woman (the editing is almost random, so that I have to reorder the pictures in my mind to get a sequence), I soon give a name—Uwe—to the boy who's sort of the star of the episode—always hard, always grinning. And in the photos of the five of them together, one boy who doesn't seem very interested in the proceedings I begin to call Franz. Then there's a little subplot in which, in a few pictures, Uwe and Franz are in bed together, kissing, as Uwe runs his hand over Franz's butt before he fucks him. But where are the other two boys? In the next bunk over, watching Uwe and Franz? And where's the buxom blonde—down the hall, on the telephone? Even in List's book of photographs, as I slowly turn the pages, the narrative of List's life begins to be reflected in the pictures he took.

Since the photos in the Boyopolis Album go back a few years, there are updates, reports, epilogues. So-and-so, who hasn't been around for some time, Michael notes, is rumoured to be seeing a therapist; Willy is living in a gay squat in east Berlin. And Kurt . . . Michael met him in a bank, where he worked as a clerk. Upon seeing a form listing Michael as a painter, Kurt began a conversation about art. "We didn't sleep together or anything," Michael says, "but he was very good about bringing other boys, friends of his, to be drawn. . . ." And Kurt's death leaves Michael looking lost in the middle of the afternoon.

"I was once into Boyopolis," Michael said, as we strolled past the half-empty cafés and shop windows of the Ku'damm, under the smudged clouds of a gathering storm. "When I did all those drawings and things. That's when"—there was the briefest hesitant gesture as he referred to an ex-lover—"when we were sorting it out." But that, I sensed, was another story, one I didn't need to know—unlike the stories of Boyopolis, which are the stuff of legend.

In the strata of Berlin, Boyopolis belongs to the 1980s. Figurative painting suddenly reappeared; art money pumped into the city by the West German state brought in foreign artists like Michael (a facet of the Cold War strategy of making West Berlin a showcase in the ideological struggle with Communism); boys who settled in Berlin were exempted from the military draft.

"But really. . . ," Michael continued, making a transition to his current affairs, and in the shift there was an undertone suggesting how tiresome those young men I was avidly seeking (I had yet to meet blond-haired Manuel at Tabasco's) really were, how limited the scope of relations with them could be. In fact, Michael's work as a painter was far removed from Boyopolis; for several years he had been engaged in producing large, seemingly formal canvases concerned with effects of light and colour scales. There was the more pressing grind of an artist's middle age to contend with—tides of fashion leaving one in its eddies, the indifference of galleries, making ends meet. Occasionally, to amuse us as much as himself, he played the Boyopolis game, taking some photos or doing a few watercolours; but he'd rather lost interest in the boys themselves. "Of course, they're very pretty," he added, momentarily recalling a golden age of Boyopolis as we neared home, "and they can be terrific fun."

"How's Markus?" I asked one morning, in the voice in which we perfunctorily enquire after members of the family we may never have met, but whom we feel we know. Markus was one of those mythic figures which such casts of characters almost invariably produce. He's the one about whom stories are told, whose relics are shown, whose opinions (however banal) are retailed with relish, about whom Michael casually remarks, "Oh, Markus came by for a little visit yesterday."

Over the years, Markus had stayed in the picture—the years since the photo in which Michael, looking understandably blissful, is pillowed in Mark's arm, while the slim boy in a polo shirt of pale blue with white stripes (I often wear one just like it) gazes almost wistfully into the camera. His look always seems to say, "This is my lot in life." Michael was not, as far as I knew, in love with Mark, though he once might have been, but nonetheless he still loved him (I have several such persons in my own life).

"Oh, he's a regular call-boy now," Michael reported. We were riding the bus to the Metropolis show that morning, the upper deck of the vehicle brushing against tree branches along the bank of the canal on Shöneberger Ufer. "Registered with the health service, and everything," he added, in a voice that echoed middle-aged English housewives talking about their daughters' marriages. Later that day, I was presented with the latest photos of Markus, now in his mid-twenties, looking rather filled out, especially across the rear end, and mugging for the camera—there was little trace of the eighteen-year-old.

In the days that followed, Markus assumed a place in the flow of events that made up our lives. I came home from a night out cruising (unsuccessfully) in the bars, and Michael was on the phone, happily and avuncularly gossiping with Mark. How pleasantly domestic it sounds, compared to the unconsumed lust of the streets. Another day, he handed me a photo of what appeared to be a skinny blond of thirteen or fourteen, in shorts, on the back cover of a magazine. "That's what Markus must have looked like at that age," Michael said. I felt as though I were seeing the archaeology of the *Knabe* body.

One night we were playing "Swim" with Michael's current friend, Günther, a factory worker in his early thirties, and a painter with the distinctive name (acquired during an earlier career on stage) of Salome. "Have you seen Markus's photographs?" Salome asked. He added, "I bought some."

"Oh, he's selling them, is he?" Michael replied.

"No sex, just uniforms," Salome reported. "American, Russian, and Nazi."

A few days later, Michael came back from the photo shop with a new set of prints featuring Markus and Dirk, a young Dutchman who cut their hair. I was sitting at the kitchen table, flipping through them, while Michael was at the stove, making dinner. The two young men were in and out of various military costumes, horsing around. Dirk, in peaked cap, high kneeboots, and a Russian soldier's uniform, was sitting in Mark's lap. Mark, in khaki trousers and a white T-shirt, was grinning radiantly from behind Dirk's shoulder. With both hands Dirk was holding onto a thick, hard cock that protruded from under his crotch, out of Mark's lap. A lighted cigarette held between Dirk's fingers gave the dildo away, but I did a double-take before I caught the optical illusion in this bit of playful blasphemy on things military. "I knew you'd get a little shriek out of that," Michael laughed, as I gazed at one of the tools of Mark's current trade. The boy who had once artlessly revealed his

pleasure masturbating now reappeared as a seasoned performer. There were also drawings from the session, large
sheets of khaki-coloured recycled paper on which Michael
adroitly pared away the flesh, recapturing a physical innocence in the now sturdy young man.

The vast flotsam of Boyopolis—imagine some portion of
the sea's surface thickly flecked with gold bits—is perhaps
best understood by the concept of *archive*. It's a notion
Michael uses for his own work. But Boyopolis is unlike
Michael's archive, which is a bulky collection of artifacts,
postcards, image banks, slides, correspondence, even com-
puterized indexes. Nor does it resemble the Bauhaus
Archiv, housed in Berlin. If anything, it's more like the old
Jewish cemetery in east Berlin, with its almost forgotten
dead crowded in ivy-covered mausoleums. Vincent took
me there one afternoon; knowing that I was thinking about
archives, he suggested I might consider that city of the dead
as such.

But in fact the Boyopolis archive is purely a work of the
imagination, a mental construction to loosely encompass all
the images and instances of pleasure and trouble its inhabitants have provided us. It is purposely unorganized, scattered; its spirit is generous, as are Michael and Vincent, its
progenitors. The boundaries of the archive are as vaporous
as the dream dissolves in movies of the 1940s; our ability to
conceive of it assures us that there are dozens of other such
archives, just as there must be other galaxies containing suns
and planets.

Since the Boyopolis archive treasures that which was
once forbidden—is still, in a sense, forbidden—it has an

aspect of political resistance. In the post-Communist world of mall culture, its pleasures and history seek, however unsuccessfully, to evade the control of both the failed command economy and the triumphant commodity civilization. I too enter the Boyopolis archive, one of its innumerable curators, docents, narrators.

At last, one Sunday morning, there's an epiphany. Mark himself arrives at Michael's, in the company of a young man who, I'm informed, is his accountant.

Mark has close-cropped sandy blond hair (gone the reddish-gold ringlets of long ago), one gold-loop earring, nicks from shaving. He's acquired an occasional mannerism of talking out of the side of his mouth, tight-lipped, imitation gangster—I *think* he says to me, apropos of his clientele, "The neo-Nazis. . . well, if you want to see some real bootlickers. . ."—and yet the haunted darkness around his blue eyes recalls him at an earlier age. The sheer physicality and brash frankness of his presence are, in a sense, more impressive than any representation of him; yet the images of him in Michael's drawings reveal a truth not available in the person. Having met Manuel by now, I am relieved of the burden of having to consider whether I desire Markus. Predictably, I'm charmed. Mark is planning a holiday in Miami ("I really need it; I'm exhausted"); his screen test for a porno movie in New York in the fall has been accepted.

After coffee, the four of us go around the corner to an upstairs gallery where an exhibition of Salome's drawings and watercolours is opening. One room features sketches of Attila, who's also there, his distinctive cackle of laughter drifting through the crowd of gallery-goers as he delivers a glass of orange juice to his boyfriend on the balcony. A side room contains sketches of an elderly actress. She arrives at the last minute in a taxi, her arms filled with a bouquet of flowers for the artist.

The main salon, however, is devoted to portraits of Mark in motorcycle gear. Moments before, I was compelled to imagine him cracking the whip above a kneeling supplicant; now he appraises the images of himself with a collector's eye, calculating the possible return on investment (at $2,000 to $3,500 a pop, no triflers, please). Mark sips his champagne, satisfies us with his cameo appearance, and quickly departs—on his way to service a client in Munich, rumoured to be a retired general of the Wehrmacht.

These are the ones who accompany us in our lives, we might say. They are the embodiments of beauty; or their beauty provides a ground by which we attend the world. It is their stirring images you now absorb, much as I look at the boys Herbert List photographed along the Baltic in the 1930s, or who appear in Tabasco's on certain evenings. Will you ask, "But is it art?"

The Cemetery

Vincent told me I'd need a hat to get into the Jewish cemetery, so I brought along a khaki-coloured, floppy-brimmed army surplus boater that I'd bought several months before, for a trip with some deer-hunters. Since I didn't have a

yarmulka handy, it would have to do. The god Jahweh
wasn't particular about what kind of headgear you used to
pay your respects.

The cemetery was located in Weissensee, a district north-
east of Prenzlauer Berg—east Berlin's artsy quarter in the
decade before the Wall came down. I'd visited Prenzlauer Berg
once with Vincent and his friend Sylvie, who'd grown up
there, to see the progress of building renovations taking place
under the direction of one of the innumerable new agencies
of German unification that had sprung up everywhere.

Though Vincent pointed out where the Wall had been
when we changed buses at Bornholmer Strasse—the only
sign of it was a short stretch of rubble-littered ground—I
quickly lost my sense of direction as the tram twisted and
turned. We got off in the middle of a busy, noisy thoroughfare, with traffic flowing in several lanes on both sides of the
tram tracks. The street was named for Klemens Gottwald, a
Czech Communist—one of many names that would disappear as the city's conservative government eagerly pitched
in for a bout of historical housekeeping.

The neighbourhood had the nondescript, clanging,
fume-smelling, slightly hectic feel of *big city*—people
dashing through traffic from the trams to the shops. But as
ordinary as it may have been, I once again sensed Vincent's
particular fondness for east Berlin. Whenever we happened
to be there together, his normally reserved manner yielded
to a noticeably warm enthusiasm. Words and abbreviations
pertaining to the now-extinct German Democratic
Republic turned up in his "word-paintings", and his friends
had gotten into the habit of keeping an eye out for old East

German objects, now out of production, that he collected.

Part of Vincent's affection for the *Ost*, I think, was rooted in his resentment of how West Germany had ridden roughshod over everything in the D.D.R., making its inhabitants feel slightly ashamed not only of their inferior products, but even of their feelings, habits, and perhaps certain civic virtues whose value was now brashly being swept aside by the technologically superior West. And when the *Ossis* attempted to display a proper enthusiasm for the glittering cornucopia of the marketplace, which they had been encouraged to worship, they were puzzled to be regarded with ill-disguised contempt by their *Wessi* counterparts, who seemed to sneer at the newly uncovered and rather vulgar material greed of their impoverished, bumpkinish cousins. Either way, the *Ossis* lost.

We turned into a quiet but broad sidestreet that tilted slightly downhill, suddenly removed from the urban bustle. At the entrance to the cemetery, where the sidestreet ended, I pulled my crumpled boater from my jacket pocket and set it onto my head. The graveyard was almost empty—of the living, that is—that Friday afternoon in mid-summer, except for a few workmen who were lazily raking the gravelled paths. Tall, dark trees lined the walkways. We took a turn, then another, slowly wandering deeper into the silence of the cemetery's maze. As one inevitably does in such a place, I idly read the birth and death dates, along with names and brief testimonials on the grave markers, memorial walls, and occasional imposing mausoleums. Loewenstein, Bloomberg, Dawidowitz; 1837–84, 1855–1911; 1883–1930.

The sun broke through the cloud cover, a bird-call star-tled the silence, a drop of sweat slithered from under my hat. I fell into a kind of trance, my awareness of Vincent, a few paces ahead of me, gradually fading.

I was first struck by the neglect of the graves compared to the relative neatness with which the state maintained the raked gravel paths. Between the sentinel rows of trees, a family plot—one medium-sized marble stone bearing a sur-name, various mothers, sisters, and children ranged below it with their life-spans etched in its russet stone face—the ground itself overgrown with weeds, grasses, and nettles. Then an open, temple-like mausoleum—the tomb of a Jewish industrialist of the 1880s—half fallen in on itself, a hole in its small dome, pillars sooted over, the whole of it covered with the ivy of neglect.

A feeling of pleasant nostalgia crept up on me. As a child, I'd been packed into the family car (a two-toned Chevrolet with finlike rear fenders) on a Sunday afternoon with my mother and father, and we'd visited the graves in a nearby suburban cemetery. The next day, as my mother made her daily round of phone calls to her sisters-in-law, I invariably heard her reporting our dutiful visit. How normal it had all been, I marvelled now. As I paused on the gravel path be-fore a memorial wall, it occurred to me that I was probably among the last generation to familiarly commune with the dead in that way, to listen as a child to serious family talk about the purchase of plots, fees for upkeep, and the like. Now, bodies were less ceremoniously disposed of (crema-tion, perhaps the scattering of ashes at a favourite spot); in the first devastating decade of AIDS it became the custom to hold memorial services some time after death, with the deceased not physically present; far fewer still visited the resting places of the dead.

When my father died in 1975, my cousin Bob phoned me long distance with the news—he had more or less assumed the role of family chronicler—and asked what I wanted done. It seemed pointless to fly several thousand kilometres; the one person I really wanted to see would be there only as a corpse. "Can you take care of it?" I asked him.

In the midst of those hazy memories, I was brought up short. Suddenly I saw why those graves lay in such a state of disrepair. My eyes darted back to the dates of death, rapidly checking, and I heard the story told by those mute stones. Though it hadn't penetrated my consciousness before, I realized that this cemetery had begun in the mid-1800s, burgeoned in the latter part of the century when the Jewish community flourished in Berlin, and abruptly ended around 1935. The graves were untended because no one was left to care for them.

If ever there was an occasion when I had an inkling of my Jewish heritage—not a particularly strong identification in my life—it was at that moment in the vast Jewish cemetery in east Berlin.

The Chicago neighbourhood I'd grown up in consisted almost entirely of Jews and Irish. A low-level current of latent tribal violence was present; when Bob Greenspan rolled around on the ground pummelling one of the Murphy brothers, it was seen as Jew versus Irish. But most days we were haphazardly mixed together, a tangle of boyish flesh, desire, rambunctious energy. In any case, I was immediately attracted to the exotic Irish, falling in love with most of the Murphy brothers in succession. No instinctive xenophobia for the tribe across the gully, over the hill, under the wooden back porches, curdled my heart. My desire was cheerfully indiscriminate.

As for Jewish observance, it was my father's concern for my intellectual freedom that determined my fate. He had suffered under his own father's tyrannical rule, compelled by thrashings to don the vestments of faith against his will— yarmulka, prayer shawl, *tefillen*. He had decided, as a father himself, not to reproduce the patriarchal resentments he had endured. As I approached my thirteenth birthday, a decision had to made about whether I would attend the preparatory training for bar mitzvah. The more devout kids regularly attended *kadar*, a Hebrew school, after the day's secular classes ended. The irresolute just enrolled for a few months prior to bar mitzvah so they could give the proper responses during the great occasion.

One day my father asked me, "Do you want to be bar-mitzvahed?" I didn't realize what a precedent-shattering question it was; a boy wasn't asked those things, he was simply shipped off to *kadar* at the appropriate time.

"No, I don't think so," I casually replied. I'm not sure what my reasons were. I know I was unmoved by what I regarded as the rather bloody-minded tribal god of the Jews, but I don't think my objections were primarily theological. My motive could have been as trivial as not wanting to cut into baseball-playing time, or just embarrassment at the thought of the fuss and fraudulence of the whole thing.

In the midst of the inevitable family storm, I went on playing baseball (not all that brilliantly) with my communion-taking and bar-mitzvahed Catholic and Jewish friends, while my father settled all debates with the irrefutable, calmly delivered announcement "He doesn't want to."

Of course, with a start like that, it was inevitable that I would become one of those Jews who drive other Jews crazy. In fact, one of the few times that I'd appeared publicly as a Jew was during a protest demonstration, on the high holiday of Yom Kippur, the Day of Atonement. Across the street from the Vancouver Jewish Community Center on 41st Avenue, where scores of people were entering in appropriate holiday attire, I was marching with a small group of protesters, carrying banners and candles denouncing a savage attack a week or so previously on a Palestinian refugee camp in Lebanon. The attack had been carried out by Lebanese soldiers, but was obviously sponsored or permitted by the Israeli government, which exercised military jurisdiction in the region.

A man in a silk suit, wearing a yarmulka embroidered with jewels and golden thread, couldn't stand it any more. He rushed across 41st until the magnificent Semitic nose beneath his flashing eyes was a centimetre from my own. After ascertaining my cultural heritage, he fulminated, "How can you do this? How dare you ruin my Yom Kippur?"

"*Your* Yom Kippur?" I snapped back. ("*Oy*, does this kid have a mouth on him," one of my relatives would have said.) "I had no idea it was *your* Yom Kippur. So, did you get it cheap?"

Carefully choosing between homicide and prayers for

atonement, he recrossed the busy street, darkly muttering to our implacable god.

Although there has been a trickle of burials in recent years, the Jewish cemetery in east Berlin died in the 1930s. The dutiful sons and daughters who had honoured their parents' memory here were asphyxiated in gas chambers, then incinerated and disposed of in mass graves. So were their own children, who had thoughtlessly played on these paths among the vibrant dead. Here was a city of the dead that had itself died. No one was left to remember them, or their grandparents beneath crumbling stones. No one except perhaps a visitor—a middle-aged man in a floppy boater, with faint identifications and strange affections—suddenly chilled by a recognition of the Holocaust beneath his very feet.

I shook myself as Vincent's lean figure came into view. Outside, I crumpled my hat into my pocket, and we headed back towards the busy thoroughfare for a late lunch in a nearby café.

Epistemologies

Once, long ago, I knew a gay activist (I attended his memorial service recently) who exercised a perhaps beneficent but nonetheless tight, if not suffocating, control over the group whose tutelary figure he was. His favourite, a blond boy, had just entered into a sexual relationship with another youth, much to his mentor's annoyance. When asked about his protégé's dalliance, he sternly huffed, "It's merely an affair of convenience."

That chilly spring of 1991, I thought I should like nothing better than exactly such an affair. With minimal instructions—though I often unfolded the waxy paper of the bulky Berlin street map to trace its dauntingly wide boulevards—I made my way to the sort of bar that attracted me, one catering to ephebes and their middle-aged suitors, located in a neighbourhood whose venerable traditions had provided a venue for such encounters since the 1920s. It was absolute beginner's luck that I met and took home a young man of such surpassing beauty as Manuel.

I'd come to Berlin to work on, among other things, problems of epistemology. I thought—against Descartes, the father of modern methods of knowledge—not that "I think, therefore I am" but rather that "desire is the body's first epistemology."

Even as I shook hands with him (or did he kiss me on the cheek?) as he was about to enter the taxi that would take him away, it never occurred to me to give him my telephone number or make a future date with him. Hadn't he said that he regularly hung out in Tabasco's? Anyway, if meeting young men was as easy as it seemed, then surely there would be others I could greet with equal certainty of desire.

It wasn't until I was talking with Michael Morris later that evening, using such euphemisms to describe Manuel as "very professional" and "versatile", that it dawned on me that I had just experienced something considerably more than a mere instance of a category of activity (i.e., sex). But by then it was the middle of the night, and I was sleepy.

The next day—reading Spender's novel about Herbert List, looking at paintings in the Dahlem museum, riding a city bus (in the wrong direction; my knowledge of the streets still shaky)—I intermittently entertained pictures of Manuel in my mind: his face; his body in underpants, lit by the opal glass lamp on my worktable, as he sat in a chair. But the bar seemed to turn a cold shoulder that night, as did the wind, shearing down narrow streets, whipping clouds across the wide boulevards. By the following evening, though I could will myself to remember that I had kissed a knee, slipped his finger into my mouth, I had to consider the possibility that it had been a mirage—an experience no more substantial than a dream during a mid-afternoon's nap.

Subsequent nights at Tabasco's only compounded my doubt. There were indeed several other young men I found attractive. One in particular, whom I saw on successive evenings, was a pale, aristocratic-looking blond, rather effete in his gestures, with long, elegant fingers. His charm reminded me that there had also been something androgynous about Manuel, the presence of which, alongside his professional, versatile sexuality, excited me.

I'd deluded myself into believing that I understood how the bar worked—as a site, or system of signs, or set of pick-up routines. Now it became clear to me, as I failed even to catch the eye of the pale blond boy (in a yellow shirt and black leather jacket), or fumbled in my response to the nod of another blond-haired, blue-eyed young man (of exactly the sort I was supposedly looking for), that I didn't understand it at all. I knew nothing. Oh, I knew how to order a drink and pay for it, though even there my German pronunciation wasn't sufficiently crisp. But whatever was going on of significance was occurring in language, signs, unspoken understandings, beyond my ken. Was the pale blond boy working part-time at Tabasco's? Hustling? In which case, perhaps he was awaiting a gesture from me, one I didn't know how to make. Or was he simply an attractive friend of the personnel who staffed the place, one of the *jeunesse dorée* who seemed to surround the barmen?

To make matters worse, among the bartenders was a handsome, friendly blond in his late twenties who obviously devoted considerable attention to the tan sheen of his skin and the taut shape of his chest, which I glimpsed through the gap in his half-buttoned shirt as he drew a beer from the tap or rinsed a glass in the sink. A few days later, I realized that I was confusing my memory of Manuel's face with that of the handsome bartender, as well as that of the pale blond boy. Indeed, I could no longer call his image to mind at all. If desire was the body's first epistemology, its short-term memory was disconcertingly unfaithful to its knowledge.

Although Michael airily reassured me, "He'll turn up, they always do," there was no persuasive evidence that I'd known Manuel at all, apart from the scrap of notepaper giving the details of *Hustlers' Lives*. Our relationship had begun with a piece of writing, and although circumstances had lately flooded my life with visual imagery ("I don't think I've seen as many pictures in years as I've looked at in the last few days," I marvelled to Michael), that written note was all I had to go on. Further, it only seemed evidential by means of a process of elimination. I looked at the words and saw that they weren't in my handwriting, or in that of anyone else I knew; the note was on my desk and couldn't have gotten there in any more plausible manner. So I must have known someone. How perplexing epistemology appeared to be.

I'd given up on him and was sitting in Tabasco's on a slow Monday night, resigning myself to a variety of other occupations (reading philosophy, looking at photos, acquiring more German). The bartender that evening was a roguish-looking middle-aged man named Henk, with prematurely white hair. He boldly asked me to buy him a drink, and since I was ignorant of the local customs I fell back on my early anthropological training (praise the food, share tobacco, don't offend the gods), and complied. He poured himself a glass of imitation champagne; I wrote it off to field studies.

At that moment, Manuel entered. He was wearing a white sweatshirt and stone-washed peel-off jeans (the effect produced by their tightness struck me as unneeded). My heart thumped. "I've been waiting for you," I said. The German verb "to wait" takes a particular preposition and an accusative object, which I had repeatedly practised in case I had need of it.

He kissed me on the cheek, seemingly pleased to find me. Naturally, there was good news and bad news. The good news was that he was free that evening. The bad news was that he was departing for Zurich the day after next. Of course, he has his own life to lead, and no doubt many cities where he's welcome. I invited him to lunch on the day of his planned departure. As we were about to leave, Henk jibed in Manuel's direction, "Oh, I thought you were looking for a *boy*." After the requisite ritual insults were exchanged between them, Henk handed us a box of matches with a photo of a boy's bubble-butt and the word "Kondom" on it, the bar's public-service reminder to play carefully in times of danger.

At home, I wasn't at all coy; I didn't want him to have the least doubt about my desire. As before, there were long, slow conversations. He told me about his "jolly aunt" from Florida, the gay scene in Hamburg, his dead parents. "Tales of woe," Michael had warned me. Afterwards we dressed, embraced, kissed; he formally thanked me (for the patronage? the pleasure? both?). Looking at him in a moment of stillness in all the movement, I noticed that Manuel is the sort of person who looks equally good in ski sweaters or his birthday suit. On the way out, he exchanged greetings with Michael, who was sitting in the kitchen in his blue pyjamas, eating pistachio nuts. Later, Michael remarked, "I don't think those jeans do anything for him." "Yes, an unnecessary touch," I agreed. How quickly we incorporate the emissaries of Boyopolis into our lives, offering solemn judgements on their fashion choices. In the shadow of the kiosk off the Ku'damm, Manuel kissed me on the mouth, said he would call the next day to confirm lunch.

Predictably, he didn't. When no word came the day after, I assumed he'd taken off for Zurich. Michael commented on the fecklessness of hustlers; in the subtext I read a discreet warning to restrain my feelings for such creatures. I was on my own, and headed to Tabasco's for a drink. In the uncodified protocols of these matters I had, I reflected, done my part, avoiding dishonour. The next move was properly his. In the bar, I moped. Around eleven, I packed it in. Michael was still up when I got home.

"Did Manuel find you?" he asked.

"No," I said.

"He was here."

"Here?" I repeated, nonplussed.

He had arrived at Michael's door, looking for me. There was something about lost papers, and he dashed off, telling Michael he would phone me at Tabasco's. And indeed, I now faintly recalled that Henk, the bartender, had taken a phone call and made a perfunctory round of the bar, looking for someone; if I had heard my name called, the fuzziness of my knowledge of the language made me too slow to respond in time. But in the dance such things are, Manuel had taken the next step—which is, after all, what the dance is all about.

Again there was an interlude. Once more, I forgot Manuel's face, even as I looked at the faces Herbert List had photographed—I was now studying, after the masked teenager and the boys playing leapfrog on the beach, a third picture, of a crouching blond-haired boy in a black bathing suit, shot from below, holding a pole in both hands, as though guiding a boat through the reedy shallows of a river. His body nearly filled the frame, sky behind his monumental figure, a minuscule puff of what might be cloud in the lower right corner. As I looked at him, perhaps as List had in 1933, from three-quarters below, I was afforded a view of the underside of his thigh and rear, the faintest blond down shadowing part of it. I'd never before seen so clearly, I realized, the part of the body denoted by the word "haunches". Should I ever find him again, I told myself, I must obtain a photo of Manuel.

North Sea, Germany, Circa 1933

One afternoon, walking past the gay bookstore, which was just a few doors from the grocery where Michael liked to shop, I noticed a new book in the window in a cover of purple and pink—the colours all the boys were wearing that season—called *Hustlers' Lives*. It was in German. I bought a copy. Possession of it was reassuring, since it confirmed that Manuel's note referred to something that existed—and conversely, the presence of the book seemed to confirm the existence of Manuel.

About a block away from the bookstore was the neighbourhood square, Savignyplatz. I sat on a park bench, within sight of a statue of a pair of naked boys, each tugging at a recalcitrant goat, and I opened *Hustlers' Lives*. Its epigraph was a quotation from the German artist Joseph Beuys: "The mysteries take place in the *Hauptbahnhof*"—the central station. The contents were rather less elevated than the promise of that aphorism, though the book was indeed about the hustling scene at the main train station in Hamburg, and consisted, in large part, of interviews with hustlers.

However, there were some immediate minor ambiguities: although the editors noted that the names of the interviewees had been changed, and Manuel had told me that he appeared as "Ingo", there was an interview with somebody named "Manuel" as well as one with "Ingo", and there was another with an ex-hustler and bartender named "Detlef", which was the name of Manuel's bartender–best friend in Hamburg. The descriptive notes at the top of the interviews only confused me more. The intro said Ingo had spent a couple of years in prison, and portrayed him as a petty criminal, none of which seemed to describe Manuel. As usual, my efforts to determine what was real bumped up against countless minute but intractable puzzles.

Nor was the interview with Manuel–Ingo particularly inspiring. He spoke in a harsh street-slang that I had difficulty deciphering. "Once, I was staying with a pal in Karlsruhe," began his tale of woe, "when a gay pig picked me up hitch-hiking and asked me whether I wanted to make a hundred marks—in the car. Although I didn't know what he meant by that, I said, 'Sure'—a hundred marks is a lot of bread. Then he said to me, 'After you jack me off, you get the money.' I did it." Later, Ingo bitterly but rather unconvincingly blamed the man for setting him on the tempting road to ruin.

"There are few, very few johns that I like," he declared. "Those I like aren't typical. With them, I can talk, because they've got something in their heads. Often they're younger than your average john, not so fat and flabby." (I winced.) "They're not just looking for a hustler, or only for sex. They want a little company. . . . But I've never had a real relationship with a john. You can buy sex, but not love. The same with friendship. Let's face it, they stay with me because of my big dick." Ingo, the cold-blooded, hard-bitten jailbird, didn't sound much like my charming Manuel.

Though it seemed like weeks, it was only days between our encounters. In the interval, I temporarily moved from the Boyopolis Chamber to house-sit Frank Wagner's apartment; Frank was off to America for a month. His place was located in Moabit, an old Huguenot quarter of Berlin just above the big Tiergarten park, whose streets were named for theologians (Calvin, Melanchthon, St. Paul. . . .)

I've barely taken a sip of my drink a few nights later when Manuel breezes into Tabasco's. The story, as we make our way home to the streets of the theologians, is about lost money, passport, ID, all of which fell out of his pocket in a cab. Zurich is off; he has to go to Hamburg the next day to deal with the paperwork. Under his multicoloured American-style team jacket there's a black sweatshirt, then a red candy-striped sportshirt, and finally a long loose white tank top that falls below the curve of his butt. When he turns around, bare-legged, his hard-on is poking out from beneath the oversized top.

The next day, after a sudden rainstorm late in the afternoon—the wind tears the petals from the blossoming trees, blows them into soggy heaps along the curb—there's a knock at the door. Manuel's been to Hamburg and back, but he's had no luck with the ID bureaucracy. He's depressed about money, and sleepy, having been up all night. I commiserate. We make plans to visit Hamburg together; I'd like to see the city where Herbert List took photographs. He strips down to lavender bikini underwear and smokes a cigarette before nodding off. He looks like a child buried in the big white comforter on the bed. I sit at the desk in the next room, reading German history. As I watch the clouds drift across the city in the early summer evening, it occurs to me that I'm having a little affair.

He fucks me sometime around four-thirty in the morning. In the cool, wet pre-dawn, there's only the sound of the S-Bahn, a block away, rumbling across the tracks over the river. When I lube the rubber he's rolled down his stiff cock with cold K-Y, he shudders. Some young men fuck discreetly, as though you were shaking hands with them at a café; others, like Manuel, fuck as if they had suddenly discovered that you were the centre of the universe.

For a few days, in the quiet streets of Moabit, we have a sort of idyll, or so it seems at the time. The world recedes.

What has happened to my project of studying the end of Communism? While we lie in each other's arms, the governments of Ethiopia, Yugoslavia, Albania, India, and Algeria fall/clamp down/impose martial law/collapse of their own weight and/or drench themselves in blood. But we are carried away from the world whose stories on other days I so avidly enter. The global cataclysms that politicians have taken to calling the New World Order are subsumed by the splendour of the Old World Order, the ancient order in which youths emerge from the bathtub to receive the adoration of their suitors.

One afternoon in east Berlin, we stop at the Pergamon museum, which contains a reassembled Greek temple in the main hall—literally the Old World Order. In the side rooms is some of the statuary that German archeologists carted back to Berlin a hundred years ago, in the heyday of Prussian imperialism. The sight of herds of German schoolboys wandering among the naked marble bodies of ancient Greek teenagers makes me sigh. Manuel seems entertained.

But in the museum café he becomes depressed about his own situation, launching into a long recitation of betrayals, rent-demanding landlords, bureaucratic obstacles to acquiring new ID ("tales of woe" exactly as Michael predicted). Besides, the Berlin hustling scene is *Scheisse*; ever since the Wall came down, the bars have been swamped with boys from the east. For a moment Manuel sounds like a typical west German taxpayer, grumbling about the costs of unification. We part at the Zoo station of the S-Bahn. He disappears for a few days. I listen to the music of Mahler, watch the clouds again.

Manuel, as has become the pattern in our precipitous affair, shows up unexpectedly, with tales of a jealous Mexican john, or of more unhappy trips to Hamburg. Another afternoon, he appears late in the day, wearing white jogging sweats and a white sweatshirt bearing the word "Florida" in gold letters. He's hungry. I go into the kitchen and throw a sausage into the frying pan while he sits in the next room rattling off a litany of complaints. Then he's off. He'll be back later, he says, but he doesn't show. The next morning, when I reach into my pants pockets to grab my coins for a trip to the bakery, I discover that the money's missing.

If Manuel and I can't even trust each other—a form of knowing—how can we know anything at all? It's not the money that disturbs me—it's a negligible sum—but rather the lost pleasures of sex, the forgone possibility of the improbable relationship—what made me think I could succeed where others haven't?—and, strangely, the sense of the incomplete narrative.

That night, on my way to Tabasco's, I get off the S-Bahn at the Zoo station, but instead of taking my usual route I walk into the main cavernous hall of the train station. Among the mysteries of the central station is Manuel, in jogging sweats, talking to a middle-aged man. After the man departs, he looks up, startled to see me standing among the pillars. It's as though, rabbit-like, he's poised to make a run for it. And if I conceive of my own body as a vessel of water, blood, and emotions, then at that moment I'm more like a sieve. Mouth dry, blood pounding, system flooded by contradictory and unexpected feeling. My body opts for desire over rage, I choose continuing narrative over a settling of accounts. We talk in the shadow of a pillar.

I become inured to his comings and goings. Ardour cools. One morning, I wake up *not* brooding about him. Instead, I look at a newspaper map of Yugoslavia, trying to sort out its multiple nations and populations. Of course, it would be nice to see Hamburg, especially through Manuel's eyes, but on the other hand. . . . I pick up a train schedule, imagine going there alone.

A friend from home writes, among other things, "Women are the mirror in which I see myself." Whereas it's not myself I'm looking for (at least, I think not); it's the *other* I'm trying to see.

In an unsteady moment, much later, I allow myself the merest suspicion that my noble, dispassionate, consuming interest in the *other* is perhaps not as pure as I make it seem. Can it be that my claim rings slightly hollow?

Yet how clearly perceivable Manuel's body is. At some point the light at dawn, creeping around the edges of the drawn curtains, illuminates the fuzzy blond hair in the crack of his ass. The down of his hindside glows in the morning. But his self presents itself to me as merely a jumble of questions whose answers are speculative, blurred in the half-comprehension of another language, or simply a blank. Is there really a "jolly aunt" from Florida arriving at the airport at four? Does the gold chain with a dog charm around his neck actually relate to dogs he owns? If so, who walks them? Where does the Swedish musician fit in? Perhaps—here's another possibility—there simply isn't that much to know about him. A friend asked, not with hostility, but as a matter of information, "But what do you talk about?", meaning, How do you get through the day with a disco-bunny?

One night, when I've come to Tabasco's from a boring literary evening held in the gallery above the Café Einstein, I'm composing in my mind one of those amusing letters (I'm going to send it to my friend Scott in Vancouver) that goes, "Well, I've just wrapped up an x-number-of-weeks, y-number-of-fucks affair with a lyin', cheatin', thievin' tramp—in short, exactly the sort of person I most adore...." That's when Manuel walks into the bar.

He takes the stool to my right. Coincidentally, the aristo-cratic-looking pale blond boy is sitting on my left. He bor-rows a cigarette from me—our first direct contact in all these weeks. Equally coincidentally, both he and Manuel are hungry, and they both order cherry cake. I can't help but be tickled by the absurd circumstance of two attractive blond boys, on either side of me, simultaneously eating cherry cake.

At home, after a further unhappy instalment of his ad-ventures, Manuel tries to get me to be a little more realistic. "I'm a call-boy," he insists. Past midnight, I settle slowly athwart his loins; he happily plugs me; I cover his chest with cum.

"Why don't we take the train to Hamburg tomorrow, and stay for the weekend?" I suggest, abandoning my nor-mally deliberative manner. I know that the next day is his friend Detlef's birthday, and that it would give Manuel pleasure to be in Hamburg for the party.

The following morning, dark and overcast, we meet in the Zoo station hall. After a night without sleep, he's falling off his feet. Minutes before our train leaves, I remember the automatic photobooth in the station and drag him over to it. He's too tired to argue. I slip the prints into a red note-book—of course, they don't do him justice—and we board the train. Once we find our compartment, Manuel immediately falls asleep for the duration of the journey.

We take a cab from the Hamburg train station (the site of *Hustlers' Lives*) to the St. Pauli district, just above the harbour, where Herbert List drank in gay bars with the boys he photographed before he left Nazi Germany for Greece. In the Florida Hotel—there's a bar on the second floor, the Exquisit, where Detlef will be working that night—Manuel has arranged a room for us that overlooks the Reeperbahn, that great sleepless avenue of casinos, sex shows, bars, and all-night greasy spoons.

After he dashes out to buy toiletries, the two of us sink into a huge bathtub filled with scalding hot water and clouds of bath bubbles. We sit face to face, our bath-oiled flesh in constant slippery contact, and this moment of pleasure seems unparalleled in my life. Is it merely the failure of memory, or are we really that much on the edge of ourselves? That is, am I "wired" in such a way that the present is almost all my body knows?

In the early evening he naps, lying naked atop the covers, his thumb in his mouth. There's a moment in the story—of a relationship, a political event, a journey—when you know that, even if nothing further occurs, it's a story. I began in Berlin, a couple of months before, with that old photograph of a boy taken by Herbert List. And now I'm in the city where List grew up, in the neighbourhood of his desire, even, with Manuel, a young man of the sort List might have photographed. The parallel ends there: Manuel is not simply an image caught in a photo; our relationship is unpredictable. Yet whatever happens from here, I sense, glancing at the thickening traffic on the wet Reeperbahn below, that the minimal requisites of the narrative have been fulfilled.

Aesthetics

When I sit lost in contemplation of those boys in the photographs, what am I seeing? What am I looking for? It's only some time later that it occurs to me that those are two distinct questions.

Desire is the body's first epistemology: that's the aphorism I've coined, the banner I carry into the fray. Every photo, said Michael, is "a story of relationships"—between you and the subject, between the picture-taker and the viewer, between the boy in the photo and the photographer, and so on.

From the moment of my arrival in Berlin, I have been in a strange if not entirely unknown place; desire is my most reliable epistemology. Seeing Manuel asleep, thumb in mouth, or the blond boy in the photo with down on his haunches, I know something certain. *We resist the plight of knowing nothing.* That is, all of us resist such a plight, and that's an observation as applicable to art as it is to sexual desire. My eyes convey to me representations of boys in photos, boys in the bar. I begin to make a world for myself.

Now, a couple of months after I was first shown Herbert

List's photos, I find myself looking at them rather more casually than I did at first. The process of looking has been something like the course of an affair, where the intense concentration devoted to the initial occasions of desire gives way to a more selective viewing of the images engendered in being together. Now I'm content just to be moved by the photographs, leaving the source of that feeling as a slight puzzlement, and simply to go on, to turn the pages. . . .

Most obviously, the advantage of pictures is that you can seem them again, unchanged, whenever you like. Yet at the same time, my viewing of pictures of boys taken long ago is accompanied by a regret that I shall never meet them as they were.

There's a photo of a young man, nineteen or twenty, sitting in the shallows of a German lake (Ammersee, *c.* 1950), his head turned away to look at something outside the frame. I notice first of all his bent knees, rising just out of the water; then his face—an elegantly lean bloodhound's look under a jumble of sandy blond hair; the way the tanned skin hangs a bit loosely about his ribs. . . . But the boy whose knees poke out of the shallow waters is a man of sixty or so, a decade older than me—if he's alive. Still, were I to meet him, he might conceivably tell me about that day at the lake, about Herbert List. What I'm seeing, then, among other things, is a little story about to begin—the equivalent, perhaps, of hearing the first notes of an overture.

We can also ask, What do the boys in the photos think of the uses made of them? When a young friend of mine appeared nude with his face obscured on the jacket of a book I wrote, didn't he seem pleased when word got around the bar that the beautiful figure was himself? For that matter, when I was twenty, I was taken to an apartment in New York where the filmmaker and photographer Jack Smith was shooting baroque tableaux of mythically costumed and nude figures wrapped in the haze of veils and embroidered cloths. I was asked to strip, and then placed within the seraglio he'd imagined for us. Could I not anticipate that I might see myself at a later date? In fact, I have, though not very strenuously, kept an eye out for the appearance of a book of Smith's photos. What would I see, should I find myself? Most likely a boy for whom I felt some desire—a sort of incestuous rather than narcissistic desire, since it would be for myself as I was—and probably a regret that I could no longer meet him as he was.

When Michael brings home his latest batch of snapshots from the photo shop, part of the excitement is that I may find myself asking, "Oh, who's that?"; I may see someone I might reasonably anticipate meeting, at a café, a gallery opening. So-and-so will be there, Michael may say, the one you liked in the photo.

Whatever it is that I know about the *other*, by means of my initial axiom ("desire is the body's first epistemology"), in short order I want to know more, and other, things. And all the rest to be known is far less certain than the knowledge born of desire, the desire that brings me to the less perfectly knowable other person.

Perhaps the certainty of desire is simply useful until other, more interesting knowledge becomes available. The city becomes familiar (I know where my favourite café is located; indeed, I *have* a favourite café); sentences in German are occasionally comprehensible; I think less about my desire for Manuel, more about the (improbable) possibility of knowing him. In sum, a more complex life gets under way.

The middle-aged List found success after the war by working for the big photopictorial magazines then in vogue—a staple of middle-class households and doctors' waiting rooms when I was a teenager. He published some books for the travel/art market, photos of Greece and Italy, in the late fifties. But the photos I'm so enamoured of were his private memories of the boys who had interested him. In his last decades—he died in 1975, in Munich, at the age of seventy-two—he gave up photography, turning to drawings and watercolours, which he collected. He had never thought—in fact, he vehemently denied, at least by Spender's account in *The Temple*—that the photos of boys had anything much to do with art anyway.

List has been rescued from obscurity posthumously and, oddly enough, by politics more than by art. In the wake of the gay liberation movement—or, more precisely, its commercialization in the mid-1970s—his photos of boys and young men were rediscovered. This was part of a project to reconstruct what was a heretofore secret history of desire, and package it in pricey coffee-table books to be purchased by middle-class gays who found the photos erotic, yet respectable or artsy enough to leave out for display.

Yet there's a sadness in the fact List abandoned the activity of photographing boys—and indeed the whole medium—by which his work would enter history. It seems like a defeat. I wish him to be alive, in his prime, to enjoy seeing the cover of his book in a shop window.

The politics of gay liberation that gave List his posthumous fame also opened the way for Herbert Tobias, whom I think of as List's successor.[3]

Tobias was of the next generation, about twenty years List's junior. Born in Dessau in 1924, he was a German soldier in the Second World War, and served on the Soviet front (some barracks photos from 1943 survive). Eventually he deserted and landed in a camp as a POW. After the war, he had a brilliant career as a star fashion photographer; there were forays into theatre and film, and a sudden return to photographs after an absence of a decade or so. With the upheaval of the 1960s, Tobias emerged as a man "of the left", compared to the politically indifferent List, who had been content to characterize himself (by the title of Robert Musil's novel) as "a man without qualities". When gay liberation made its appearance, Tobias's photography was also radicalized, as evidenced by the explicitly homosexual photos he made in Hamburg from about 1975 to his death at age fifty-seven, of AIDS, in 1982. What had been a representation of longing, in the line of homoerotic photographers extending from Baron von Gloeden in the late nineteenth century to people like Tobias himself into the 1960s, became a frank portrayal of homosexual desire and sexual practices.

On a ramp in the old fishmarket hall on the Hamburg waterfront, a young man backlit by daylight filtered through walls of frosted glass windows leans forward on a rust-caked, wrought-iron railing. He's wearing a military cap with a shiny visor, a black leather jacket bunching up on his shoulders, and leather boots whose tops fold down, buccaneer style. He is otherwise naked from mid-torso to calves; the cold, flat daylight falls across his strong thighs, narrow waist, the offering of his bare ass.

Hamburg, 1975

In a photograph Tobias took in Paris in 1952, a nude man sits on the wooden arm of a wicker-bottom chair before the floor-to-ceiling french doors of a hotel room. The glass door is covered by a patterned mesh curtain; the man's right arm, resting on the back of the chair, pushes aside the heavy drape. The man, in his late twenties, I'd guess, is turned away—you can't see his face—towards the high, narrow doors. What stands out is the lower half of his body, tautly balanced on the arm of the chair, so that one notices the indentation in his buttock, the tensed calf muscles, his arched bare foot.

Decades after the picture was taken, it finally comes out that this was Tobias's first lover, an American named Dick who had given him a camera, with whom Tobias lived for a while in Paris. That belated knowledge—available only because I, along with others, stood at the barricades in 1969 (or whenever)—doesn't alter the photo, but lends a certain poignancy to the way I see it.

I'm overwhelmed by the thought of thousands of historically invisible loves, couplings, affairs, furtive encounters, which were thoroughly suppressed, whose spoken memories were confined to select circles, unmarked by announcements, declarations, narratives. (*The Temple* was put in a drawer for half a century; before that, so was E.M. Forster's *Maurice*.) Even today, information in the mainstream media about our desire—as opposed to commercially produced but semi-clandestine male porn—is so sparse that I've often noticed, in the homes of my friends, that they've cut photos of striking youths out of the newspaper (I do this myself) and taped them to the refrigerator door, as if the newspaper had published a news story headlined "Here's a desirable boy." The tales of past relationships reappear among us as randomly as a bottle with a message cast into the sea; someone discovers a photographic negative; a diary or letter turns up.

The photos of Herbert Tobias that most fascinate me were taken in Berlin in the mid-1950s. There are two pictures, more or less unremarkable, of Eisenacher Strasse, around 1954. In each one, children are in the foreground, sitting on the intact curbs, while the camera stares down a long vista of the bombed-out rubble of the empty street—shells of gutted buildings, slopes of heaped-up bricks tumbled towards the curb. Part of my interest is simply the recognition that this is what Germany looked like, even a decade after the war. Then there's the minor coincidence that a few metres from the intersection of Eisenacher and Fugger is Tabasco's bar; in showing the photo to someone, I might say, I know that street, I've walked down it a dozen times, as though it really were a small world.

In a photo (also Berlin, 1954) taken in a hotel room, a naked youth sleeps belly down, seen from behind a clutter of objects on a night table. I find myself craning my head around a glass vase of half-wilted roses, past a curious round shape made of leatherette—perhaps a piece of luggage, I think, or maybe a hatbox, until I figure out that it's a portable record player—and I lean over the edge of the table to get a better look at how the light from an unseen window slides up his body, as if daylight itself were his lover.

Some pages farther on in Tobias's book, there are two facing photos, taken in 1957. In the photograph on the left, a woman in an off-the-shoulder Persian lamb stole is about to enter a car on a Berlin street at night; the manicured nails

of her hand reach across her body to adjust the collar of her
fur, revealing a bracelet that looks like plastic embedded
with gold filigree, and matches her headband (perhaps the
photo is for a jewellery ad). This demure goddess of capitalism appears as an icon of returning postwar prosperity, of, as
they said, the German "economic miracle".

Berlin, 1954

On the facing page, a boy-man wearing denim shorts
and slippers leans almost insouciantly against a hotel room
door. He has short, chopped black hair, smouldering dark

eyes, an unlit cigarette dangling from the pout of his lips. His hands are brought together at his midriff, thumbs tucked into the waist of the tight shorts; as the weight of his solid, bare torso leans against the doorjamb, one leg is casually crossed over the other, which has the effect of pushing his genitals forward so that his cock is clearly outlined, and

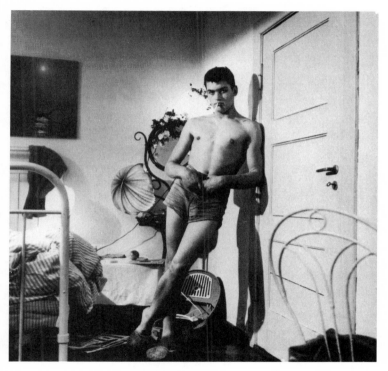

Berlin, 1957

of proclaiming a sexual confidence so sure of itself that it doesn't require a defensive posture.

As the young man dominates the tableau, every object in

the room, even the room itself, flutters around his presence. The half-slippers he wears appear to be of woven straw; in the foreground there's the white wrought-iron delicacy of a café chair, behind him a mirrored dressing table, the mirror wreathed in (possibly artificial) flowers. Newspapers are strewn half under the bed, whose striped duvet is an unmade pile; a pair of jeans is draped over the painted metal bedstead. Even his shadow, which undulates up the wall, is more boyish than its owner. Just as I'm falling into infatuation with him, I notice that on the floor behind his feet is a round-shaped leatherette object, its top open to reveal a white grille. I have to look again to see that the grille is in fact a sound-speaker, that the hatbox-shaped object is a portable record player, the same one that appeared in Tobias's photo three years earlier, of a naked boy sleeping in a hotel room.

Immediately, the tiniest narrative opens before me, of Herbert Tobias moving from one hotel room to another, carrying, amid his luggage and cameras, a leatherette-encased portable record player. If I follow that story, facets of it enlarge. For instance, later I found another photo of that black-haired boy—whose name, I learned, was Manfred—shot on the same roll, or at the same session—moments later, apparently, because the cigarette is now lit. In this shot the seeming toughie looks entirely different—somewhat "fruity" even. When I showed it to Michael, he immediately said, "How unfortunate"—one of his favourite words for softening a negative evaluation. Yet I rather liked it, or at least liked the idea of Manfred being rescued from his iconic status, reinstalled into the everyday reality of that Berlin hotel room.

Then, at the opening of a photography exhibit at the Men's Art Gallery in Berlin, about a year after I'd become interested in Tobias's photos, I met Hans Eppendorfer, a playwright and critic who had known the photographer and owned several of his works. Upon learning of my interest in Tobias, Eppendorfer invited me to visit him at his home.

So I returned to the city where I'd gone with Manuel, where List had lived in the 1920s and Tobias a half-century later. Eppendorfer greeted me at the door of his apartment, wrapped in a kimono, apparently just arising. He'd returned late the night before from Brussels, he explained, where a play of his was having a revival. He magisterially showed me through room after room of art works—from Japanese scrolls to drawings by Cocteau; a few Tobias photos were among the collection; in one room sat an aged tiny woman (possibly his mother)—and at the end of the journey was a small sitting room where we would have coffee. At the last minute, as though producing a rabbit out of a hat, Eppendorfer called out and there appeared a dark-haired boyfriend with the build of a soccer player, about twenty, who was just buckling the belt on his jeans. Again I had entered the precincts of Boyopolis.

The boyfriend, named Peter, promptly went off to brew a pot of coffee. I tried to get Eppendorfer to tell me about Tobias. He had employed the photographer in the mid-seventies, when he edited a gay magazine in Hamburg. He reached into a bookshelf and offered me some issues containing photos by Tobias—mostly, I saw, not very distinguished beefcake shots. The photographer had obviously been down on his luck, reduced to doing hack work.

Eppendorfer's brief account was somewhat dismissive, describing Tobias as the sort of person who borrowed equipment from other photographers and seldom returned it—a hotel-room transient. Indeed, my host wasn't particularly interested in talking about Tobias; he was happier to turn the topic to himself and show off his boyfriend, whom I certainly had no objection to looking at. And all the time I marvelled at the invitation that the story itself seemed to offer, if only its reader would notice a small portable record player.

"Art is life's only twin," I dutifully record in my red notebook, quoting the unforgettable aphorism of poet Charles Olson. Not the imitation of life but its twin, its *only* twin.

Coda

I sometimes imagine Boyopolis as a city devoted to boys, like those places of the past dedicated to the gods, or kings, or the dead. Of course, I know that it is just an idea, a game invented by Michael and Vincent to celebrate and mourn the evanescence of a particular form of human beauty.

This city, created by a phalanx of talents from artists to clothes designers, would contain everything from public boy monuments to running shorts. There would be Olympic-length swimming pools, afternoons drinking milkshakes in Donatello's David Café, and so on.

Something odd occurs when I imagine Boyopolis. I get bored. To relieve my boredom, I begin to imagine it more "realistically". It occurs to me that its culture might increasingly consist of the trashy action pictures, video games, and pulsating music collages that entertain adolescents today. The boys become men, some of them turn into paunchy businessmen. The lucky ones, that is. Some of them don't become men, they become disfigured corpses.

Wait, this is all going wrong, I say. I rewind the tape, attempting to smooth out some of the inherent contradictions in my imaginings. Still, at best, Boyopolis might be rather boring. Even if the boys themselves weren't boring, I suspect that, ultimately, any utopia is.

One afternoon, when Manuel and I were staying at the Florida Hotel in Hamburg, we came back to the hotel and popped into the little room that was being used for breakfast while the bar was undergoing a renovation. For a moment, I thought I saw Boyopolis as it actually is.

The room was thick with smoke; the men and boys had been sitting around the handful of crowded tables since morning. The staff, perhaps hustlers pressed into temporary kitchen service, drifted in and out of the room, as did the construction workers —who may have had other connections to the establishment than carpentry and drywalling. There were dregs of coffee in the cups, crumbs in the bread baskets and on the linen tablecloths. The customers sat in the late-afternoon gloom in the postures of people who had accustomed themselves to purgatory. They were men and boys who knew each others' bodies. Their conversations were slow and desultory, familiar. I was staring into the cosy horror of eternity.

Boyopolis fails as a Utopia, probably, because there isn't really a *polis*, a city, at its heart. It is no more than a striation

of desire, beauty, and laughter that runs through the streets
of our actual marbled cities.

DeCoda

I have an old friend (and fellow writer), Brian Fawcett, who,
like you, is reading these stories. He sends me urgent messages about them that go bump in the night across conti-
nents and oceans. Of course, nowadays, they don't really go
bump, but come slithering out of the maw of a fax machine,
or glow in cyberspace.

What worries him about some of what you've read so far
concerns the nature of homosexual desire, or at least my representation of it, and how such a depiction might work
against and undercut the other subject matters of these tales.
Although Fawcett doesn't share my "sexual preference"—as
these things are euphemistically known—he respects this
passion as a source of knowledge. But I portray homoeroti-
cism, he says, as though I were writing about the lives of
the saints—"hagiographically"—rather than in an accurate
manner, or "anthropologically". As he urges, "You're going
to have to step outside of your own erotic procedures and
look at them as a self-ethnologist."

What exactly, he asks, do I mean by "falling in love", as I
sometimes suggest when describing an infatuation with one
or another of these boys? After all, we're often talking about
hustlers here, young men who sell their bodies for money,
and we usually don't anticipate much affection under such
conditions. "Is it to adore from a slight distance," Fawcett

asks, "to engage in brief and carefully impermanent sexual relations, to have a relationship in which one is always aware of where the exit is?" (My first mischievous impulse, I must confess, is to reply, "Gee, that sounds pretty good," but I know that won't do; I'm required to adopt a sober mien.) "I'd call it," Fawcett proposes, with respect to such a relationship, "an 'active infatuation'."

Further, isn't there a *prima facie* political problem in a work that tells "post-communist stories" from the perspective employed here? "You're attracted to the transient commodity of youth and inexperience, not to the persons in and of themselves," he accuses. "It's a problem in Eastern Europe, since, frankly, similar qualities are what makes Eastern Europe of interest to capitalist entrepreneurs." Unless some sort of case can be made out, some explication provided, he warns, "Your relationship with these young men looks pretty awful." He suggests there "hides a huge darkness within this form of desire, before which you *must* stand judgment and answer . . . else how can you be a leftist, an egalitarian, a democrat, and all the things you claim to be in every other way?"

I doubt that I can manage anything quite as grand as my earnest guardian angel imagines necessary, but since I, too, believe that the stories we tell are important, let me, then, as the author rather than the narrator (the difference is, admittedly, paper-thin), partially step out of my story for a minute. Luckily, we're in the midst of a part-narrative/part-essay about art and desire and their relation to the world, so my interruption shouldn't be too jarring. If this is hardly the time or place for the treatise that might be required to explain all, then at least a decoding device is warranted, which, as one writer I know proposes, every text should have.

I realize that the overwhelming majority of people who might be reading these pages has little direct knowledge of either those whom I desire or of the social system(s) in which they move, especially the demimonde of prostitution. My gay friends would never think of questioning my attraction to Manuel and others—to them, it's obvious and unproblematic; my friends in Berlin, since they live in a non-puritanical culture, would consider it *gauche* to look askance upon an encounter that is neither illegal nor morally vicious.

Nonetheless, I'm uncertain as to who my readership really is with respect to these issues. The larger stories I'm telling are, of course, for anyone who might read them, anyone who happens by, who has an interest in the world. But this excursus isn't indiscriminate—for example, I'm not out to persuade the Family Values division of the Christian Coalition to loosen its ideological grip. Thus, I'm talking not to a hostile "them", but to a relatively friendly "us"—an "us" not beset by fundamental(ist) objections to homosexual desire, an "us" sophisticated enough in its recognition of the diversity (and mystery) of the sources of desire to tolerate my image of eros, focused in the particular way it is. It's an "us" that might say, at most, Odd, isn't it, that your desire is confined to those young men? An "us" to whom I might reply, in a voice as non-judgmental as their query, Yes, they're obviously the boys from my adolescence, from my neighbourhood, the sandlot where we played baseball. In sum, the Imaginary Reader I'm inventing is, if anything, simply unfamiliar with an exotic territory. He or she merely wants to know how it works, and wants a measure of reassurance that we're at least in the same moral universe. That is reasonable.

So first, and most obviously, I'd better clear up any misconceptions that might exist about my usage of the word "boy". The "boys" designated here, hustlers or otherwise, have all arrived at the legal age of consent to sexual activities. None of the youthful males who appear as figures of my desire is a "child"; I'm neither an advocate nor covert promoter of the practices of pedophilia. While there can be some argument about precisely *what* the age of consent ought to be (in Europe, it tends to be around sixteen; in North America, about eighteen), I don't think there can be any serious argument against the notion that there is, in fact, an age of consent. If the precise age is slightly uncertain, we're at least sure that there are some ages at which meaningful consent to sexual activity isn't possible. While the boys and young men here are adults, they are of course developmentally contiguous with post-pubescent boys who aren't; conversely, while these boys are adults, they're distinguishable from the men they will become. That I feel compelled to spell this out is a measure of the heated character of the contemporary North American debate about "children" and the "abuses" to which they might be subject.

In any case, let me underscore the fact that the boyish young men who are my idea of the erotic are all legally adults. While I don't mind people disapproving of my notion of desire, I would indeed object to being thought one of those demons who make the headlines of the morning tabloids.

A more arcane bit of anthropology concerns prostitution. Again, I'll begin by emphasising that we're talking about a legal activity (prostitution is legal in Canada and the other places referred to in these stories), so if there's an issue here, it's one of morality or taste rather than legality. For the moment, though, my preoccupation isn't moral but, rather, informational. The sole point I want to make is that male prostitution, or hustling, is different from female prostitution.

The differences are as follows: unlike prostitution involving women, generally speaking there are no pimps in the realm of homosexual hustling (and thus those engaged in it are more independent, less under threat); sexual acts between males—this is true of homosexuality generally, and also applies to hustling—tend to be more reciprocal or equal than those between men and women (I'm especially thinking about acts of anal intercourse, and their symbolic as well as actual effects) and thus some of the disparities of power in the encounter are more likely to be evened out; the question of desire in homosexual prostitutional encounters is more complex than our stereotype of unreciprocal desire in heterosexual prostitution; finally (and this is more of a generalization based on my observations than an established fact), relationships between customers and young men in homosexual prostitution strike me as more "sociable" and "romantic" than relationships in heterosexual prostitution.

In schematically laying this out, I'm not concerned to diminish whatever moral opprobrium might attach to prostitution in general, or to the customers of prostitutes. I'm simply arguing that there are structural and qualitative differences between homosexual hustling and heterosexual prostitution that one would have to take into account in, say, making a judgment about the damage caused to "victims" of prostitution. These increased complexities are further coloured by the fact that everything that occurs under the rubric of "homosexuality" takes place within an antagonistic, if not outright homophobic, political condition (notwithstanding the increased tolerance homosexuality has achieved in broadening social circles over the past quarter-century of debate). Just as all heterosexual prostitution by definition contains an aspect of male sexism, so all homosexual prostitution occurs under a regime of whatever oppression is applied to homosexuality generally. Our increased sensitivity to "sexism" inclines some people to want to equate homosexual and heterosexual practices. The objection often takes the form, Isn't what you do the same as what middle-aged heterosexual men do who seek out young women hookers? But in my view, the circumstances are not symmetrical precisely because of both the general differences between homosexuality and heterosexuality, and the actual differences between hustling and heterosexual prostitution.

Although I think it's useful to make explicit these facts for friendly readers unfamiliar with such subjects, I'm struck by how earnest the tone becomes as soon as one starts talking about them. We're immediately enmeshed in a political discourse that's curiously reductive of desire. That is, we find ourselves seeking to disentangle moral ambiguities, to come up with solutions, to establish rules of order. On the one hand, I'm attracted to such talk. To someone (like me) for whom ideas of citizen, community, civil society and civilization resonate, it's only natural to be engaged in such discussions.

Yet that talk fails to fully recognize the character of desire. To bestow upon passion an extreme aphorism: there's a sense in which *desire is nature*, and as such is indifferent to, if not subversive of, civil society as presently constituted, though we of course seek to reconcile the two (through institutions, moralities, decencies; and of course I'm not suggesting that desire is purely nature, or that civility is devoid of desire). Still, desire resists reconciliation, for if an aspect of it is indeed best understood in terms of nature, then by definition it's anarchic, playful, out(side)law, contrary to much of conventional sociality. Worse, homosexual desire especially outrages present forms of conventional society for, unless severely domesticated, it seems to threaten the institutions of family, fidelity, procreation, and much else. I'm not sure if homosexual desire, in and of itself, proposes a political reform of conventional society. Quite possibly, but that's outside the scope of what I'm arguing for here. Perhaps I'm pointing to no more than the existence of a genuine and contradictory dualism between nature and civilization, which unexpectedly shows up in the borderlands I inhabit and describe, and whose tensions, as they apply to desire, merit recognition.

So, to put it as unoriginally as this sentiment deserves, I desire in a world that I didn't make. Where "we" see a morally problematic relationship, I experience an encounter with another person in a relationship whose morality will be tested only by what we make of it. Some friends—I pestered all of them in contemplating this—indeed urged me to take a "worldly" view of the moral problem of relations with hustlers. What's there to say? they shrugged. The boys are beautiful and capable of consent, you desire them, you're otherwise not a monster, they're there (in a bar), conditions are proposed which you're prepared to meet (the famous cash nexus), why be so bourgeois as to accede to the qualms of those who refuse to recognise the ways-of-the-world? And anyway, you're older now, longer in the tooth, and your knee hurts. It's a tempting view, but just as I'm about to be tempted, the other side of the dialectic, the human city, invariably hoves into sight.

Of all the warnings Fawcett offers, I notice that the one I'm most defensive and anxious about is the suggestion that I might be attracted only to the "commodity of youth and inexperience, not to the persons in and of themselves." Underlying that anxiety, I think, is another current bias in North American discussions of relationships, one against any trace of the "objectification" of other people. Immediately, I begin mentally scrambling to secure details to "prove" that I'm attracted to the specificity of the person, that I don't experience him as merely a cipher for certain qualities, that I don't regard my infatuations as interchangeable. But the exercise strikes me as a bit strained, if not futile. The narrative either persuades you that I regard the other as a unique person or it doesn't.

Perhaps there's one more thing to say about the problem of whether or not I regard those young men "on the stroll" as persons in and of themselves. Once we drop the characterising term ("hustlers", "male prostitutes", "whores")— and it should be dropped—it immediately becomes easier to see them as simply boys, young men, persons with names, *other people*. Forgetting to see them as people is a consequence, however unconscious, of retaining a conventional stereotype about hustlers; often a well-intentioned liberal concern about their "plight" ends up masking an unintended, but demeaning view of them as persons.

It also occurs to me that I may be making too big a deal about this. Why not admit to simply liking boys, as if they were a *genus*, a species? I think of heterosexual men I know who are attracted to a certain sort of woman—someone in her thirties or forties, with a recognizable sophistication, style or cast of mind; I even begin to recognize the subsidiary "type" that So-and-so likes. Perhaps we make too much of all this. Certain things about those we're attracted to *are* interchangeable; so what? That doesn't eliminate their particularity.

But with respect to those I do in fact desire . . . is it love, or as Fawcett suggests, adoration from a slight distance, "brief and carefully impermanent sexual relations," "a relationship in which one is always aware of where the exit is"? But why can't that be "love", too? "Mini-love"? Does it matter what we call it? Or, what if I'm prepared to cede "love" to adultophile sharers, whether of homo- or heterosexual persuasion, of long-term monogamous domesticity? Let them make of love what they will; I'll retain my *amateur* status. If not "love" then, should I take up Fawcett's designation of "active infatuation"? It sounds like some kind of unpleasant viral infection. I think I'd prefer something that better captures both its enchantment and its finitude. How about *enamourment*?

More important than all this philological tussling, I should note that those enamourments have an element of being self-induced, though the inducement seems to require no special effort on my part. As Fawcett observes, one of my motives for "falling in love" is that "it's a way of holding Berlin and your life in an eroticized, slightly romanticized nexus." That is, it's procedural, a way of becoming sufficiently attentive to see what else is going on in a given location. Desire, apart from its own pleasures, serves as an initial epistemology for politics.

But it's not only my own desire that's at issue. One might also inquire about that of the boys as well. From the outside, one only gets the sociology of it. A Berlin bi-weekly, running one of those periodic "Boys of the *Bahnhof Zoo*" cover stories, melodramatically asks, "Hustler-misery or Sexwork?" "Naked self-defense, fast buck, or wild adventure?" it enquires, not terribly sincerely, of the post-Cold War emigration of Polish, Romanian and Czech youths to the murky street behind the train station.

However, experienced from inside the relation, something else is noticeable. As I noted earlier, one of the differences between hetero- and homosexual prostitution is the greater complexity of desire in the latter. This isn't all that surprising. For some hustlers, it's of course simply a business, but others—and remember, this all takes place under the general social proscription of homosexuality—are themselves gay or bi-sexual. Recurrently observing the actual pleasure of the other person, or experiencing some human feeling in the encounter not bound by the economic transaction, I had to consider that the form his desire took wasn't the same as the shape of mine, which specified him, but that nonetheless I was in the presence of not merely my own, but also *his* desire.

But now it's time to come to close quarters. The issue about hustling, if I haven't utterly deluded myself, isn't boys or love or enamourment but, using the word in an old-fashioned Marxist sense, exploitation. The world assembles the boys in whatever site, primarily (though not solely) through economic circumstances; if the world gave them jobs as clerks or mechanics or philosophy instructors, they most likely wouldn't choose to be in a rent-boy bar. There is an enormous number of arguments designed to evade this point—what might be called arguments for mitigating circumstances, and I've heard most of them—but finally, I don't think any of them avoid the residual aspect of exploitation. The customer—or "suitor" as it is in German—has an advantage over the hustler; it isn't merely a simple exchange. To participate in such conditions is to perpetuate them. The john is free, in a way the hustler isn't, not to participate in them.

When I get to the nub of it, then, it appears to me that my position is this: that of all the possible evils before me—some of which, short of saintliness, we engage in, freely—this is the one I choose to be stuck with, and thus perforce— since there's no way around it—accept the implications it has for, as we used to say, the state of my soul. In sum, confession rather than *apologia*.

Another friend asks, is it evil or sin or merely a moral failing on my part? Well, not sin, since I don't believe in that. Or, if it were a sin, then a venial rather than a mortal one, as

the Catholics so thoughtfully distinguish. But, yes, personally, a moral failing. Of course, pardonable sins and moral
failings don't obviate our ability to be citizens. However,
the systematic exploitation to which even venial sins con-
tribute is no mere failing, but an evil.

All of this—the calculation of a moral logic or "the com-
ical physical union our arms like briars are wrapped around"
—goes on while I'm, for example, riding the Berlin subway
over to Tabasco's. And along the way, I'm noticing the most
unexpected bits of life—the unreproduceable beauty of a
passerby I'll never see again, or a magical item in a shop
window, or the way a particular linden tree looks in the evening light as I'm turning into Fuggerstrasse—while at the
same time realizing that surely I'll forget this or some other
wonder of the world before the night is out. But when,
later, the desired one undresses, those informing undercur-
rents, troubling riptides, dissolve. I may even idiotically proclaim, "Boys suit me. Period." But I don't for a moment
assume that I'm exonerated, or that things don't go bump in
the night.

On Certainty

Between the anticipations of the evening and the loss of the
day's memory (and more, no doubt), we occupy the present
tremulous moment. While Manuel sprawls in sleep above
the gathering traffic hum of the Reeperbahn in that interlude dividing the end of the afternoon from the early evening, I, having woken from our nap before him, sit reading

at a small dressing table at the foot of the bed, pausing occasionally to glance up at his tousled hair.

I first happened upon Ludwig Wittgenstein's *On Certainty* while reading Ray Monk's biography.[4] The essay is, like almost everything Wittgenstein wrote, unsystematic, fragmentary, and unfinished. It was also the last thing he wrote; he worked on this topic right up until two days before his death in April 1951. My admiration was roused by the fact that Wittgenstein simply kept on, scribbling thoughts into his notebook, to the very end: "I do philosophy now like an old woman who is always mislaying something and having to look for it again: now her glasses, now her keys." There's really nothing else to do. Impending death ought not be treated as something out of the ordinary, he seemed to imply.

On Certainty was, as well, about exactly the subject that was most on my mind. I was immured in the mixture of my body's certainty of desire for Manuel, and my puzzlement over almost everything else, from the identity of the other person to that of the new societies emerging from the wreckage of the Communist states. Wittgenstein seemed to offer at least another way of asking about what we knew.

In addition to Manuel, there was another person in my life, Alexander Goertz. He was the one with whom I had begun reading *On Certainty*. Goertz (everybody called him by his surname) was a rosy-cheeked, blond-haired music student in his early twenties, of Hungarian-German parentage, whom I had met indirectly through Michael Morris, perhaps a week or two after I'd met Manuel. There wasn't anything sexual to our relationship; Goertz was, insofar as these terms

apply, heterosexual, and often lamented his misadventures in
the minefields between the sexes. It had been intimated to
me that Goertz might in some fashion become my intellectual companion in Berlin; I immediately saw the need for
such a person in my life, and his arrival was welcome.

Goertz's interests in music ranged from the medieval
composer-nun Hildegard of Bingen to the obscure American musical inventor of the 1940s Harry Parch. Goertz was
in his period of walking down stairs backwards; he was a
vegetarian, so we regularly went for lunch at a cheap Indian
restaurant on Grohlmanstrasse; he was one of the few people
who could recount a dream in such a way that I wasn't bored
by it; he invented devices to purify the sound of electric guitars, and so on. Though some regarded him as merely
quirky, I had no difficulty in recognizing his genius. More
important, when I mentioned Wittgenstein's name (I'd just
read the biography), Goertz at once declared his interest.
Thus we began reading *On Certainty* in Berlin—sitting in
the Boyopolis Chamber—puzzling out the book's fragments
rather randomly, since the form of its composition seemed
to lend itself to such a reading.

The problem Wittgenstein set himself was roughly as
follows. In 1939, the English philosopher G.E. Moore published an article, "Proof of the External World", in which
he claimed to *know* a number of common-sense propositions, such as "Here is one hand and here is another." In an
earlier paper, "A Defence of Common Sense", he made
similar claims: "The earth existed for a long time before my
birth," and "I have never been far from the earth's surface."
Moore was attempting to defeat philosophical scepticism

about objective reality by a number of "obvious" assertions.

Wittgenstein replied (in his notebook), "If you do know that *here is one hand*, we'll grant you all the rest." The sweep of that opening gesture delighted me. The question he posed was "Now, can one enumerate what one knows (like Moore)? Straight off like that, I believe not—for otherwise the expression 'I know' gets misused," adding, "We just do not see how very specialized the use of 'I know' is."

Instead, Wittgenstein turned the problem of knowing around: "What we can ask is whether it can make sense to doubt it." He meant that quite literally. "Do I, in the course of my life, make sure that I know that here is a hand—my own hand, that is?" Then he tried to explain why such an announcement would be most odd, and to think of conversational examples where such a claim might make sense.

Now, pondering *On Certainty* in the Florida Hotel, I wondered if its author might be amused to know that he was being read in a brothel (for it was slowly dawning on me that that's what the Florida was). Or perhaps it was simply I who was pleased that philosophy could be at home here.

That evening, behind the Exquisit bar in the hotel, Manuel's best friend, Detlef, was the host of his own birthday party, pouring drinks for the men and boys who filled the bar stools while deftly accepting little gifts from new arrivals—they were buzzed in to the second-floor establishment through a locked steel door—as well as taking phone calls offering best wishes on his thirtieth birthday.

Detlef was a solidly built, dark-haired man in a denim shirt and jeans, the edge of his butt perched on a tall stool, legs confidently spread. I was introduced to him, and he poured Manuel and me glasses of champagne with which we toasted him. I could see what he must have looked like at eighteen. Had some of the middle-aged men who now crowded the bar once slept with him? He was taciturn, cool. His style was more *noblesse* than *oblige*. Manuel's enthusiastic greeting was returned rather indifferently, I thought. When Manuel asked if he should take up my invitation to visit me in Canada, Detlef dismissively replied, "Sure. Why not?", as though he had left the invitations of men far behind him, as though he knew exactly what they were worth. He soon turned his attention elsewhere. Manuel had told me that he and Detlef had never slept together, that they were just friends. I wondered if their friendship was as close as Manuel supposed.

After a while, Manuel suggested that we visit the other gay bars of Hamburg. Outside, in the cold drizzle, we hailed a taxi that took us to the St. George district on the far side of the train station. We aimlessly traipsed from one bar to another—the Universum, the Club König—each slightly differing in decor and demeanour, but all of them strangely empty. Back at the Exquisit, Detlef's party went on. We had a nightcap before going upstairs at midnight.

When we went downstairs for breakfast in the morning, we discovered that the entire bar had been ripped apart and was in the process of being renovated. Wiring dangled from the ceiling. The furniture had been piled up against the walls. To Manuel's annoyance, the breakfast room was temporarily housed in a suite off the corridor; the coffee was cold, the bread stale. We escaped the wreckage, taking a cab across town, where we found a basement bar that was just opening. There was hot coffee, and a pinball machine to amuse my guide in this labyrinth.

Oversized windshield wipers swept away the rain pelting the smoky grey windows of the tour bus. When Manuel had asked, "What do you want to do?" I had said, "Let's see Hamburg." It was one of those standard city sightseeing tours for visiting strangers, probably boring for Manuel, who knew Hamburg, but I liked it; I liked being inside out of the rain, being with Manuel, not having to do anything, while the city—narrow, villa-lined streets, a fountain in a lake—floated by us in a wet haze.

At the harbour, where there was a shopping stop as the tour more or less ended, we got off the bus, hunched under a small umbrella. I was too cold to imagine that I was looking for List or Tobias, the ghosts who had brought me to Hamburg, although I wanted to see the places where they had made their daily rounds. I could barely make out the harbour cranes and anchored ships through the mist and slanting rain. Certain jumbled streets that angled towards the slate-coloured water tempted me (was I looking for some long-gone bar of the 1920s—The Parrot's Perch?—where List had gone?), but I saw that Manuel had had enough.

On the Reeperbahn we searched for an open restaurant—not easy to locate on a street that only awoke with dark—until, just as we were about to give up, we stumbled upon a place that served a traditional plate of *Eisbein* (hamhocks on a bed of spicy sauerkraut). A television mounted high behind me was showing a Chinese comedy film. Manuel watched it with pleasure, while I enjoyed looking at him and his grey-blue eyes following the slapstick. We had no idea in the world where we could go from here.

Though the surfaces of the city were cold and wet, inhospitable even, I was nonetheless deep inside it looking out, rather than the other way around. Manuel was attentive to my desire; his manners charmed me. I could never have found my own way into and through that garish maze. If I had entered the Exquisit myself (using one of those gay guides that offered the symbol "R" for "rent-boy"), I would have been faced with the opaque backs of the men at the bar, or by Detlef's cool demeanour. Instead I had been led by the hand. But to where? In one sense, to no more than a slightly shabby waterfront sex hotel. But in another, was it not into the heart of the heart of the body's, or the city's, secrets? Back in our room, we lay in the tangle of white sheets in a brothel sanctum.

Manuel liked me to impale myself astride his condom-covered erection. He said he got hot seeing me jack off onto his belly as he came inside me. It amused him to watch me cry out with pleasure as I reached back to place my hand on his bare thigh, feeling the convulsion of its muscle as his groin bucked up into me. Afterwards, he napped.

I sat naked in a chair by the little table, once more looking out over the Reeperbahn as I returned from the animal world to the uniquely human one that Wittgenstein wrote about. My body involuntarily quivered, still shaken by its recent fucking, so that it took an effort of will to keep my hand steady enough to read the page.

At first, when I was reading *On Certainty* with Goertz, we dipped into its passages playfully, in no fixed order. "Suppose

some adult had told a child that he had been on the moon,"
Wittgenstein speculated, thinking of Moore's claim that he
knew he had never been far from the earth's surface. "The
child tells me the story, and I say it was only a joke, the man
hadn't been on the moon; no one has ever been on the
moon; the moon is a long way off and it is impossible to
climb up there or fly there.—If now the child insists, saying
perhaps there is a way of getting there which I don't know,
etc., what reply could I make to him?"

Goertz and I liked the unintended irony of that passage.
A decade or two after Wittgenstein's death, the impossibility
of being on the moon had itself been dissolved. That season,
they were playing a song in the bars that included, amid the
blur of techno-sound and the interstellar static, the voice of
Neil Armstrong, proclaiming in slightly botched grammar,
"One small step for [a] man, one giant leap for mankind."

I had been reading *On Certainty* as though I were seeking
the answer to a Zen riddle, but in that hotel room—my
body, the ground of first knowledge, still alive to the place
where it had been so recently penetrated, and the boy who
had done so now innocently asleep—I came as close to understanding Wittgenstein as I would.

Since Wittgenstein saw the human realm as residing in
language—the rest of the world being an unspeakable mystery—doubting and certainty were simply possibilities in the
practices of language. "A doubt about existence only works
in a language-game," he proposed. "We should first have to
ask: what would such a doubt be like?" Certainty, Wittgenstein says, is, "*as it were*, a tone of voice in which one de-
clares how things are...." Later he adds, "Do I want to say,

then, that certainty resides in the nature of the language-game?"

That is, "it's not a matter of *Moore's* knowing that there's a hand there, but rather we should not understand him if he were to say, 'Of course I may be wrong about this.' We should ask, 'What is it like to make such a mistake as that?'" Because "the *questions* that we raise and our *doubts* depend on the fact that some propositions are exempt from doubt . . . certain things are *in deed* not doubted." In the end, "If you tried to doubt everything you would not get as far as doubting anything. The game of doubting itself presupposes certainty."

It was not that I knew something with certainty, but that my doubts depended on my not doubting certain things. I had thought I was looking for a Cartesian kind of certainty. What Wittgenstein wanted to show me was that there was no separating certainty from doubts; what were of interest were the doubts, and the set of undoubted propositions— the language games or, simply, the "background"—necessary to sustain them.

If I had translated my desire for Manuel into the equation "Desire is the body's first epistemology", Wittgenstein solved at least half the riddle of how we know anything. I had still to discover the other half of the maxim that I sensed might complete my declaration about what the body knew, or where its knowledge led.

That night the bars were again a failure. At midnight on a Friday, they yawned in emptiness. I was uncertain if the explanation—for which various bartenders offered their versions—was to be found in a seasonal economic downturn,

or the lateness or earliness of the hour, or was simply an un-
accountable mystery.

Manuel and I sat up in bed till three or four in the morning, gossiping through the baffle of language. Those leisurely
conversations—in the middle of the night, or dawdling long
after breakfast—were what took the relationship from urgent
desire to a more diffused enamourment. Manuel claimed to
make a good living from hustling, and held up Detlef as
a role model, a possibility of how one could make the successful transition to a later stage in life. Detlef was how he
imagined himself ten years down the road. But since I didn't
seem to fit the picture of one of those lavish-spending gentlemen from whom he drew sustenance, what was he doing
with me?

"Because I said I would go to Hamburg with you," he
replied. I asked him if he had any regrets. "Not at all,"
he said. "You like doing sex?" I asked. "Yes," he answered,
"like you love writing books." (Did he really say that, or had
I misunderstood, mistranslated?) When he asked, just before
we fell asleep, "What do you like best about Hamburg?", I
answered "Making love in Hamburg with you."

When I woke in my familiar bed on a cool, cloudy Berlin
morning, feeling the little aches and pains of middle age, it
was a reminder that Manuel was twenty. The thought of him
bore with it reflections on the transience of our intimacies.
About twenty-four hours before, I'd been fucked, and yet
now it was utterly forgotten by my body, while *I*, on the
other hand, remembered that he had taken my pen, written
my name on the bottom of his big toe, then his own on the

bottom of the other one, and brought his feet together, pressing our written-on-flesh names against each other, making me laugh. But what was this "body" I separated myself from? Who was this "I" that I thought about apart from the body's sensations?

Meanwhile, life went on: I obeyed the orders of the day. At dinner with Michael and Vincent, I pondered the difference between pornography and the erotic, and Michael showed me his latest snapshots. Goertz turned up for lunch and again we attempted to untangle a passage of Wittgenstein. I made myself at home at Frank Wagner's apartment and explored the streets of the Moabit district.

One night, as I walked part way home from the bar, I turned into the Ku'damm and found the great boulevard jammed with honking cars. There were crowds several people deep on the sidewalk, gazing up at the huge electronic news screen on the corner as it announced the narrow vote by which Parliament had chosen Berlin to be unified Germany's capital once again. Where the Wall had transformed the formerly thriving Potsdamer Platz into a wasteland, Sony and Mercedes were planning to build their new corporate towers. The post-Communist future was unfolding.

Manuel and I appear in each other's lives casually. In the middle of the afternoon, as I stand on a busy street-corner across from the Zoo station, dithering over something trivial, he materializes out of the blue—actually, out of one of his favourite hangouts, the Presse Café, which is right next door to the international press shop where I've just bought a newspaper. "Are you free?" I ask him. He laughs. "You're simply impossible," he says, a phrase I particularly like because it's the same one he admonishingly addresses to his erect cock, shaking a finger at it, as though his body too were distinct from himself. And in minutes we're on the S-Bahn, riding home.

After we play for a while, he asks for a rubber. Then he's inside me. I reach behind, cupping his ass in my hand, to press him deeper into my body. Later, while I lie on my back, his teeth nip at my groin as I come. Even later, after he's gone—to meet his jolly aunt from Florida? to hustle in the Zoo station?—my body doesn't remember. As is my habit, I seek an aphorism to encapsulate that peculiar dualism I experience: *the body fucks and forgets; I remember and write*. I'm left with inconsequential details of our couplings —the disposal of a used condom, the sight of cloud formations when I open the curtains again.

But what does it mean to say that the body forgets? It experiences the pleasure provided by Manuel but shortly afterwards, as the sensation dissolves, it's almost as if it never happened. I, having an identity, remember what happened to me—even if memory is unreliable and cuts out at odd moments, like a power disruption—but the body is indifferent to identity. It's concerned solely with sensation, is *sense-full* and thus "senseless". It doesn't contemplate life or death; I do.

My dualism, I notice, seems to divide in a rather different way from the standard philosophical terms of "body/ mind" (or "mind/brain", as it has become in contemporary debates). For me the set is "body/me", where "me" is a language-rooted (Wittgensteinian?) concept. "I" or "me" is not mind, not brain, but that which is associated with the words identifying myself. In a way, my dualism skirts the question of whether mind can be reduced to the material(ism) of the brain; instead, "me" is more like a fictional character.

And indeed that's how *fictional dualism* seems to work. I can use the body's memories for only a very short time, and then I have to "make up" what it feels like to be in the bubblebath with Manuel in Hamburg. Memory without fiction is incoherent.

For the moment, I see dualism everywhere. I've begun to learn reflexive verbs in German, which makes considerably more use of that grammatical device than other languages I know. "I remember", in German, is *ich erinnere mich* —literally, "I remind me", thus implying, at least in terms of syntactic logic, that there is a "me" for "I" to remind.

But if I have a use, as a writer, for what I remember, then what do other people do with the bits and pieces left over from the experiences that the body, perforce, forgets? While we (artists) make art of it, for others it goes into gossip, anecdotes, ways of presenting themselves, summing themselves up; reminiscing; in short, pretty much what the rest of us (artists) do with it. Is the difference between us—other than artists make art, non-artists don't—merely tautological?

Of course, one can't go on believing "fictional dualism" for ever. But I could go on, for as long as it might last, seeing Manuel, reading philosophy, watching the sky over Berlin, meeting Goertz for lunch.

One afternoon, some weeks later, Goertz came by with his guitar. The windows and balcony door were open onto the courtyard and the thick foliage of the chestnut tree. By then I was again staying at Michael's, in the Boyopolis room; it was warm and muggy though the sky was thick with rain-clouds. Goertz played some pieces by Leo Brouwer, a Cuban whose name I'd mentioned to him. I thought about the obvious fact that I liked Goertz so much more than Manuel, notwithstanding the fate imposed by desire. Listening to the sounds, watching Goertz's fingers on the strings, I was astonished that someone could do that, that it could be done at all—the skills involved seemed so difficult compared to what I did in making sentences or constructing and deconstructing philosophical puzzles.

"I'd better play some Bach," Goertz joked after playing one of Brouwer's works, "just to make sure I'm not frightening the neighbours." As he played, it began to rain. In the middle of the afternoon, the storm gathered in a fury I'd never seen or heard before. The noise of the deluge, pelting the chestnut tree, echoing in the courtyard, drowned out the music. We sat and listened to its consuming roar.

Manuel phoned one night, late, from the bar. I was sitting at the black-topped desk, looking into the night sky, which was filled with the whop-whopping of unseen helicopters. There'd been choppers over Berlin all day, occasioned by the arrival of a flock of foreign dignitaries from NATO. Perhaps he was bored at the bar (I could hear its disco rhythm in the background); he said he'd come over in half an hour and spend the night (I didn't ask why he couldn't sleep at his own place). When he hadn't shown up an hour later, I fell asleep in familiar puzzlement. I'd never understand his appearances, his no-shows. He'd been agitated of late. Things were going badly, I assumed. Landlords, creditors, bureaucrats, were all demanding payment.

At a quarter to three he woke me. I didn't understand all the details of his tale about getting stopped for riding the S-Bahn without a ticket. He crawled into bed with me and quickly dropped off into exhausted slumber. A great deal of the pleasure I took with Manuel, it occurred to me, consisted in simply looking at him while he slept; it was a pleasure I connected with that of looking at the moving clouds. He threw the comforter off, and I was filled with wonder to see his naked body.

Manuel slept until noon the next day. Then I gave him some money to go to the bakery for pastries while I laid out the plates, put on the coffee. From the kitchen window I watched him come back up the street, recognizing even from a distance the bakery's familiar wrapping paper, a package balanced in his hand.

After breakfast, he asked, "Do you want to go swimming?"

"I don't swim," I said, puzzled.

"In the bath," he laughed.

In the warm soap-bubble froth of bathwater, we slid across each other's bodies again. We towelled off and went back to bed.

I'd said earlier, over breakfast, that I wanted to go to the Zoo station to pick up a newspaper and smokes. He proposed that he sleep a bit more, that I wake him when I came back and we'd have coffee and the rest of the pastries before he went off to "work". Maybe I could get him a copy of the local tabloid, *B.Z.*, he suggested. There was a parting sentence as he lay in the comforter, but I missed the verb. He may have been asking if I trusted him enough to leave him alone in the apartment. The thought had crossed my mind.

The errands took a half-hour. When I came into the house, I noticed from the corner of my eye, passing through my workroom into the room where we slept, something amiss on my desk. Something white on its black surface, something red out of place. The bed with its tangled comforter was otherwise empty. The place where I kept cash, tickets, passport, and traveller's cheques had been disturbed. There was an instant of bodily thrill, a rush of adrenalin, at taking in so instantaneously what had happened.

Yet I felt strangely cool about the theft, unlike the first time he had stolen money from my pocket. Then, when it was far too early for a real narrative to have formed, I'd simply experienced the emotions of someone who had been robbed. Now I also saw it as a final "plot twist" in the story. I began to assess the damage methodically, going first to the maroon-coloured bag where I stored my money and documents, but remembering the disarrangement on the desk, of white, of red.

The cash (again a relatively small sum) was, of course, gone. But what about the traveller's cheques? Some were there, scattered about as he'd hastily rifled the bag. If he'd taken any of them, that meant a dreary sorting out at American Express. I took the handful of cheques with me into my workroom to match the numbers against those I'd written in the back pages of my red notebook. Only the cash was missing.

The white object left on the desk was a note. As I was about to glance at it, I realized that the red notebook itself had been left on the desk, out of its usual place amid the stack of books that was my current reading. Though I was relieved that the notebook was still there, its placement meant that Manuel, for some reason, had been into it.

I went through its pages until I found what was missing: the strip of photobooth pictures of him that I had pasted into the back cover. Was he trying to make it harder for the police to find him, in the unlikely event I should call them?

I turned to his note, written in German, in capital letters.

DEAR STAN,
I'M SORRY I HAVE TO DO THIS. I'M REALLY
STUPID. I'M NOT DOING IT BECAUSE I WANT TO,
BUT BECAUSE I'VE GOT NO OTHER CHOICE.
WE'LL NEVER SEE EACH OTHER AGAIN.

TSCHUSS,
MANUEL

At last, certainty filled me. Something had happened, and while there were perhaps doubts about Manuel's conflicting motives (at least, I hoped there were conflicting motives), there was no doubt about the event. At that moment, sometime in the early afternoon, a new batch of clouds rolled in, and the sky darkened again.

The certainty (and doubts) before me seemed curiously distant from the things that Moore claimed to know and that Wittgenstein doubted. The material damage was relatively minimal. I still had my documents, my traveller's cheques, and my irreplaceable notebook. His arithmetic was odd, though, since he would've made more money by sticking around.

Did I doubt that this was my hand and that was my other one? It was possible that he had enjoyed the sex and nonetheless decided to steal from me. It was even possible that he liked me, though that was in the realm of uncertainty. He had given me a surfeit of bodily pleasure. What sort of thief left you sexually content, and apologized for stealing from you? A damn elegant one.

Had I been to the moon? I was charmed that our encounter had begun and ended with writing. All that summer, I had been deluged with visual images—the photographs of List and Tobias; Michael's drawings; snapshots, porn, ads—even as I insisted on words. I'd feared I would forget what Manuel looked like, and now that he had taken the only pictures of him that I had (although, oddly, they had not helped me remember what he looked like while I had them), all I had by way of remembrance were words. The bibliographic details he had written out on the first night we met, the note of apology at the end.

Had the earth existed for a long time before I was born? I might run into him again, but this felt like a natural end to the story. But what was the nature of that narrative, that I'd sought to fulfil by choice and interpretation of accident? Certainly there was no preordained story that wanted me to do "x"—go to Hamburg, or fall in love with a blond-haired boy—no other, greater source that overrode the secondariness of my personal life compared to the primacy of the world. Nor was there a narrative independent of us, discerning some shape to seemingly haphazard events. But our seeing a story made life something it wasn't heretofore.

If desire is the body's first epistemology, the knowledge to which I aspire at last is the story.

I loved the wildly romantic boyish despair of that last line: "We'll never see each other again."

Well, of course we would. Or at least hear each other again. A few days later, Manuel called from Cologne (or that's where he said he was; I was only certain that it was he). The rest was lost in the blur of language. "Why did you steal from me?" I managed. "I don't know," he said. He was going off with the alleged jealous suitor to Mexico. He'd call me again.

That night I was drinking sweet vermouth and soda in Tabasco's, while Henk listened to one of the customers at the bar tell his tale of woe. A dark-haired boy with a faint, downy moustache wandered in and ordered a beer in heavily accented English. I had been vaguely expecting to see a blond boy I'd noticed in Tabasco's once or twice before.

When whoever it is (invariably unexpected) begins the conversation—he's Portuguese, his name is José, he's travelling in Europe, wants to know if I'm looking for a good time —all that matters is to recognize: this is what I requested from the world. Many miss it altogether, deny they've asked for anything, mistakenly decide that this is not exactly what they asked for.

He sits naked astride my thighs, his medium-sized hard dick nestled under my balls, the light from the night-time street outside glowing on his smooth torso. My cock slides up and down in the grip of his fist, he tips his head forward and aims a stream of saliva he's built up in his mouth so that it lands where his hand provides a spit-slickened groove for me.

When I walk José to the main drag so that he can get a cab back to the bar, there's a low-key full moon over Paulstrasse.

The next day, comparing notes with Michael on the telephone, I mention the Portuguese visitor.

"Portuguese? Mmm, sardines on toast," he says, exaggeratedly smacking his lips. "I could go for some of that."

Meditation
in a Moonstone

How do we distill ourselves
into a text, how does the text
arise from our texture?
— *George Konrad*[I]

Text, Texture

SEVERAL TIMES during our conversation that evening
in Budapest, Andras B. Hegedus—he insisted on the
middle initial so that we wouldn't confuse him with
a former, discredited Hungarian prime minister of the same
first and last name—referred to the room in which he,
Tom, and I were talking. My sense of being present at a
historic moment—and not just one to which politicians
attempt to lend gravity by declaring it historic—was deep-
ened by being in a place that had been one of the sources of
that history.

"In this room . . . ," Hegedus said, and then later, in reference to something else, "Yes, right here, in this room," and
once again, towards the end, when the grandfather clock in
the corner chimed the quarter-hour before seven in the

evening, reminding us it was time to go, one of us asked (I can't remember if it was Tom or myself), "Did that happen here?", and he said, "Yes, in this room."

It was a long, high-ceilinged, sumptuous room, lined on three sides with overfull bookshelves. You entered Hegedus's apartment, on the fourth floor, from a courtyard balcony. The door, bearing a small metal nameplate with the distinguishing middle initial, was located at a corner angle of the balcony that ran high above the entire edge of the garden below; when opened, it gave onto a dark foyer inside. The large library room was on the right, the rest of the apartment off to the left. In the middle of the room there was a big worktable with piles of documents spilling over—the work of the Committee for Historical Justice, of which Hegedus was the secretary—and beyond that, comfortable armchairs and a low coffee-table upon which cups, saucers, ashtray, notebooks, and tape recorder were eventually assembled. In the near corner, the elegant standing clock chimed the quarter-hours and, more lengthily, the hours themselves.

Hegedus, a man of about sixty with long, swept-back grey hair, wore a plaid shirt, tan corduroy pants, and slippers. He was a veteran of the Hungarian Revolution of 1956. Perhaps there could be no more poignant moment to think about the event which had figured so largely in his life than on that particular Sunday evening towards the end of March 1990. That day, Hungarians had gone to the polls in the first multiparty election in almost half a century.

Tom and I had spent the morning and early afternoon with a woman who was our guide to the city. We observed her marking her ballot; afterwards she took us sightseeing and we ate a chestnut purée confection in a café in the hills overlooking the Danube River, which divides the two parts of Budapest. In the early evening we had arranged to meet Hegedus, to whom we had an introduction from an academic friend back home, and afterwards we would go to one of the election headquarters to get the first returns.

Once more, as elsewhere in Central and Eastern Europe on similar occasions in the wake of Communism, names of the dead were invoked, names that meant something perhaps only to Hungarians—maybe only a certain generation of them—and to a diminishing circle of international intellectuals.

Of all the communisms in Eastern Europe after the Second World War, few had a more brutal inception or a more deceptively soft decline than the one in Hungary. The country had never experienced anything resembling twentieth-century democracy. In the entirety of its thousand-year history, from near-mythical tales of the adventurer Arpad and his horsemen sweeping in from the Transylvanian hills to the collapse of the Austro-Hungarian Empire at the end of the First World War, its sole bright political moment was associated with the proto-democratic revolutions of 1848, which sent a momentary tremor through the European monarchies. In a taxi that scooted along the shore of the river—it was on the day of our arrival—we'd caught a first glimpse of the statue of Sandor Petofi, the young poet whose death was linked to the events in Budapest in March 1848.

Unlike Czechoslovakia's incipient democracy, or Germany's social democratic, if chaotic, Weimar Republic, between the great wars of the present century Hungary drifted from the aristocratic conservatism of Admiral Horthy's regency to its own brand of Arrow Cross Fascism, complete with virulent anti-Semitism. In the end it sided with Hitler, and suffered the fate of the Nazi debacle.

After the country's consignment to the Soviet camp at Yalta, the gyrations of Soviet affairs determined political life in Hungary. By 1947, any nascent semblance of postwar democratic government had been squeezed out by the Communists, led by Matyas Rakosi and the Muscovite faction of the party. When Tito's Yugoslavia broke with the Soviet Union in 1948, an enraged Stalin demanded the unearthing of conspirators throughout his extended empire. Rakosi, who proudly dubbed himself "the best pupil of Comrade Stalin", readily complied, producing as the chief Titoist traitor Laszlo Rajk, the Minister of the Interior he had appointed to replace Imre Nagy, one of his Muscovite rivals. Rajk was tortured, made to confess, and executed. In the terror that followed, between 1949 and 1953, some 150,000 of Hungary's ten million citizens ended up in prison or labour camps. Rakosi purged his own ranks, ensuring an atmosphere of suspicion and the penetration of a corrosive cynicism to every level of society.

When Stalin died in 1953, and was replaced by a collective leadership eventually dominated by Nikita Khrushchev, the internal rivalries of the Hungarian party were thrashed out in Moscow politburo rooms. The ensuing unsatisfactory compromise permitted Rakosi to retain his party post, but elevated Imre Nagy to the office of prime minister. Yet the local party apparatus, jealous of its privileges, resisted, even as Nagy enforced a general liberalization that included the release of imprisoned former party members (the most prominent being Janos Kadar), tolerance for a group known as the Petofi Circle, and even an attempt to form an extra-party "patriotic front" to oppose the power of the appa-ratchiks. Rakosi counterattacked. Within two years Nagy was ousted, though the Soviets would not permit Rakosi to reimpose a reign of terror.

But again external events intervened. The Soviet deci-sion to patch up its feud with Yugoslavia in 1955 effectively doomed Rakosi. In February 1956, Khrushchev delivered his secret denunciation of the crimes of Stalin to the Soviet Party Congress. By June, Rakosi was retired to the Soviet Union, replaced by a longtime henchman. That autumn there was the first of a sporadic series of political eruptions in nearby Poland, and in October the Hungarian party re-buried a posthumously rehabilitated Laszlo Rajk. Two weeks later, university students and workers demonstrated in the streets of Budapest, demanding reform. Stalin's giant statue was toppled. The secret police opened fire. The Hun-garian Revolution had begun.

"The Petofi Circle," Hegedus explained, "was a discus-sion club of young intellectuals. The first times there were a few people, then hundreds; at the climax, there were some thousands. The problem was, Do we have a possibility of reforming the whole system or not? We have to say that we thought, between 1953 and 1956, that the system was reformable."

"This was reform within a Marxist context?" I asked, still uncertain of his party status.

"You can say within a Marxist context," Hegedus said

with a shrug, "or in a socialist context. But all right, I can say within a Marxist context. Between 1946 and 1956 I was of this party, naturally, as was everybody who was on the left. I was very active in 1956. Not in the revolution," he carefully noted, "but before the revolution. I was never in the fighting."

The Hungarian Revolution was crushed by the Soviet invasion in November 1956. Imre Nagy and several of his associates were executed, then secretly deposited in unmarked graves. Janos Kadar was installed in office—the beginning of a thirty-year regime—by his Russian masters. How ghostly to hear Hegedus, in his thickly accented English, mention the names of Rakosi and Rajk and Nagy in passing, presuming a rudimentary knowledge on our part. To me, as a fifteen-year-old, the Hungarian Revolution had meant little more than the cover of *Life* magazine. I found myself trying to recall the image that the magazine cover had portrayed. Was there a tank in a cobblestone-paved square laced by metal tram tracks? And people photographed from above, running diagonally across the glossy sheet—blurred traces of them, like birds darting through one's field of vision?

"How did you live all these years?" Tom asked, bringing me back to the man in the room.

"I did a lot of things," Hegedus replied. "I was arrested, two years; after that I did everything. From 1963, I was for fifteen years a mechanical-industrial economist. That was not bad, it was a normal life."

"You talked about making politics in this room," Tom prompted him.

"In the sixties, the seventies, I was passive, because we had no possibilities. I went back to politics in 1979, when there was the signing movement for the Czech Charter '77. I undersigned this declaration for Vaclav Havel. And after this action, this absolutely minor action, I lost my job, but I got my salary. I was banned from the institute, I didn't work. That was very bad psychologically, it was a hard situation," he admitted.

In the late eighties, as the Kadar regime quietly expired in what would become a general wave of Eastern European revolution, Hegedus and some colleagues formed the Committee for Historical Justice.

The committee had sought what Hegedus called the "rehabilitation of '56"—that is, political recognition that the revolution was not merely an outburst of "Fascist hooligans", as the party had long branded it. It also proposed the reburial of all those who had been executed, whose memory had been effaced. In the last year, the veterans of 1956 had succeeded beyond expectation.

In June 1989 the committee conducted the reburial of Imre Nagy, more than thirty years after his execution. An ailing Kadar died three weeks later. The reburials of the others were continuing still. In fact, a reburial a few weeks before had been attended by Vaclav Havel, for whom Hegedus had signed the declaration of support a decade earlier.

"I never thought when I signed it that I would be with Vaclav Havel ten years later. I never thought that Havel would be President of Czechoslovakia. So, that was really a nice moment." Then he added, "Morally, it was not uninteresting."

The phone rang. Hegedus got up and fished among the papers on the worktable, pulling out a cream-coloured cordless telephone, and then ambled through a doorway I hadn't noticed in the bookshelves on the far wall.

Hegedus's son Istvan, a man in his early thirties whom we'd seen at a press conference the day before, was a candidate for the youth party—Fidesz, or the Young Democrats. It, along with the dissident-based Free Democrats, the centre-right Hungarian Democratic Forum, and the reformed but discredited Socialist Party, was among the likely contenders for the night's vote. When Hegedus came back into the room and mentioned that the call was from Istvan, I asked him about his son's party.

"Fidesz is a hard question," he allowed, "because—well, that's my son. What's my opinion that my son is a candidate? I think that the new generation has the right to shape its own image, and we, the older generation—not only those in their sixties, but those in their forties too—are full of personal and political contradictions. Of course, I'm very far from my Petofi Circle ideology, but I have a *nostalgie* for the generation of 1956. Fidesz are very well educated, very talented—but it is also my son, what can I do?" He offered a fatherly shrug. "We discussed, in this room, the problem of his being a candidate. I think I trust this generation, they have to try it. I lost trust in my generation. That's the reason."

"What made you sign the declaration?" I suddenly asked.

"Pardon?"

"What caused you to sign in defence of Vaclav Havel and the Charter '77 people?"

"*Why* did I sign it?" There was a longish pause. "It was a

must," Hegedus finally said. "I think it was a psychological must. Two young gentlemen came in this room, and it was ... I thought it would be a shame not to sign." He was silent again. "Sometimes we have to say a yes or a no to something. Even if it has eruptive consequences."

Standing in the foyer, putting on our jackets, we had a last backward glance at the room. In the long absence of public places, it had provided a private space for public affairs. No doubt it would be used again, if not with the same urgency. The grandfather clock chimed once more.

The Young Democrats' election returns centre was a large third-floor meeting room in a building on Molnar Street with cubbyholes on the floor above for press interviews, and a general bustle on the floors below. Upon entering, I was immediately stunned by the sight of a young man, about twenty, whose beauty was as strange and memorable as any I'd ever seen. What's more, it was a uniqueness that stood out from a remarkably attractive gathering.

There were a couple of hundred people in the hall, the majority young men, most of them pressed towards the front of the room, where the election returns were being presented amid a bank of monitors and microphones.

The most extraordinary feature of the dark-haired young man—as I would discover in a moment—was that his beauty was set within a viscerally frightening disfigurement. I made my way to him almost without thinking—he was with a younger friend, a plump boy who had costumed himself in jeans and a tuxedo shirt and bow tie for the evening's festivities—and as he spoke English, we effortlessly entered into conversation. Against the running narrative of the election returns that he provided, punctuated by cheers when the crowd was pleased, we exchanged the sort of information common to strangers meeting for the first time.

"Szabolsc," he said, when I asked his name. He had to repeat it several times before I got the pronounciation approximately right ("Za-*bolsh*"). I had been standing for a minute or so alongside this athletically graceful young man, with longish, flowing jet-black hair which he shook back from time to time with a quick flip of his head, when we happened to turn to face each other.

His functioning eye was dark brown, a rich, glowing colour; the other was a milky near-blankness, like a dully lucent moonstone. There was the faintest circle of grey where the pupil should have been. Upon seeing it, I experienced a tiny wave of nausea as I involuntarily imagined one of my own eyes being blanked.

I hadn't heard the name Szabolsc before.

"It's old Hungarian," he said. His family, he added, had originated in Transylvania.

Szabolsc was unselfconsciously outgoing, friendly, at ease with foreigners. He was a student, of economics, I think he said, wearing a loose-fitting white T-shirt and worn jeans. But he seemed to convey or even embody—through his remarks, his interest in politics, his cosmopolitanism—a sense that Hungary was entering a new and larger world that evening, and that he was one of the young New Europeans determined to be part of it.

I found his mannerisms charming. When he was temporarily stuck for a word in English, his face creased with self-critical annoyance, his hand plunged into his mop of thick black hair and he scratched furiously, as though he might extract the missing word from his mane. When he went off on a brief errand, his younger pal in the mocking tuxedo top trailed after him with a puppy's adoration.

I returned again and again to that eye with its milky lucence. Unlike the squinting slit of a missing eye, or the fixed gaze of a glass eye, it declared its absence of vision. If anything, it enhanced the power of his beauty. One's attention shifted back and forth between his striking form and the deformity of the eye that made one momentarily forget the beauty.

The crowd was excited, but the initial returns were somewhat less encouraging than might have been hoped. The centre-right Democratic Forum led with about a quarter of the counted vote, followed closely by the Free Democrats. A party allied to the patriotic-religious Forum, the Smallholders, was next, while the revamped Socialists and the Young Democrats were neck and neck with about ten per cent.

We were together for a couple of hours. The final results wouldn't be known until the following afternoon, and even then there would be a second round of voting two weeks later. As Tom and I were leaving I had a moment of anxiety that I would lose Szabolsc, but we ran into him and his friend on the staircase on the floor below, and I stopped to say goodbye. Was it he who asked if we would see each other again? In any case, he gave me his phone number and we made a tentative lunch date for a few days hence.

In the cool night air Tom and I made our way along the river towards the sublet apartment where we were staying.

There were lights on several of the bridges that spanned the Danube, and the castles and the Matthias Church high up on the ramparts of the Buda side were bathed in an illumination whose golden reflection played on the river. I thought about the distorted vision of the generation Hegedus no longer trusted, and the optical illusion of beauty with which Szabolsc had surprised me. In the country of the blind, a one-eyed youth is king.

The apartment on Raday Street, a couple of blocks back from the river and near the fume-spewing traffic roar of Boraros Square, had been obtained for us through the same academic friend who had provided our introduction to Hegedus. He had put us in contact with a friend of his, Vera Szelenyi, who had arranged for us to sublet the place of a friend of hers, Klara, who would meanwhile stay with Vera.

The address on Raday was for one of a series of tightly ranked five-storey late nineteenth-century apartment buildings. From the narrow street, packed with traffic, you entered through a small door into the merciful hush of an enclosed courtyard. Klara's was a tiny two-room flat on the third floor. I sank into a rough ochre-coloured armchair, determined never to be dislodged, while Tom energetically boiled water for coffee, unpacked his bags, made forays into the square for food, and decided on morning jogging routes that would allow him to avoid asphyxiation.

"This used to be the club of the secret police," Vera had told us when we met her that afternoon in the lobby of the art-nouveau building being used as the election press centre. She was employed by a Jewish film festival or magazine, or perhaps both—in the tumult of the Hungarian economy, everyone who worked seemed to have three or four jobs, of which translating for the foreign press was only one of Vera's. She was separated from her husband and their child lived with her, but we didn't need to know that now because she had arranged a little party for the following night, Saturday, where we would meet everybody.

In the second-floor theatre, decorated with plaster putti and an art-nouveau goddess whose flowing hair was painted in gilt, there was a running press conference. Miklos Haraszti, one of the best-known of the former dissidents, was on the stage, fielding questions for the Free Democrats. We settled in.

Most of the weekend was spent in Vera's company. Dinner at an elegant restaurant, the party at her house—her former husband, a psychologist, among the guests—Sunday morning voting, press conferences where we met reporters and swapped "war stories" (there had been a recent violent clash between Hungarians and Romanians on the border), unhurried wandering through the fifteenth-century streets of Buda, with frequent café stops. Vera seemed pleased to find that I was more interested in coffee and cigarettes and what she laughingly called the "national intellectual drink", an alcohol whose brand name is Unicom, than in trudging through three floors of paintings in the national gallery.

Through it all, there was a sporadically told story of life during the later, "soft" period of the Kadar regime, when intellectuals lived in its shadow in their own patchwork "civil society", as it was known—a creation of the unofficial opposition. Vera referred to the "charm" of the repression, as she described semi-illegal lectures and large parties held in private apartments.

"We could define ourselves against the limits of the regime," she remarked, adding, "It was quite enjoyable in a way." Now there was more uncertainty; the weight of dealing with unstable jobs, money, existence itself, produced daily stress; people were suffering from "nervousness" in the midst of the country's democratic transformation. Vera conformed to my vague stereotype of the sophisticated, beautiful, approaching-middle-age European woman. She was instantly recognizable to me as someone from what I jokingly referred to as the Hermes Agency—a mythical international body that provided the people in your life who took you from one world to another.

The world she guided us into was Budapest itself. Every time we stepped out of an interior, we seemed to encounter the sinuous river, spanned by its bridges, as it coursed through the city, dividing the two old towns of Buda and Pest. I tried to commit to memory the series of crossings, from north to south: Arpad, Margaret, Chain, Elisabeth, Freedom, Petofi. And above the city were the church named for the fifteenth-century king Matthias Corvinus, the rococo embellishments of the Gellert Baths, the orange-gold lights that lent night-time Budapest an air of faerie timelessness. Yet its beauty was not inhuman. The narrow streets and busy squares, the walk along the riverside strip of luxury hotels and sidewalk cafés, the clanging trams, the nineteenth-century art-nouveau buildings being eaten by auto pollution, all had a feeling of being used, touched, trodden upon.

Budapest was more like a city encountered in dreams than any other I had experienced. Even in strolling along the twisting streets or entering the closed face of an apartment building, I had a sense of tunnelling, burrowing upwards to emerge in a courtyard. Coming out the mouth of Raday Street into Boraros Square, I felt as if I had surfaced on the shore of the Danube, as though the city were somehow underground, while the river represented ground level. And the underground city was itself composed of deeper historical strata. The innocent square whose traffic we now dodged had once been traversed by Russian tanks; beneath it were Petofi and the 1848 Revolution, all the way down to the marauding Arpad.

If Budapest felt like a city explored in dreams, the Rudas Baths, where Tom and I went the Monday morning after the election, seemed to be a sensuous extension of its dream architecture. They were located on the Buda side of the river, just off the Elisabeth Bridge, and dated from the sixteenth-century Turkish occupation.

A newsstand stood at the entrance to a long, vaulted hall where a cashier in a boxed-in cubicle was selling admission tickets. There were openings in opposite directions, presumably for men and women, and she pointed us at one of them. On the other side of a curtain, a beefy attendant issued us gauze loincloths and towels and led us through a maze of small wooden locker-rooms.

After we changed into the loincloths, we passed through a low, rounded portal and entered a massive grotto. A large circular pool steamed under a high dome that admitted shafts of dim light through bits of coloured glass. As my eyes adjusted to the gloom, I saw many men, mostly older and a little ghostly in the faintly sulphurous air, either in the depths of the thermal pool or seated around its edges, immersed to the neck. The light from the dome commingled with the rising steam.

While Tom went off to explore—there were smaller pools in the corners, massage rooms, a shower—I picked a spot to soak on the steps of the big pool. Two young men appeared, sank into the pool, emerged shimmering, then seated themselves on a little platform not far away. One was blond, with longish hair and a double button earring; he was smooth-limbed, the lines of his lean flanks unbroken by the skimpy loincloth that covered his front. His companion was stockier, more athletic.

They were almost dream-figures, bubbling up from an erotic unconscious, as were the other male bodies farther off, some reading newspapers at the edge of the pool, others meandering through the fog-wisps of the thermal waters. We were deep below the earth, in an earlier place, a different time.

As Tom and I emerged from the baths, a chill morning drizzle slanted against us. We vainly tried to find a cab to take us to the press centre on the now hazy Pest side of the river. There was an hour or so of bone-chilling travel hell—the temporary total loss of all direction and meaning that wanderers inexplicably fall into from time to time—before we arrived at the art-nouveau building tucked into a hidden street behind Roosevelt Square.

The press-conference theatre was packed to overflowing as the leader of the Hungarian Democratic Forum, a distinguished conservative named Jozsef Antall, responded to questions. The press corps had already determined him the winner, notwithstanding the electoral formalities still ahead. The mood of the journalists was different from that of those who had covered the East German election with deadline excitement in Berlin a week ago. Here, the reporters were already bored with the Hungarian affair. Many papers, in fact, were using wire-service reports rather than sending their own correspondents. The electoral validation of the fall of Communism was now a foregone conclusion; the complicated distribution of voting percentages was reduced to a mention of "minor parties"; the phenomenon of Fidesz wasn't even noteworthy. The reporters, in short, were packing their bags.

Tom had struck up a conversation with a young investment banker named Randall Dillard, and now he pulled me from the armchair-lined corridor and introduced me. The three of us went downstairs to a café. Dillard worked for a Japanese firm, Nomura, "the largest investment bank in the world," he quietly boasted. Contrary to whatever image I had of international bankers, he was casually dressed in jeans, white shirt, dark sports jacket. Although he was in his early thirties, he looked considerably younger. By the time I'd located a waiter and ordered coffee for us, Tom had begun a brisk journalistic interrogation.

"What's the labour cost look like in Eastern Europe compared to Japan or North America?"

"I can't say about Japan," Dillard replied, "but compared

to Europe, you're getting one in five—it's one-fifth the cost. You can get it down to one-tenth, if you really want to go down to the bottom of the barrel, just labour-labour."

"So that's one of the appeals for investment," Tom suggested.

"Sure. Anything should be structured on the labour-intensive continuum."

"The Marxist theory of labour value strikes again," I said, adding a wry chuckle to make it clear that I wasn't, of course, one of those who might advocate such a thing. Dillard missed the nuance. "Yeah, the first thing you have to add is labour," he replied.

Tom reported that when he'd asked a woman we knew—he must have been referring to Vera—about the changes taking place, she had replied, Yes, things have changed this year: we're much poorer.

"That's true," Dillard agreed. "Now that the subsidies are gone. I mean, what the old government did is, they would subsidize everything, and they would borrow to subsidize and give people an illusion of material comfort, and they were producing nothing." Dillard seemed a bit appalled at the notion of producing nothing, although he had noted that Nomura didn't "produce" either, "we only arrange access to capital, we charge a fee for that; that's basically what we do." But "the IMF will not give aid unless they stop these subsidies, and everything's going to whack out, and that means they actually are going to be poorer in the short run. And the only thing that's going to stop that from being a complete freefall is new aid, and forgiveness of lumps, otherwise it's a total spiral."

Dillard was from Florida and had gone to Cambridge on a Fulbright scholarship, where he'd acquired a Ph.D. in international law, clerked for the European Court of Justice, and then joined a big London law firm, doing debt rescheduling.

"I liked international law and banking, not because the ideas of international were so sophisticated, but I liked to travel, meet different people, and I thought, well, maybe I should try to focus on a lifestyle rather than technical interests, and you can't become international in America, so I moved over." He had done mergers and acquisitions through the rapacious 1980s, and that led to a stint with Merrill Lynch, "but they were just too erratic. So then I moved over to Nomura. Nomura—I probably shouldn't say this—they have very low technology, but a lot of money, and the interest. So I had the technology and Nomura had the time, and we found a good fit."

While the press scrum was trailing a potential prime minister upstairs, we were seeing the future of Eastern Europe. The bright-eyed advisers from the privileged West could tell newly democratic governments to sell equity— "give it away if you have to, to get investment here, and get it off the budget deficit," Dillard urged—and at the same time innocently conceive of themselves as "focusing on a lifestyle", "finding a good fit". They were "intensifying coverage" of Eastern Europe as naturally as Arpad's horsemen rode in from Transylvania.

Dillard told us about Tungstrom, a Hungarian lightbulb company that was one of the first sell-offs of state-owned enterprise. "Gyro Centrale, an Austrian bank, bought a majority stake in Tungstrom and paid cash for it. They then went out and sold it to General Electric and immediately made, in six months, a forty per cent return. Now, one could argue that that's capitalism, that's the ugly face of it, but everybody was shocked. I mean, they wanted companies like Tungstrom to go into private ownership, but the idea that somebody would make money other than the government bothered them. To some extent, they're right."

It wasn't clear whom Dillard was referring to by "they". But within a few months, back home, I would see a GE television commercial celebrating the purchase, complete with exploding fireworks over the illuminated Chain Bridge, and the faces of happy, freedom-loving, post-Communist Hungarians.

"The banality of evil" was a phrase coined by the philosopher Hannah Arendt in connection with the Nazi extermination of the Jews. I doubted that genocide could be banal, but the banality of global capitalism seemed to pose fewer problems of discernment. A popular novel had appeared in America a year or two before, in which aggressive Wall Street stockbrokers and bankers were referred to as "the masters of the universe". Randall Dillard didn't seem much like the cocaine-snorting, luxury-car driving, sexually restless figures whose adventures adorned the bestseller lists. The real-life masters of the universe were well mannered, educated, affable even. After all, why shouldn't they be?

A few doors from our apartment on Raday, on the opposite side of the street, was a tiny, lighted entrance under a sign that said, Orpheus Drink Bar. We hadn't noticed it until we were coming home that night. Tom, who didn't drink, urged a Unicom on me before we turned in.

The oval sign above the door was crudely hand-painted, and around the words were childish dabs of black paint in a rough circle. Inside, there was room for a dozen customers at most, a television set (a sports interview was on), and an imitation stained-glass window containing an image of Orpheus, lyre in hand. Again I was surprised by the magic that greeted us as we turned a corner, by the story within the story that insisted on digression. Drinking a bittersweet Unicom, I suddenly and clearly saw the face of Szabolsc for the first time that day. I had tried to recall it unsuccessfully at various moments, but now he was before me, moonstone eye and all.

When we got home, I phoned him.

"I know we're supposed to see each other for lunch in a couple of days, but I was wondering," I quickly asked, "if you were free for dinner tomorrow night." He was.

Szabolsc was waiting for me outside the Alfoldi restaurant when I arrived the next evening. It was a crowded student eatery with a brace of wooden booths down the centre. Vera, who had recommended it, told me that the word *alfoldi* meant "the earth". But as soon as we were seated, I realized I had made a mistake. Whereas I had wanted to display my interest in Budapest by going to a restaurant with traditional Hungarian food, he was disdainful of the familiar, the local, irrespective of its authenticity. Szabolsc was attracted to the foreign, the new, the world beyond. We would have done just as well eating at the Budapest

McDonald's. Similarly, if I longed to see his body, my remark about the thermal baths, designed to entice him into a similar visit, merely elicited an indifferent scowl. The baths were old-fashioned, too Hungarian. "I only go there to go swimming," he said.

Szabolsc was a normal twenty-year-old, interested in cars, travel, R.E.M. (a rock group then popular in America). My infatuation with him was of course rather self-willed, something I would only allow myself to recognize after the fact. When he mentioned that he had been to Greece with his family and I expressed some surprise, he lifted his aqua-green sweatshirt to show me his T-shirt as proof. The white T-shirt had Greek calligraphy on it. I could read the letters, but had long since forgotten most of the words. They were the first lines of Homer's *Odyssey*:

> *Tell me, Muse, the story of the resourceful man*
> *who was driven on far journeys, after he had sacked*
>   *Troy's sacred citadel.*
> *Many were they whose cities he saw, whose minds he*
>   *learned of....*

I imagined our life together, an impossible mixture of reading Homer, swimming, listening to R.E.M. on a Walkman. . . .

After dinner, though Szabolsc might be the New European, he walked me through the streets of old Europe, past the shops of Vaci Street, along the corso by the Danube, across various squares with their statues of historical figures. Though he had more than a touch of that affliction the old regime denounced as "cosmopolitanism", he was also a

Magyar youth whose late adolescence had casually included participation in the public events that spelled the end of Kadar.

When we walked past the statue of Petofi in the small park just north of the Elisabeth Bridge, he mentioned that he'd been here in the ecology demonstration a couple of years before, or that over there was where Fidesz had held an important rally. Across the river, the lighted castles high up on the Buda bluffs spilled their reflections into the water. On Vaci Street he paused before a shuttered toy store, and recalled how important it had been to him to buy a model train there when he was fourteen. He remembered the day at grammar school—he was twelve—when the students had been assembled for an important announcement.

"They said Brezhnev, the leader of the Soviet Union, had died that morning," Szabolsc said. "I was very frightened. What would happen, I wondered. Would there be a war?"

Through it all there was that shifting head, almost like double-exposure photography, as I saw one eye, then the other—the brown one, deep and wild; the moonstone one, vacant and milky.

If Szabolsc was the New European, the Last Communist was Peter Bihari, who lived out in a residential district of nearly identical rows of concrete buildings, not far from where the city had preserved a patch of woods. Bihari could see us between four and six in the afternoon, after which his wife would be coming home from the hospital with their newborn.

It would be our last full day in Budapest before taking a train to Bucharest the next evening. A rumpled but enthusiastic philosophy professor had come over to our place for coffee in the morning, and he and I had talked amiably about our mutual profession. At noon Tom and I had dashed over to the Buda side of the river, and met with some trade unionists in an office overlooking the tram-clanging Martirok Avenue below. We just had time, in the early afternoon, to interview a representative of the tiny Green Party in the elegant nineteenth-century rooms of the Angelika coffeehouse.

Bihari was cleaning the freshly painted apartment in preparation for his wife's arrival when we got there. His in-laws were taking care of their other child, a two-year-old, he explained. He was a lean man in his thirties in a green polo shirt, prematurely balding, with a closely cropped black beard. He set aside a mop and pail, and seated us on brown corduroy chairs around a low, glass-topped table.

I'd been shown a letter a few months before, which Bihari had written to an economist friend of mine, which provided a Marxist analysis of political developments in Hungary.

"I got the impression from your letter," I began, "that it must be rather depressing to be a socialist in Hungary these days."

"Yes. Yes it is. It's a very strange situation," he said. Bihari had a quiet voice which I had to lean forward to hear, but which nonetheless precisely articulated his words in English. "I said in this letter that the left is dead in Hungary, but things have changed a bit since then. Of course, no one on the left will be in power once the elections are over. The future government will be antisocialist," he conceded.

"On the other hand, the economy cannot change that quickly. Privatization is a dear idea for many, but it is not very easy to do." Conditions for privatization—such as purchasing power or savings—didn't really exist. "Hungary is not an attractive place to invest," he pointed out, ticking off the reasons. "It is not cheap—it is more expensive than East Asia, for example; infrastructure is underdeveloped; union rights are strong. So I don't really see quick privatization. And if this doesn't happen, it will mean that the economic power and the political power will have some contradiction. That's my forecast." Bihari's prediction was not all that different from the one we'd heard from the young American banker.

"So, democratic poverty rather than authoritarian poverty," I suggested.

"Mmm, yes," he said, and then, as if the flippancy of my remark had stirred a thought, added, "My other feeling is that this democracy—first of all, it's very fragile, and of course these days there's no return to the former system, Stalin's or—well, I don't buy this description of Hungarian society as a neo-Stalinist system. I don't think it was a dictatorship in the ordinary sense of the word."

"Not a dictatorship of the *nomenklatura?*" I asked, referring to the formerly privileged ranks of the Communist Party.

"No," he decided after a pause.

"How would you describe it?" Tom asked.

"I don't have a good description," he admitted. "I'm trying to find the terms. 'Distorted socialism' or . . . or 'underdeveloped socialism'. I don't deny that the *nomenklatura* had too much power, and it was all overcentralized, and there were limitations on individual freedom. I don't deny this. My problem is that I'm not sure we've really moved from whatever it was to democracy. Formally speaking, it's democracy in the Western sense, which means everyone can form a party, join a party—"

"Which was prevented previously," I interrupted. In the back of my mind I registered a sense of unease about the way he had slid over "limitations on individual freedom" so casually.

"Yes, which was prevented previously," he agreed. "But my problem is that the current situation includes a very strong moral intimidation of people. I don't know if this word exists, I'm inventing a word—"

I missed it. It sounded like "radicalization".

"Ridiculization," he repeated.

Tom and I laughed, getting the point of his neologism. But then he offered a curious example. "I wrote this article for, it used to be the official newspaper of the Communist Party, now it is called *The Socialist Daily*, on a proposal made by representatives of Fidesz. Their position was to remove all Lenin statues from public squares and to establish a special park and to put all these statues into this park—"

I involuntarily burst out laughing as I pictured the park.

"—and build a big fence around this park, and all those who are friends or followers of Lenin, they say, could go into this park and have their meditations."

Yes, it was an example of "ridiculization"—but, as my ill-suppressed chortling revealed, it hardly seemed a threat commensurate with those the party had visited upon the nation. Our whole conversation seemed coloured by a similar emotional dissonance, perhaps largely of my own making. Bihari was a serious, quiet, thoughtful man, though capable of a quip. When I asked at one point, "Where is Marxism left?" he laconically replied, "Well, Marxism is left behind." He wasn't a political hack; he had been critical of the Communists, as he was of the post-Communist socialists, while remaining faithful to his own understanding of Marxian socialism. "I would make a very sharp distinction," he insisted, "between Marxism, what I mean by it, at least, and the system or politicians who continuously referred to Marxism."

Yet I was irked by what I took to be his complacency about the enormity of the failure of Communism, as if it were a matter of a few technical adjustments, an avoidable miscalculation, and not a moral bankruptcy of historic proportions. Even his repeated reference to "the previous system", his resistance to characterizing it as a dictatorship, struck me as an evasive euphemism. Still, ours was an argument of colleagues, not necessarily opponents.

Though we talked about economics, Marxist theory, the causes of the fall of Communism ("the party miscalculated the depths of the crisis," he said), it was, oddly, not the broad overview but Bihari's insistence on local, specific details that reminded me of his seriousness. His remarks criticizing those who now mocked the ideas he believed in reflected not merely the petty, self-interested complaints of someone who had something to lose, but a profound intellectual distaste for distortions of objective reality (the very criticism, perhaps, that I was making of him).

Near the end, he returned to the question of the Young Democrats. "The Fidesz people are very clever. I happen to be the teacher, at the university, of some of them." I laughed at the inadvertent implication, which Bihari hastened to correct. "This is not the reason they are intelligent, but I mean I personally know they are intelligent."

In one of the Fidesz campaign posters—we were talking about the semiotics of the political campaign—there was an arresting split image. The top half of the poster showed one of those classic Communist leadership bussings, Brezhnev kissing the former East German party chief, Honecker, while the bottom half counterpoised a photo of a young, attractive couple in the midst of a passionate kiss. When Bihari cited it, I allowed as how it was no doubt a bit simplistic, even childish.

"No, I don't object because it's childish," Bihari insisted, "but because it is a lie. The alternative is not this, either we young people are kissing each other, or we are going to get that. You don't have to overthrow the system to get rid of Brezhnev and Honecker, especially in Hungary. This is false propaganda, a manipulation."

Bihari's sense of objectivity was offended. I was thinking of a one-eyed boy frightened at the announcement of Brezhnev's death.

We stood in the crowded doorway, shaking hands—simultaneous greetings and goodbyes—with Bihari's wife, new child in arm, and the relatives who had brought her home. In the procession of generations, a new, undefined one had arrived.

We reached Raday Street just in time to get Vera's phone

call. We had hoped to have a farewell dinner with her, but a domestic disaster had intervened. Her twelve-year-old son had locked himself in the house, gone to sleep, didn't respond to her frantic pounding on the door. It was a tale comprehensible to fellow parents like Tom, who commiserated and said he would check in with her by phone the next morning to get her assurance that all was well.

I'd resolved not to make the same mistake again. When Szabolsc got off the tram at Boraros Square, I suggested that perhaps we could have lunch at a Chinese restaurant I'd noticed along the Dunacorso.

"It's very expensive," he at first demurred, though I saw that he liked the idea.

"Not at the rate of exchange we tourists get for our Deutschmarks," I said.

"And I'm not dressed for. . . ." He was in a denim jacket, white T-shirt, and jeans, carrying a mathematics text and a three-ring binder on which he had pasted a sticker bearing the slogan of the times, "Just do it."

At the Szechuan restaurant, I instructed Szabolsc in the mysteries of using chopsticks (he took them with him as a souvenir of his first Chinese restaurant). After lunch we took a walk. He was to meet his math teacher at four, but was ill prepared, he admitted.

"Why didn't you study?"

"I talked too long to my girlfriend on the phone," he laughed.

We walked across the Chain Bridge to the Buda side of the river. On the shore, workmen were laying turf in preparation for spring. A passer-by on the bridge carried a spray of lilac. A hydrofoil bearing a boatload of tourists churned up the Danube beneath us. We made our way up the narrow streets to the castle, stopped at a café for a soda; by the time we'd wandered back to the bus stop it was mid-afternoon. He rode back with me to the Dunacorso. On the crowded bus, I noticed a small boy, with the unselfcon-scious curiosity of children, staring in wonderment at Szabolsc's glazed eye.

We said goodbye at one of the tram stops along the river. I watched Szabolsc board, schoolbooks in hand. Before heading back to the apartment to pack for the train trip that evening, I stopped at one of the luxury hotels to pick up an American paper. The late election numbers hadn't changed; the various parties of Hungary were dancing around the question of possible coalitions.

I noticed, perhaps a few seconds late—I was no doubt indulging myself in a last sigh for a boy with a moonstone eye—that I was being cruised by a blond young man in a tan raincoat. He was standing by the iron railing overlooking the tram tracks that ran parallel to the river. I slowed, ob-serving out of the corner of my eye that though he main-tained the posture of someone absently contemplating the river, one foot up on the lower rung of the railing, he'd also craned his head around in case I should chance to look back.

There followed an extended parrying, a dance of stops and starts. I paused by the railing. He ambled past, behind me, stopped a few metres away, glanced in my direction. He looked like the lean blond I'd seen in the Rudas Baths, though at this closer range he seemed somewhat older—

maybe mid-twenties. He was rather more worn, but nonetheless possessed of those fine, small facial features and that blond hair that I'd come to recognize as a particular Magyar type.

I was confused by his signals as we sauntered. He looked at me directly, but didn't move to approach. He put his hands into the waist of his baggy pants and there was a hint of a sensual gesture, but I couldn't read it; he rolled his tongue within his mouth.

Finally we were at a tangle of streets at Freedom Bridge, where a pack of tourist buses was parked. I had to make up my mind. I crossed the street to where he was standing. In a second I passed from dreamy, chaste romance to the coldness of desire. There was no mutual language that we shared, so we worked in the no man's land between languages where a word that sounded like "zex" explained everything. His name was Zoltan.

As we were climbing the stairs of the building on Raday Street, Tom was coming down. He had diligently spent the last day interviewing an anarchist.

"I'll need about an hour," I said.

"No problem," Tom chuckled, offering a friendly half-salute to signal his almost infinite indulgence of me.

When Zoltan stripped, I saw that his lean body bore various scars of its use, long-healed cuts, a small tattoo. In a first, long, tongue-exploring kiss—I was happy to discover he wasn't shy, and his kiss also served to reduce my anxiety about dangerous strangers—I inhaled the strong, not unpleasant smell of his body. Reaching between his legs, I felt the satisfying weight and heft of his cock, thick, sheathed by foreskin. We wandered through the bodily passages as though we were in the labyrinth of wooden cubicles at the Rudas Baths.

Afterwards, as I reminded myself to pack the cum-stained towel, Zoltan and I engaged in a brief, complicated calculation of currency and cigarettes designed to satisfy us both that neither had been cheated. He seemed amused by the novelty of the Canadian money I handed him. The sweat dried on my body.

When Tom returned, he delivered his report on the interview with the anarchist; I could listen to the tape later. Vera had gotten back into her house and sent me her farewells. And finally, Tom had learned that there was to be a Fidesz-sponsored demonstration at the Russian consulate to protest the Soviet treatment of independence-seeking Lithuania, an hour before our train to Bucharest. We'd have time for a coffee before the taxi arrived to take us to the demo.

I had spent happy hours, many of them sitting in the golden-ochre armchair, its bristly material cut into a floral pattern. In that chair I had read my guidebooks, newspapers, maps, thought about everything, listened to the now familiar sounds of the apartment, pictured the face of a one-eyed youth. As we left, I could imagine a ghostly body of myself continuing to sit there, about to inaugurate another, slightly different life.

Outside the Soviet consulate, a crowd of several hundred people, and a cordon of police beyond them, gathered around a flatbed sound truck to listen to Istvan Hegedus and another Fidesz representative deliver brief speeches. Bouquets of Hungarian and Lithuanian flags flourished among the demonstrators. At the end, there was a co-ordinated burst of chants. "Russians go home," the young Hungarians insisted, as had their fathers and mothers before them.

Script, Postscript

> *Dissidents, who have led this exodus, this desertion of the City, now find themselves in the wilderness.... We cannot describe it, since the public words capable of speaking of things that are not personal, were exiled, together with all of us, when we left the City, all together.*
>
> — Gaspar Tamas[2]

> *... not infrequently our views can be read "between the lines".... Observers might well imagine that here is long-awaited proof that art is an adversary of the establishment...*
>
> — Miklos Haraszti[3]

The Angel Bar wasn't at the address listed in the 1993 edition of the Spartacus Gay Guide, which I had checked before leaving Berlin for Budapest. In the narrow street off Rakoczi Avenue, a shuttered shopfront whose business I couldn't determine had replaced the Angel, if it had ever existed. I mentally shrugged. Finding the Angel wasn't a priority; I was, for the moment, sufficiently consumed by a romantic affair in Berlin. Checking out Budapest gay bars was more of an anthropological curiosity than an urgent interest, another way of measuring the changes in Hungary since the fall of Communism.

I re-entered the early evening traffic of Rakoczi Avenue, walking back in the direction of the Elisabeth Bridge, mingling with the strolling crowd who had come out now that the daytime summer heat was giving way to a slightly cooler night. The Angel Bar might have provided an evening's diversion upon arrival, but the reason I had returned to Budapest, apart from wanting to see its streets again, was that I'd read a lucid, bitterly self-critical, classically conservative essay a few weeks before, in Berlin, where I was spending several months that year.

The author of "The Legacy of Dissent: How Civil Society Has Been Seduced by the Cult of Privacy" was a philosopher and opposition member of the Hungarian Parliament named Gaspar Tamas. Accompanying his article in the pages of the *Times Literary Supplement* was a 1988 photo of him being arrested and led away by the police.

"In today's Eastern Europe, the dissidence of the 1970s and 80s is not popular," his piece briskly began. The former anti-Communist heroes were increasingly marginalized in the political arena, often decried, however ironically, as Communists themselves. "In the Hungarian Parliament, any mention of dissidence is greeted with laughter, catcalls and jeers from the government benches," Tamas reported. Its very existence as a historical fact was not only belittled, but sometimes even denied.

Tamas could comprehend part of the backlash. "The attempt to create a respectable pedigree and the embarrassment felt by the present democratic leaders, who nearly without exception had been collaborationists, former Communist Party officials or at best pusillanimous 'sleepers' (having spent the past fifty years saying nothing), are understandable," he not unjustifiably sneered, then added, "Nevertheless, the general antipathy felt towards dissidents calls for some explanation."

If anyone could explain what had gone wrong, Tamas appeared to be the one. It proved easy enough to get a telephone number for him, he was at home when I called, my unfeigned enthusiasm for his essay appeared to please him, and he generously invited me to visit him when I got to Budapest.

That something *had* gone wrong in the years immediately after the Eastern European revolutions of the late 1980s was not in question. While parts of the new Europe were painfully transforming themselves into capitalist democracies (more painfully than anticipated), elsewhere the end of Communism had produced chaos and horror.

The Soviet Union had ceased to exist, collapsing into its component national parts, and was daily threatened with further splintering, wherever a local militia could be assembled to raise the flag of a new Abzurdistan, as such entities were sarcastically dubbed by the media. The former Yugoslavia had been turned into a multinational pit of ethnic terror. At the less extreme margins, a post-Communist socialist party had wrested electoral power from nationalists in now-independent Lithuania (and another would soon do likewise in Poland); whether former Communists controlled the governments of Romania and Bulgaria was a matter of dispute. Even in otherwise pacific Germany, neo-Nazi violence was rising in response to the great waves of emigration under way in Europe, and the costs of German reunification had proved to be vastly more expensive than promised, even as the country struggled with economic recession and unemployment. Now people spoke of the process of change requiring a generation, rather than a mere, if bumpy, two or three years. It was the matter-of-factness rather than the prospect itself that was notable.

I'd gone a block or so, undecided whether I should check out the Dunacorso to see if it still had a hustling scene, when one of two young men going in the opposite direction hailed me with a classic "Say, don't I know you?"

I stopped as the pedestrian traffic flowed around us.

"Sebastian, remember?" he asked hopefully.

"I don't think so," I said. Sebastian was dark-haired, the shorter of the two. His pal, Todor, was a sturdy blond. They were both around twenty.

"What are you doing tonight?" Sebastian asked, after we established the various places where we hadn't met. It was quickly obvious what their interest in passing tourists was.

"Well, I was looking for the Angel Bar," I said, making it equally obvious what my interests might be, "but I couldn't find it."

"Oh, we're just on our way there," Sebastian told me. It had relocated onto Rakoczi, just a few blocks up.

The building we arrived at had an entrance that led into an open courtyard around which various shops and businesses were located. The Angel Bar was in a basement at the back of the courtyard. There was an electric sign that you could see as you came in off the street

Sebastian kept up a steady patter. As we entered the

courtyard he said, "See this?" He held up a bulge of material somewhere around his waist. At first, in the gloomy light, I thought it might be a genital display. Then he added, "Want to see my gun?"

We had gone only a few steps into the courtyard, but it suddenly seemed a long way from the street. It was dark. I looked around. "You're joking," I said, hoping that he merely had a quirky sense of humour.

Sebastian lifted the corner of his T-shirt for a second, flashing the top of an aerosol can. "No, it's only a can of Mace," he amended. "It's for the Romanians. Lots of dangerous Romanians around. They're everywhere. You can get mugged, you better be careful."

We had reached the door of the Angel. Todor, who hadn't said anything during Sebastian's routine, mumbled to me, "It's just deodorant." I preferred his quiet reserve to Sebastian's pressing, more than faintly menacing come-on. A stairway led down to the basement.

The Angel Bar, newly reopened, was mirrors, shiny metal and harsh lighting, round tables and high stools, a crew who didn't seem particularly attentive but from whom I eventually coaxed a couple of beers for Todor and Sebastian. There was a café in the next room, a dance floor beyond that, and, in between, a corridor that led to some porno-viewing booths. Customers gradually drifted in.

Todor went off to the can, while I pumped Sebastian for information about living standards for hustlers and the general populace. The average wage, he reported, was presently between three and four hundred Deutschmarks a month, while a package of coffee—for some reason that was the economists' "basket of goods" item I picked to measure the cost of living—was about three Deutschmarks. I did the calculations as we sipped our beer. That meant that coffee was attainable, but relatively expensive compared to the Berlin price of ten Deutschmarks out of a German wage about ten times the Hungarian one.

Sebastian made a couple of half-hearted propositions to me, but abandoned the effort in the face of my evident lack of interest. When Todor came back from the bathroom, having run a wet comb through his wavy blond hair, Sebastian drifted off in the direction of the porn booths. Todor explained that he was Romanian, from Bucharest, and had been in Budapest for five months; that accounted for Sebastian's earlier jokes about "dangerous Romanians". Todor was pleasant company, and we had another beer before I made my way out of the basement of the Angel into the dark (but no longer threatening) courtyard.

I quickly caught a cab. What had still been Lenin Boulevard my last time in Budapest was now renamed Terez. As we crossed the Margaret Bridge, I got a long glimpse down the river to the illuminated, semi-Gothic nineteenth-century Parliament building on the Pest foreshore, before I was deposited before the battered apartment building on Leo Frankel Street where I was staying.

Christoph, the proprietor of the apartment I had the run of, was an impoverished but visionary composer. The flat had been leased as a studio to a painter named Ursula, who was off to Vienna for a week with her kids and her husband, an airlines executive, before making a quick stop back in

Budapest (I'd perhaps get to meet her then) prior to taking off for a family holiday in Florida.

She was a friend of Michael Morris, who had made the arrangements for my stay. When I talked to her on the phone, she explained that she was just in the process of giving up the lease but that I'd be looked after by the apartment's owner. It was easy to fit me into the loose network of acquaintances and collegial relationships that wove through the flat on Leo Frankel. Christoph lived at the top of the building in a half-finished garret, where he wrote his scores, while wealthier artists provided some sublet income.

At seven in the morning the stone floor of the balcony was cool to my bare feet as I took a cup of fresh coffee out to a wicker table where I could pile my morning reading. The front rooms of the apartment, protected from the summer heat by slatted wooden shades, were above the tram tracks running down Frankel Street, and looked out at the river a block or so away. The balcony faced west, into a leafy courtyard and other apartments beyond which were the rising green hills of Buda. The cloudless sky was a purer and deeper blue than any I'd seen in several months in cloudy Berlin.

"Dissent was an anomaly," Gaspar Tamas wrote in the essay that I was reading for a third time. "The minority within the body politic which was aware of 'dissident activities', as they were called, felt ambivalent about them. This was because the dissidents . . . questioned the tacit assumption that all resistance was so dangerous that it was impossible, thus challenging the moral stance of those who had been silently opposed to the Communist regime, but did not dare to do anything about it."

The guilty "sleepers" were the ones most prejudiced against the dissidents afterwards. "The essence of dissent was, or so the intellectuals in the 'reform dictatorships' believed, the Silent Reproach," Tamas said. "According to them, dissidents were not so much telling the leaders of the regime to 'Go to hell!' as saying 'Shame on you!' to the majority of bystanders." Tamas admitted that he had been so frequently accused of this that he'd begun to entertain some doubts about his own motives. More important, and "in reality, 'dissident activities' also challenged another common East European assumption, namely that all politics are dirty, *civisme* does not exist, the law is only for the strong; it therefore followed that anyone who was prepared to make visible sacrifices for their political beliefs must be mad."

I studied the photograph of Tamas positioned in the centre of the *TLS* page. He was a heavily black-bearded man who might be wearing glasses that had been knocked slightly askew (I couldn't see the detail in the photo's graininess), wearing a short-sleeved white shirt and suspenders for his jeans, being quick-marched, one arm twisted behind his back by one of two uniformed cops, across a patch of open asphalt.

Tamas offered a mocking self-portrait of himself and the other dissidents who resisted the Communists but had since been marginalized. Still, "at a time when 'thaw' and détente made Soviet systems seem almost acceptable, the lonely voices of dissenters from beyond the Iron Curtain had some impact. Feeble voices, of course, but they proved, simply by having spoken, that the quest for liberty and justice remained universal, that state socialism was not a permanent fixture rooted in the ineffable traditions of the East, that the *dilemmas* of mankind were at least interrelated."

I had the tail-end of the weekend to wander about the city in what was intense, if premature, summer heat. Beyond the Margaret Bridge, I made my way along the river for a while, then started up the hill on which the Matthias Church stood, following its hairpin turns until, soaked with sweat and half-dazed by the sun, I staggered into a sidewalk café for a cool drink. The rest of the afternoon I seemed to be walking over the bridges that spanned the Danube, crossing the Chain Bridge to the Pest side and, later, the long Margaret Bridge back to Buda. A few hundred metres past the apartment was a quiet square, where I had a lonely traveller's dinner at an almost empty neighbourhood restaurant called the Melodia.

When I got back home, Christoph was in the kitchen, having a late supper of buttered bread, pickles, and sausage. He was a thin, pale, strangely intense man, in his early thirties, with round rimless glasses. We did a little French-style fencing over politeness—he apologizing for disturbing me (the kitchen and bathroom facilities in his attic, which he was installing himself, were not yet functioning), I apologizing for occupying his apartment.

"Is this the apartment where you grew up?" I asked.

I didn't get all the details, but the question led naturally to the tangled history of his family, which included a sister, who was now married and the mother of children, who would soon be claiming the apartment for her expanding brood, something that Christoph felt he could hardly deny her. But the major event of his youth had centred around his brothers.

"I have two older brothers," he explained.

"Do they live in Budapest too?"

"Oh no, they've been in America for many years."

If it was many years, that meant they had fled during the Communist period.

"It was in 1975. They waited until the death of our mother. The next year, they fled to Italy, just like that."

"Do you mean you didn't know they were going?"

"They didn't say a word," Christoph said.

"You must have felt rather abandoned."

"I was sixteen," he said. "Well, of course, there was my father and sister." There were also, as a consequence, the police, since the state had the right to seize the property of those who chose exile over the Soviet-inspired brand of socialism available. "The police came and inventoried the furniture, even though it belonged to my father." They also imposed a five-year ban on passport privileges for remaining family members.

Christoph hadn't seen them again until last year, when he had travelled to America himself. One of his brothers lived in San Francisco, where there was a music publisher to whom Christoph had sold some of his songs.

"Well, that must have been something," I said, somewhat neutrally, vaguely sensing emotions that weren't yet fully apparent.

"Not really. We're very different. They're interested in material things, cars, business, and I'm, well, more spiritual, I suppose. I felt estranged."

"Yes, of course."

"And then, all those years," he went on, "even though they were doing well, they sent nothing back to us." His mouth tightened. I grunted sympathetically. "When I arrived, I think he thought I simply wanted something. That I was, you know, a poor, primitive Hungarian."

"Well, at least there was the success with your music," I said, awkwardly trying to dispel the memory of familial bitterness that I had inadvertently called up. "What sort of works do you write?"

"Oh, you must come up and hear it," Christoph offered, brightening a bit. "It's a new kind of music, very different." I missed the term he applied to it.

"Like the Renaissance. A reflowering. I call it *Refulgence*," Christoph said, repeating the word, and warming to an explanation that I was unable to follow, about fifths, sevenths, various chords. He was a seemingly timid man, his emotions kept carefully in check, but when he spoke of his compositions there was a childlike sunburst of delight mixed with fierce absorption.

"Well, once I hear it," I said, as if that would clear it up.

"Yes, you must," he urged.

When I'd made my mid-week dinner date with Tamas, he had asked, as an afterthought, "Oh, by the way, when are you arriving?"

On the weekend, I had told him.

"Ah, then you can come to the symposium with Richard Rorty on Monday evening," he said. "I'm one of the respondents. It's the inaugural event of the Budapest Kollegium."

"Rorty will be in Budapest?" I asked. "Then Budapest really is the centre of Europe."

Rorty was one of the most prominent philosophers in America, a protagonist in the current (and recurrent) "end of philosophy" debate. By coincidence, I had been reading his most recent book, *Contingency, Irony, and Solidarity*. It was, unlike a lot of philosophy, a surprisingly readable text, in which Rorty argued—contrary to conventional belief—that there were no unconditional moral grounds for preferring good over evil, kindness over cruelty, and so on, though of course he, as a liberal democrat, would choose the former rather than the latter in each instance. The best we could do in our quest for democracy, as well as anything else, he asserted, was to offer justificatory arguments for one course of action over another. There was, in his view, no ultimate truth, universal foundations, or even reason, to which we might appeal. There was only the pragmatic persuasiveness of what he called our "final vocabularies"—that is, the latest arguments that might be convincing in the current debate.

The Budapest Kollegium was located on the same hilltop square as the Matthias Church and the Budapest Hilton Hotel. As I entered the square around five in the afternoon, two men were coming out of the Hilton. The taller man, with white-thatched hair and wearing a summer suit, was recognizable to me from the author's photograph on his book. The other man was a rumpled, wild-haired professor I had interviewed the last time I'd been in Budapest.

"Are you Richard Rorty?" I asked the taller one upon approaching them.

Yes, he said. I introduced myself and we shook hands.

"And you're Professor Woyda," I said to the other. "We met in March of 1990."

The three of us entered an ancient, refurbished building just off the corner of the square. It was a beautiful two-storey villa with an enclosed garden. The monastic arcades around the garden and its thick, freshly whitewashed walls provided some protection against the summer heat.

By the time the formalities had begun, the upstairs room where the colloquium was being held had filled to capacity. The crowd consisted of philosophers (I recognized a couple of the more prominent ones), students, and various dignitaries. I just had time to say hello to Tamas and reconfirm our dinner date before the proceedings began.

The cultural attaché of the U.S. embassy was produced to perform the introduction of the visiting American philosopher. The attaché praised the building and the "glorious new cultural tradition in Hungary" that was being inaugurated; none of the philosophers in the audience seemed to be worried about the oxymoron of a "new tradition".

Rorty nodded benignly in the direction of the young American diplomat. "My title this evening is 'Universality and Pragmatism'," he began. "What I'll be reading is the beginning and end of a rather long, rambling paper which I wrote in preparation for a get-together with Habermas."

Germany's Jurgen Habermas was a political philosopher as internationally prominent as Rorty himself, if not more so. Habermas was also considered to be an "anti-foundationalist"—that is, someone who didn't believe there was an ultimate truth—but one who attempted to save those crumbling foundations by a notion of "communicative reason"—our human intersubjectivity that determined whatever truth there was.

"Is the topic of truth relevant to democratic politics?" Rorty asked the recent democrats of Budapest's intelligentsia. Although he was about to tell them that, contrary to most of their own intuitions, it wasn't, he admitted that the question of whether there were any beliefs or desires common to all human beings was only interesting in terms of a democratic community, "a community that prides itself on the different sorts of people it welcomes, rather than on the firmness with which it keeps out strangers." Most human communities depended on pride "in not being other sorts of people—people who worship the wrong god, eat the wrong foods, or have some other perverse, repellent beliefs or desires." The nearby former Yugoslavia was enough on the minds of his audience that Rorty didn't have to belabour the point.

Seated behind a table, and flanked by Tamas and the rumpled Woyda, Rorty was a tall man with a moon-face under his thatch of white hair and, as in his book-cover photo, a just perceptible Cheshire Cat smile of self-satisfaction. He talked philosophy with the casualness of the guy next to you in a bar chatting about baseball scores. Still, he spoke in the cadences and accents of the secure patrician classes, and at the edge of his intonation, there was just the tiniest bored irony about the alleged truth of the *idées reçus* he was about to puncture.

"One of the desires said to be universal by philosophers interested in democratic politics is the desire for truth,"

Rorty said. He disagreed. He thought that the notion of truth didn't make any sense, that it was one of those "impossible, indefinable, sublime objects of desire". What you could reasonably aim for, in his view, at least with respect to democracy, was justification. "We shall never know whether a given belief is true, but we can know, for example, that nobody is able to summon up any residual objections to it, that everybody agrees that it ought to be held." Truth was to be replaced by consensus. But what if consensus wasn't achieved, or what if agreement was arrived at by coercion, manipulation, deception? Well, that's life, Rorty seemed to be saying. The truth "is too sublime, so to speak, to be recognized or aimed at. Justification is merely beautiful, but it is recognizable, and sometimes, with luck, justification is even achieved"; however, he added, "that achievement is only temporary since, sooner or later, with luck, new objections to the temporarily justified belief will be developed."

He went on for forty-five minutes or so, skilfully turning a phrase, speaking as casually as a man talking about sports and yet subtly signalling, if anyone was inclined to challenge that offhanded tone, that the most technical distinctions of the field were also at his fingertips.

His opponents, Rorty observed, were anxious "to avoid what they called 'relativism', a relativism which seems to them to put democratic politics on a par with totalitarian politics. They think it important to say that the former sort of politics is more rational than the latter. I don't think we should say this.... I think that we should admit that we have no neutral ground to stand on when we defend democratic politics against its opponents. . . . It would be franker, and therefore better, to say that democratic politics can no more appeal to such presuppositions than can anti-democratic politics, but is none the worse for that." That is, the totalitarian politics from which the people in the room had so recently emerged were indeed, in some sense, on a par with the uncertainties of the democratic politics upon which they had lately embarked. Abandoning the idea "that knowledge is the distinctively human capacity," he urged, "would make room for the idea that democratic citizenship is better suited for that role. The latter, I think, is what we human beings should take most pride in, should make central to our self-image, and should cease trying to ground on anything prior."

It wasn't clear who exactly Rorty thought might make "democratic citizenship" central to our self-image. I hadn't noticed much emphasis lately on democratic citizenship in the entertainments of the society I had come from. There was trivia, amnesia, consumer behaviour in abundance, sponsored by corporations whose insignia every child wore on a T-shirt or jacket, but little discernible in the way of citizenship.

Downstairs, there were glasses of wine set out for us, along with food to nibble on. We drifted into the arcade-lined garden in the prolonged light of a summer evening. How curious to come here to be asked whether truth mattered, or even existed.

If the first time I had come to Budapest, at the beginning of the decade, it had seemed to me like a city encountered in dreams, those dreams had had a tactile, bodily quality. Budapest still seemed—as we stood in a medieval garden, all civility, tinkling glasses—like a place found in dreams, but its dreaminess this time was distinctly cerebral.

Towards the end of his book *The Velvet Prison*—in Hungarian it had the more pointed title *The Aesthetics of Censorship*—Miklos Haraszti discussed "the space between the lines".

I'd first heard of Haraszti in the 1970s, when an English edition of a manuscript he'd written had been published under the title *A Worker in a Worker's State*. It was an autobiographical account of working in a Hungarian factory for a year, in which, in elegant and pungent prose, he disabused his readers of any illusions they might have of the "dignity of labour" under socialism, or the notion that the "worker's state" represented the workers who worked in it. It had affected my thinking about Communism. Its publication had also caused a small international fuss, since its author had been detained by the authorities and put on trial, occasioning petitions of protest from intellectuals in many countries. As often happened with the dissidents of Eastern Europe, Haraszti then slipped from our view.

It was only in the 1980s, sometime before the fall of Communism, that the second book by Haraszti had appeared in the West. Though I had eagerly looked forward to reading it, I was, for some reason since forgotten, inattentive to it. I missed whatever his dark point was, and put it aside.

At the time of the Hungarian elections, in 1990, I'd briefly seen Haraszti, who was one of the dissidents-turned-parliamentary-candidates, at a press conference for the Free Democrats. Afterwards I'd gone up and introduced myself, making an appointment to interview him the next morning. However, still entangled in electoral affairs, he'd been unable to appear.

Now, headed to Budapest, I'd taken along my copy of *The Velvet Prison* for something to read on the plane. As I noted on the copyright page, it had sailed under several flags. The French called it *The State Artist*, the English version had been given a typically catchy American title, but the original name forced you to consider that "censorship", which we in the West thought of as a brutal club, might have its own aesthetic—that it might be a system *of* art. In my reading of it this time, in the airspace between Berlin and Budapest, it became an illuminating manuscript whose point I at last grasped.

Haraszti accused readers in the West of taking some pride in reading "between the lines". We scanned the pale parables that the censors had permitted to appear in print, and imagined ourselves as co-conspirators with the daring authors who had inserted subversive messages in the space between the lines.

"Observers might well imagine," wrote Haraszti, "that here is the long-awaited proof that art is an adversary of the establishment, even in its period of abject servility. What else would one find between the lines other than restrained protest, signs of cautious independence? The fact that one can read protest between the lines is, it is said, a concession of censorship that will all but defeat it . . . state culture's decay, in this view, becomes unstoppable the moment that art achieves the freedom of diverse interpretation—even if only between the lines."

If there was collusion in all this, he argued, it was not between authors and readers, as we had, with a touch of vanity, assumed, but between state artists and censors. "Censorship is no longer a matter of simple state intervention. A new aesthetic culture has emerged in which censors and artists alike are entangled in a mutual embrace. Nor is it as distasteful as traditional critics of censorship imagine . . . it is not that one does not encounter state meddling in the arts; rather, such meddling is no longer used to silence opposition to the state but to ensure that intellectuals will perform their proper role." And if we thought that artists regarded this as onerous, all we had to do was eavesdrop on their conversations at any of the "country villas reserved for intellectuals, or on the chitchat of high-ranking functionary artists after an official conference. One would be surprised to hear the satisfaction with which they tell each other about their 'misadventures' with the state. For censorship is the final glaze that the state applies to the work of art before approving its release to the public. . . . The artist and the censor—the two faces of official culture—diligently and cheerfully cultivate the gardens of art together."

Haraszti declared that "many prefer to believe that the poet will write a poem that he does not like because of the threat of imprisonment instead of accepting the much simpler truth: art is not wedded to freedom forever and always."

That was the heresy at the heart of his thesis, which made it not just a clarification of a fallen past, but a challenge to the post-Communist present, and it was as unsettling in its way as the philosophical proposal that we might do without truth, universality, reason.

"Rumour has it that freedom is an essential condition of art," Haraszti went on, "that anything which severs art from its anti-authoritarian essence will kill it; that the true artist is an individual who is independent, at least in his own creative process; that art is false unless it is autonomous; that art means boundless sensitivity, unrestricted imagination; that art is the graveyard of prejudice, the fabulation of reality, form that thinks itself . . . a mysterious magic lantern, a door slammed for the sake of the sound; that art is permanent revolution."

In fact, he reminded us, "these notions are actually quite recent. Only since the middle of the nineteenth century has art been seen as synonymous with anti-authoritarianism. . . . That artistic autonomy could be an end in itself was part of the promise of bourgeois civilization. . . . We have only to recall the art of the ancient Egyptians and Greeks to realize that art without anti-authoritarianism is possible. Does it make sense to complain of a lack of freedom in the art of medieval Christendom?"

In any case, "the figure of the independent artist is now to be found only in the waxworks museum, alongside that of the organized worker," Haraszti declared. "Independent art is impossible because there is no independent audience. We live in a society in which anti-authoritarian art would be rightly condemned as anti-art."

If there was no independent audience for independent art in the regimes that had recently dissolved, how independent was the audience outside the late state socialism that Haraszti pilloried? How free was our free-market art? Most people in the societies of North America no longer found art relevant to their lives. Could we still describe as art those products whose final glaze was applied by "entertainment" rather than "censorship"?

Whatever the intention, in the end one had to ask, What was, in truth, in that "space between the lines"?

According to Haraszti, "it is public life itself that is the space between the lines". In viewing the hidden, subversive meanings in seemingly orthodox texts of the past, a gloomy Haraszti muttered, "Surely, I have no reason to consider totalitarian socialism's double talk any more destructive or short-lived than that of its predecessors. Communication between the lines already dominates our directed culture." Not only artists, but bureaucrats as well were specialists in the technique. "Real communication takes place only between the lines."

He warned, "The reader must not think that we detest the perversity of this hidden public life and that we participate in it because we are forced to. On the contrary, the technique of writing between the lines is, for us, identical with artistic technique. It is a part of our skill and a test of our professionalism."

In the end, then, the messages between the lines "are suggestions sent to the same state and the same public that our official lines continue to serve.... This is the true function of this space: it is the repository of loyal digressions that, for one reason or another, cannot now be openly expressed."

At best, those who wrote between the lines were only the state's conscience. "So even when we are critical between the lines we never try to hide anything we would express had it been allowed. Actually, we have no idea what our message would be if it could be freely articulated."

Haraszti's own message was not only a breathtakingly bleak admonition to his compatriots of a decade ago, but perhaps one that also resonated in the post-Communist present. If it was leavened at all, it was only by the barest hint. The one taboo of the state-directed art was the exclusion of any art "that might suggest that reality is, or sometimes is, nonaligned, indifferent, aimless, absurd, intangible, deaf, dumb or blind. . . . [State] art neither hates or worships reality: it merely denies reality the chance to be mysterious."

The photograph on the cover of *The Velvet Prison* showed a prematurely balding man with a moustache and scraggly beard lying back, half exhausted, in a chair, even his shirt seeming to sag against his torso. The lively, cleanshaven man with dark eyes and black hair before me bore no resemblance to the photo.

In an office several floors up in a white marble-sheeted building—it may once have been the Communist Party headquarters; now it was at the disposal of members of Parliament—I showed Miklos Haraszti the cover of the English edition.

"Who is that?" I asked about the man in the photograph, a person readers might assume was Haraszti himself since the edition carried no author's photo on the back.

Haraszti, who had seen it before, said, "I don't know, it must be the designer's idea. I think the designer thought that this was a typical East European intellectual."

We both began laughing.

"He looks like he's just suffered a complete intellectual collapse," I said.

"Yes, exactly," Haraszti chortled. "And look here," he

said, pointing to a blur where the man's wrist met the arm of the chair, "the faint suggestion of a handcuff. Do you see it?"

"Yes!"

"As if his being handcuffed to the chair should be felt in your subconscious," Haraszti joked.

We had talked for an hour or more. Haraszti was now a parliamentarian preoccupied with party politics, and had written no books since *The Aesthetics of Censorship*. "Predictably, I got the criticism that I exaggerated," he said, "that it wasn't that deep a mental slavery, it wasn't that unconscious."

Mostly, we talked about the theory of "civil society" that the dissidents in Poland and Hungary had evolved, the notion that a self-generated parallel culture would gradually force the Communist regimes to accept the compromise of a social contract. He regarded the theory as a failure, or at best a moot point. By the time the regimes were prepared for such a contract, "they were already so weak that it wasn't needed any more." For the past three years he had been embroiled in the debate over the independence of radio and television. By his account, it was a losing battle.

Before the arrival of democracy, his dissident politics and literary engagements meshed; they were, as he said, "a good solution to my schizophrenia". Now his life was "a melange of useful engagement, personal discontent and, well, some personal satisfaction too." But no, there weren't any new books.

When I got back to the apartment on Frankel Street that afternoon, Christoph was on the cool balcony outside his apartment, with a well-dressed woman and two children.

The woman was Ursula, the former occupant of Christoph's apartment, just back from Austria and leaving for Florida the next morning. She'd brought a bucket of raspberries from the countryside, and a bottle of champagne which we sipped as she showed us photographs of her Austrian relatives.

After Ursula and her children departed, I followed Christoph up to his attic, under the eaves of the building. The half-finished kitchenette and toilet were a tangle of rough plaster and gypboard. Inside, the single room was more than half occupied by a black baby grand piano. I wondered how he'd been able to winch it up and into his tiny nest.

When he sat before it and played, however, Christoph was transformed from the shy, emotionally careful person he presented in other circumstances. As he struck the keys, there was a power in his forearms that I hadn't noticed before, a set to his jaw; his eyes gleamed. The music was without any of the dissonance that the twentieth century had explored. It was a mixture of nineteenth-century melodies and the ethereal sounds of what was known as "New Age" music, a brew of mysticism, fabricated ancient voices, and reincarnational determinism. I liked some of it, but I was more immediately impressed by his skill at the piano, and by the sound of "live" music, which, I realized, I hadn't heard for some months.

Even the slightest encouragement, more politeness than enthusiasm on my part, was sufficient to launch Christoph into what was both a technical discussion—he played samples of Beethoven's late piano sonatas to show me how he resolved certain problems of chords in his own work—and a messianic announcement of the Refulgence movement. The music sought a metaphysical balance between the technical and the spiritual; he could imagine a new Golden Age unfolding.

His madness seemed inoffensive enough that I invited him to dinner at the Melodia. On the way, he took me into a neighbourhood basement wine bar that I had passed several times without noticing. Its low ceiling was held up by rough-barked timbers; the Riesling was decanted into tureen-sized metal containers.

After dinner, walking home in the dark, Christoph again stopped to show me something I would otherwise have missed. It was an apartment building, set back from the tram stop in the square but not particularly different in appearance from its neighbours. An ornate metal grille gate opened into the courtyard, around which rose several floors of apartments. There were lights here and there, laundry hanging to dry, bits of sound, the normal life of a block of flats. But in the centre of the courtyard, instead of a tree or patch of cement, there was a squat, round building.

"What is it?" I asked.

Its window frames of crumbling cement held a Star of David motif, as did its locked entrance.

"A synagogue," he said.

"Really?" I was surprised. "Do they still use it?"

"Yes, I think so."

In the darkness we walked halfway around it. Again I had the sense of encountering some depth of Budapest I

wouldn't possibly come to know. Old Jewish neighbourhoods, crumbling remnants of a long-past community life,
bitter histories, all of this just glimpsed for a few moments in
the night.

My return to Budapest, supposedly intended to survey a
fledgeling post-Communist democracy, had taken a rather
different turn. I'd ascertained, of course, that its parliamentary government was, if unloved, nonetheless sound enough
(there were preparations for future elections as the first four-
year term wound down; Haraszti was contemplating running again); I had some idea of its standard of living
(impoverished compared to Western Europe, precarious
even, but not in utter ruin, as was the case with several of
the republics that had emerged from the former Soviet
Union); and there was sufficient pluralism that a zany composer could imagine that his melodies might be the fount of
a movement.

Notwithstanding those bits of empiricism, the story
whose spoor I followed seemed to be that of the fate of a
thought. What had happened to the ideas of the dissidents,
to the theory of civil society? This tale, which succeeded
that of the moonstone-eyed boy named Szabolsc, was dis-
cursive, its brief moments of "action"—a drink in a bar, the
playing of a piano—merely stitched together lengthy passages of exposition, reflections on the unexpected outcome
of the fall of Communism. In between the contemplations
of that thought, there was only an endless, aimless, dreamy
perambulation through the streets and over the bridges of
Budapest in the hot sun.

On Molnar Street, a block back from the Danube, I arrived, in my usual overheated state, at Gaspar Tamas's apartment. He led me into a study lined with books from floor to ceiling. Not only were the shelves full, but piles of books and journals occupied every available surface, spilling onto chairs, tables, a small day bed against the wall. I mopped my forehead with a handkerchief.

"Here, let me," he said, hauling away a tottering heap of volumes to make a space for me to sit down. Tamas was thinner than in his dissident days, his once bushy beard carefully trimmed, his fluent English tinged with the accent of an Oxford don.

I had spoken with Haraszti about the dissidents' theory of "civil society", and he had dismissed it in a single, backward glance. Tamas was not content with that. After all, it had informed the resistance to dictatorship not only in Hungary but throughout Eastern Europe, from Poland, where Adam Michnik had expounded its tenets, to Vaclav Havel's Czech Republic, which had been peacefully severed from Slovakia at the beginning of 1993.

Tamas's essay about the legacy of dissent may have begun with an enquiry into the post-Communist "general antipathy felt toward dissidents", but his deeper interest was in the dissidents' own understandings and misunderstandings about a number of central ideas—namely, civil society, democracy, and the resistance to the Communists that George Konrad had dubbed "anti-politics". What he found profoundly disturbed him.

The idea of a civil society held by the Eastern European opposition had been inherited, Tamas duly noted, from

Enlightenment liberalism in the West. The classic problem in Western liberal society, where the power of the state was weak compared to the absolutist monarchies that preceded it, had been to fashion a civil society in which the initiative necessary for self-government could be sustained through the activity of citizens in voluntary associations. "In other words," Tamas put the question, "how were they to hold society together in the absence of a pre-ordained hierarchy?"

But the problem faced by East European intellectual critics of Communist regimes was entirely different. If Western theorists had to figure out how to "persuade the autonomous individual in a free society to be a citizen . . . my generation in Eastern Europe had to counter the crushing preponderance, the all-pervasive omnipresence of the police state. Our fear was not . . . that individuals would become 'atomized,' disoriented, amoral, oblivious to duty. We were afraid that without diversified, pluralistic voluntary associations the dutiful citizens of the totalitarian state would become *automata*."

The East European idea of civil society, Tamas argued, had been pitched *against* the state. If the Western idea of civil society was political, "the East European dissident idea was anti-political. The East European idea was, as can be seen from the works of Havel and Konrad, to avoid politics altogether with the aid of a straightforward morality which would stress the beauty of everyday life, integrity in small matters, sense of humour, self-deprecatory modesty and above all, *authenticity*." Havel had called it "living in truth". The result was a deep suspicion of institutions, including the state. Tamas thought that such anti-political disdain for "institutional discourse, the imposition of codes of behaviour, ideas of justice, and an abstract universal language" were contributory factors to the present disarray.

Given such a view of society and state, it was not surprising that the dissidents had focused on a campaign for human rights. The campaign had been successful to a point. Since Communist states had signed international human rights accords, they were faced with the dissidents' question: Why can't people say what they believe to be the truth?

"There was no good answer to that question," Tamas wrote, "for the simple reason that in principle communists did not condone mass murder, or even the radical deprivation of liberty. Hitler never said he was a humanist, but the Bolsheviks did, and this was their undoing. Liars are not heroic, and exposed liars lose their authority." The dissident critique had had at least some effect.

Still, the human rights for which Tamas and others had fought, he now thought, had been selected "so as to be anti-political, to interfere little with the existing structures of administrative, economic, military and cultural power." Perhaps it was understandable, given the exigencies of Soviet power and Western acquiescence to the status quo of a world divided by the Iron Curtain. But it also reflected the view that "civic community, the state, the law were all suspect for most dissenters. They smacked of regimentation, indoctrination, domination. Freedom seemed to reside in individual moral action. In Eastern Europe, dissenters believed, human rights would leave public action to a very small state manned by administrators."

In the end, those rights would "nullify any conceivable claim of the City on its citizens: the exodus of the citizen from the City would be completed. Dissidents, who have led the exodus, the desertion of the City, now find themselves in the wilderness. They find themselves faced with a body of opinion which fails to recognize any institutional authority, any civic duty, any political obligation, any idea of the common good, while at the same time impatient with disorder and squalor."

It was a withering critique, I thought, and one not without its application to the societies I knew, where the retreat from politics was as widespread as Tamas claimed it to be in post-Communist society. The sources of disaffection might be different—consumerism, entertainment, trivia, a media-driven disdain for the "City"—but the results were not dissimilar.

"It seems to me that this is a very lacerating self-criticism," I said about his essay, once I had settled myself into the crowded study.

"Well, that's what it is, yes," Tamas agreed, as he wedged a window open to stir the sticky, warm air of the room.

I was curious to know how he had made the journey from the dissident insistence on individuals "living in truth" to views that seemed to sail within sight of Plato's Republic. Tamas had begun as something of a libertarian, and now he was a parliamentary representative of a centrist party, even a left-centrist party, but his thinking had brought him to an ancient, full-fledged conservatism.

"Well, we went through this period of self-admiration," he began, then, as if impatiently brushing it away, added, "and we've had quite enough of all that. It was time to find out what had happened to us, and what happened to this country, to establish the part of responsibility we share for what I see as a flop of these Eastern European democracies."

He underscored the word "flop". "We shouted on the streets of Budapest, 'We want democracy!' Not rule of law, not liberty, not justice, but democracy." And now one could see what that idea of democracy had amounted to, simply by looking at what people presently considered anti-democratic. "Imposition of political will by an elite (law) is anti-democratic. Coercion used to elicit uniform behaviour (public order) is anti-democratic." And the list continued, through representative government and the redistribution of wealth through public taxation—all were seen as anti-democratic. What was left but "an overwhelming desire for the obliteration of the public realm"? In his essay, Tamas invoked a passage from Hannah Arendt's *The Human Condition*, which admonished us that "this enlargement of the private, the enchantment, as it were, of a whole people, does not make it public, does not constitute a public realm, but, on the contrary, means only that the public realm has almost completely receded."

Tamas looked back on it all ruefully. "We were all part of the great web, weren't we; the heroic times, thank God, are over, a new world begins, a world of creative disorder," he said, ironic to the end. But despairing also. "We cannot describe it, since the public words capable of speaking of things that are not personal, were exiled together with all of us, when we left the City, all together."

It was late when we left the stifling study and walked

through the dark, empty streets, past the sealed courtyards of apartment buildings that lined the neighbourhood.

Tamas had been raised in the Transylvanian city of Cluj, a member of the Hungarian ethnic minority in Romania. His father, a descendant of the petty nobility, had been the manager of the local provincial theatre there. His mother was Jewish. Tamas described the city of his youth as a place frozen in the past.

"I did things in childhood like Austrian children did in the nineteenth century," he remembered, as we walked towards a nearby restaurant. "Sunday afternoon visits where children were seen and not heard. My father came home every night in a hansom cab. This was in the 1960s, mind you."

"You mean, with a horse?" I asked, trying to imagine the backwater from which this cosmopolitan philosopher had emerged.

"Yes, of course. It wasn't for tourists, it was the real thing. It was creaky and old and it smelled." Tamas wrinkled his nose. He had studied philosophy in Cluj, and managed to get in trouble with the Romanian authorities for "refusing to conform, rather than doing anything in particular. So I just had to go." He had emigrated to Hungary when he was thirty.

But it was not his own student days that were so much on Tamas's mind as the views of his students at the institute where he taught. "I see the new generation of students," he said, "and their perception of the democratic changes and mine are diametrically opposed to each other. What do they say? They say that the present-day democracy is an abdication. They think that there was a socialist dream, which was beautiful, but human nature is so depraved that we just cannot live up to that vision, and so we have to face the prose of everyday life, the sinful nature of man."

"My students say the same thing," I commiserated.

"And they're bored," Tamas added.

The restaurant was an expensive, opulently appointed basement establishment. Tamas was known to the management, who fussed over him. Across the crisp linen, we shared a bottle of rosé wine through a procession of dishes. When the brandy arrived at the end, we were still engrossed in the image of the endangered City.

"There's a shyness and taboo everywhere when it comes to thinking about the state," Tamas insisted. He cited as examples the bloodbath in Bosnia, the lawlessness of Russia. "The warriors in Bosnia don't say that it's their right. They don't say that their culture is superior. They say, If you don't give way, I'll shoot you. That's all they say. An inarticulate, personal, individualistic idea which has nothing to do with the state, with institutions. And this is compounded by the demise of the state itself," he went on. "Look at Russia— the problem with Russia is not that Russia has a state which has failings of this or that kind; Russia doesn't have a state— the state has just disappeared, sucked into the black hole. Are the Russians free? I very much doubt it."

"Essentially you're saying that, insofar as you had an influence, you created a city without citizens," I said.

"So it unfortunately seems," he concurred. "My fear is that there will be no city. No city can survive for long without citizens."

At midnight, we emerged from the underground eatery. The air was still warm. The streets were empty; shadows flitted along the façades of the silent buildings. We had come to the surface of a city that seemed, for the moment, to be literally destitute of a citizenry. It was not the Ancient City, but our own. If Gaspar Tamas was right, then the floodlit ruins of the abandoned city were not only to be found in Budapest.

I walked across the Margaret Bridge a final time on my last evening in Budapest. Though I was uneasy with heights, a fear compounded when they were situated over water, for days I had trudged back and forth over bridges. I averted my eyes from the water far below, fixing my gaze either on the tram tracks that ran down the centre of the bridge or on the ornate Parliament Buildings along the shore. At the end there was a pedestrian tunnel that dipped under the road, emerging either at the tram stop in the busy centre of the avenue, or on the walks to either side of it.

We had agreed to meet at nine, but he hadn't arrived. I watched each of the trams unloading, looking for him. The light was going; the day's heat still lingered. I dodged through the traffic and stood across from the tram stop by a flower-seller's kiosk. After about fifteen minutes of scanning the faces of young men descending from the trams, I began to think that either I'd gotten the meeting place wrong, or he had stood me up.

The first time he passed, at a distance, we missed each other. Then he spotted me, and crossed over from the tram island to where I was standing.

"I'm sorry to be late," he apologized, shaking my hand and shifting a small knapsack from one shoulder to another.

"Szabolsc," I said. I hadn't yet quite reconciled the beautiful boy I'd briefly met three years ago with the young man before me now. I had written to him a couple of times, delicately hinting at my infatuation with him, and he had phoned once or twice. The calls, I'd recognized, weren't really to me personally; they were like the larks of youngsters who had somehow commandeered a phone and were excitedly phoning foreign countries. When I got to Budapest I phoned his house, and his father gave me his number at work. "Well, let's get a drink," I proposed.

"Yes, of course, but I'm afraid that I can't stay very long," he said. "I have to be on the other side of town by ten-thirty."

It was only after we found a basement pub and were seated on stools having a beer that I began to see him. His hair was drawn back severely and tied in back. His green shirt bore a design of black arrowheads. The skin stretched tightly around his high, broad cheekbones, like a drum surface. His looks seemed to derive from another, distant civilization, Mongolian, or American aboriginal. Facing him directly, I saw both eyes at once, the dark, sighted one and the blank, milky one.

"Well, what's happened to you since we last saw each other?" I wanted to know. "What's the place you're working at?"

"It's an advertising agency," he said. I missed the name, a set of initials.

"What do you do there?"

"I'm in charge of the computer system," he explained.

"Computers," I said.

"It's quite a big place," he said. "Over thirty people work there. The directors are two women. They're really nice, it's very non-hierarchical."

It must pay pretty well, I thought.

"Well, I'm working long hours, but the pay is good. It's about $500 a month. In fact, I'm a little embarrassed because I'm making more money in three years than my father who's worked at his place for twenty years."

And was there a girlfriend?

"She's an American. She was teaching English here in Budapest a couple of years ago, but now she's back in America. I've visited her there a couple of times."

He had been to New England. He was impressed by its unspoiled nature, and the cleanliness, but he didn't think he could live there. "The cultural differences, I think, are too great for me. I'm hoping she'll come here."

"It sounds like love," I joked.

"Yes, perhaps," he allowed.

"So it's all worked out for you pretty well," I said. "What about Fidesz, is that still your political party?"

"I think it's still the best party, yes," he said, and recited the most recent opinion poll figures.

He related one or two anecdotes about the hectic pace of work, then glanced at his watch. "We have this ten-thirty dinner meeting with some Austrian clients. They've come from Vienna. It's about a new software accounting program."

"Well, it's been really good to see you again," I said, as he lifted his knapsack onto his shoulder. I walked him back to the main street, where he could catch a cab to his dinner meeting. It was dark, and the avenue was bustling with night-time traffic.

"Do you remember," I asked him, just before we parted, "when you told me three years ago how frightened you had been as a boy the day they announced Brezhnev's death?"

The memory made him laugh. In the darkness, his laughter sounded familiar. I almost saw the one-eyed boy who had enchanted me.

"That was a long time ago," he said, perhaps referring not only to the death of the former leader of a former empire, but to three years ago as well. The cab took him away, quickly swallowed by the surge of traffic as it disappeared into the city. I turned towards the bridge.

The Springtime
of Nations

I N 1989 I read the phrase "the springtime of nations" in
an essay by the British journalist and historian Timothy
Garton Ash.[1] The phrase originally referred to the European revolutions of 1848, which had challenged the absolutist state, but in the *annus mirabilis* of 1989 Garton Ash
applied it to the mixture of reform from above and non-vi-
olent revolution in the streets below that was then under
way in both Poland and Hungary. Within months, a seeming chain reaction of uprisings would bring down the Berlin
Wall, transform Czechoslovakia and Romania, and shudder
through the rest of Eastern Europe.

Now it was a few springtimes later—spring 1993. Those
ebullient seasons of the early 1990s had given way to warier,
wearier ones as the mid-nineties approached. One might
still refer to the end of Communism, as one commentator
did, as a "historical event comparable in importance to the
fall of the Roman Empire", but increasingly I found myself
thinking of other empires, other tyrannies—the Hapsburgs,

the five-hundred-year Ottoman Empire—which had become but dim memories. Maybe the fall of Soviet Communism would assume a similar, much diminished place in the historical record. Communism (perhaps I should say *that* communism, so as not to foreclose the possibility of future ones), although predicated on an idea of human freedom, had irreparably ruined the lives of at least two generations of human beings.

As early as mid-1991, Vaclav Havel wrote in *Summer Meditations*, "The return of freedom to a society that was morally unhinged has produced something . . . which has turned out to be far more serious than anyone could have predicted: an enormous and dazzling explosion of every imaginable human vice.

"Thus we are witnesses to a bizarre state of affairs: society has freed itself, true, but in some ways, it behaves worse than when it was in chains," said Havel, echoing Rousseau's celebrated paradox in *The Social Contract*, "Man is free, yet everywhere he is in chains." "Criminality has grown rapidly," Havel continued, "and the familiar sewage that in times of historical reversal always wells up from the nether regions of the collective psyche has overflowed into the mass media. But there are other, more serious and dangerous symptoms: hatred among nationalities, suspicion, racism, even signs of fascism; politicking, an unrestrained ambition, fanaticism of every conceivable kind, the rise of different mafias; and a prevailing lack of tolerance, understanding, taste, moderation, and reason. . . . Demagogy is rife, and even something as important as the natural longing of people for autonomy is exploited in power plays, as rivals compete in lying to the public. Many members of the [Communist] party elite, the so-called *nomenklatura* who, until very recently, were faking concern about social justice and the working class, have cast aside their masks and, almost overnight, openly become speculators and thieves. Many a once-feared Communist is now an unscrupulous capitalist...."

Despite that litany of woes, Havel insisted, "As ridiculous or quixotic as it may sound these days, one thing seems certain to me: that it is my responsibility to emphasize, again and again, the moral origin of all genuine politics, to stress the significance of moral values and standards in all spheres of social life, including economics, and to explain that if we don't try, within ourselves, to discover or rediscover or cultivate what I call 'higher responsibility,' things will turn out very badly indeed."[2]

I went to Zagreb, Croatia, in 1993, to see the writer Slavenka Drakulic, and—I don't know how to put this other than awkwardly—to get closer to the war. Not to get *into* the war, mind you—I'm not given to mock heroics, nor was I tempted by the tales told by reporters in Berlin about donning flak jackets to wander through the Bosnian shooting gallery. I simply wanted to get to an edge of it where I might be able to appreciate, second hand, the moral enormity of what had befallen the former Yugoslavs.

Had not Drakulic herself written, in a book called *Balkan Express*, of the misunderstanding and indifference of Western outsiders, of their refusal to regard the present barbarities as a war *in* Europe? "Astonishment gives way to anger, then resignation at the way Europe perceives this war," she wrote, "—'ethnic conflict,' 'ancient legacy of hatred and bloodshed.' In this way the West tells us, 'You are not Europeans, not even Eastern Europeans. You are Balkans, mythological, wild, dangerous Balkans. Kill yourselves, if that is your pleasure. We don't understand what is going on there. . . .'" The assumption of belonging to European civilization was gone. "We have been left alone with our newly won independence, our new states, new symbols, new autocratic leaders, but with no democracy at all. We are left standing on a soil slippery with blood, engulfed in a war that will go on for God knows how long," Drakulic lamented. "The accumulating deaths make the wall dividing us from Europe and the world even higher and more formidable, placing us not only on the other side of the border but on the other side of reason too."[3]

When I asked the telephone operator in Berlin to connect me to Zagreb, she said, in a concerned and unoperatorlike voice, but one that confirmed Drakulic's claim of European confusion, "Isn't there a war going on there?"

"I hope not," I said.

The next night, when I had to phone Drakulic again in Zagreb, I happened to get the same operator.

"Didn't I talk to you last night?" she asked.

"Yes, that's right."

"Well, I found out that there isn't a war going on in Zagreb," she said, relieved for both of us.

Zagreb was an unexpectedly beautiful city, but also cold and bitterly windy for the end of March. I don't know why

I found its beauty unexpected. In fact, I don't know what I was expecting— perhaps that it would be like Berlin.

That spring I was living in a small, coal-heated, white-washed studio in the back of a run-down four-storey walkup in Berlin's Schöneberg district, a busy commercial neighbourhood of Turks and Germans where the local red-brick Gothic church (St. Paul the Apostle) and nineteenth-century *Jugendstil* edifices were jumbled amid copyshops, cafés, and dilapidated heaps of plaster-faced apartment buildings.

Zagreb, by contrast, presented a certain grandeur, and it was laid out with a clarity that immediately alleviated the irrational terror I always felt upon confronting the maze of an unknown city. The airport was south of the city, and the bus that took us in passed through Zagreb's outer precincts, with the neo-Stalinist, neo-modernist architecture that increasingly seemed to be a feature of cities everywhere. But once we reached the imposing nineteenth-century railway station at the south end of the city centre, it became clear that we were in an elegant metropolis of the last century, with a grid street plan, spacious parks, and solid public buildings decorated with loggia-like balconies, art-nouveau goddesses embedded in corner alcoves, and muscular caryatids bearing the weight of tiled mansard roofs. The northern edge of downtown was occupied by Jelacic Square, a large expanse of stone and marble where the tram lines all converged, tangles of embedded rails carrying the pretty blue-and-cream streetcars in various directions.

Behind the square, above an open vegetable market, narrow streets wound upwards and through twin medieval hill

towns on the Medvenica uplands, where the present city of
more than a million people originated more than nine hundred years ago. Above the city the dual spires of St.
Stephen's Church were wrapped in construction nets and
scaffolding for repair.

In Jelacic Square, in addition to the crowds waiting hud-
dled for trams in the late afternoon, knots of people gathered
in conversation despite the wind—among them the occasional unarmed soldier in neatly pressed camouflage fatigues,
the only sign that we might be in a semi-war zone. Fronting
the square were large coffeehouses. To escape the battering
wind, I ducked into the Gradska Kavana, a cavernous room
with plentiful tables and a broad, red-carpeted staircase leading up to a mezzanine. Once the hot milky foam of a cappuccino touched my lips, I felt safer. My "fool's errand" of
coming to Zagreb to see a writer for an hour or two seemed
slightly less ludicrous.

Slavenka Drakulic was, to my mind at least, one of those
writers who had addressed the most difficult subject matter
possible. Although she primarily thought of herself as a novelist, Drakulic had written two remarkable works of literary
non-fiction since 1989, *How We Survived Communism and
Even Laughed*, and *Balkan Express*. In a later edition of the
first book, after the Yugoslavian wars had broken out, she
conceded that the title was all wrong. "We have not yet survived communism," she amended, "and there is nothing to
laugh about." Other than that, nothing in either book had
been superseded by subsequent events. Both books were, in
effect, a single piece of work—consisting of, as she herself
had described it, "short half-stories, half-essays," dispatches

from a shifting and often interiorized "front"—which, as I'd seen from further newspaper publications, was ongoing. I had been sufficiently moved by both the pain and the beauty of her writing to want to seek her out.

I reached her by phone from my room in the Hotel Dubrovnik.

"Zagreb is surprisingly beautiful," I announced.

"Well, why not?" Drakulic said, in greeting. She couldn't see me until the following day. "There's a birthday party for a friend of mine that I have to go to. She's forty."

"Forty," I repeated.

"So, what will you do tonight?" she wondered.

"I haven't thought about it yet."

"Well, the movies are in English," she suggested.

"Maybe I'll wander up the street off the square with all the bars," I said noncommittally, although the cold, slate-grey sky didn't look very inviting. She said the name of the winding lane, which I had seen on a map but couldn't pronounce. I was thinking that the logical place to be was at the birthday party.

"Perhaps the thing would be for you to come to the party," she said.

"Yes," I agreed.

"Well, I have to call Vesna—it's her birthday—to see if it's all right to invite you. If it is, I'll call right back." Then she thought of the other possibility. "But if it isn't, then I won't call back because, well, I'll be too embarrassed." I laughed.

But a minute later the phone rang. "Vesna says that any-one who has come all the way from Berlin to Zagreb to see me deserves to be invited," Drakulic reported. She gave me instructions for finding my way there.

At night the dark, empty streets were forbidding. The wind blew down their length without letup. At the east side of Jelacic Square there was a fork in the road, where one tram track curved to the south while another went straight ahead. I bore to the left, as I'd been instructed. I tried to shrink inside my jacket, but the wind chapped my face. At a major intersection, where a stoplight swayed in the gusts, I found the diagonal Rackoga Avenue that Drakulic had told me to look for. The instructions contained one odd bit that somehow humanized their functionality, a detail one wouldn't invent for a story: when I found the name on the doorbell—I had to take out my cigarette lighter and hold it in a cupped hand to see the name—I was to stick a pen into the hole where the button had broken off in order to ring the buzzer.

A man in a bow tie and tuxedo jacket greeted me at the door.

"You're the one who's come to see Slavenka," he said. He was the husband of the woman whose fortieth birthday it was. Suddenly I was inside, safe in the warmth and light of a large urban apartment.

The man led me down the entrance hallway to a black-gowned woman whose wrists were decorated with gold-coloured bangles. Drakulic and I shook hands. She was strong, friendly, elegant; a wave of her long hair swept down over an eyebrow onto her shoulder. "So, you'll see a little bit of Zagreb intellectual life," she said, immediately taking me into the living room and introducing me to her friend Vesna, to whom I offered birthday greetings. In a larger room beyond, a buffet—ham, salads, cheese, breads—had been laid out on a long table. Vesna's husband brought me a whisky and soda. I was presented to a succession of people—a woman from a foundation, an engineer, a bearded historian, a young visiting Englishman who taught political science—their names going by me like the night wind. Slavenka and I agreed to meet at the Gradska the next afternoon.

I settled on the bearded, hefty, cigarette-smoking, whisky-drinking historian, who had wedged his bulk into a space at the end of the hallway, at a juncture between the living room and kitchen through which the party-goers continually passed. We shared an overfull ashtray perched on the ledge of a set of shelves.

"Can you give me some idea of how things are?" I asked.

His body lifted in a gloomy shrug. His name was Zoren and he was associated with the opposition party. Indeed, he assured me that no one here was one of those nationalists who monopolized the news accounts I had no doubt read. When the precarious federation of states that had made up Communist Yugoslavia under Josip Broz Tito, from the Second World War to the latter's death in 1980, was finally swept under in the wave of 1989, the north-western republics of Slovenia and Croatia quickly declared their independence, and succeeded in securing recognition throughout Europe, notwithstanding the opposition of Serbia, the dominant state in what remained of Yugoslavia. The elections in newly independent Croatia, however, had not produced democracy but a right-wing, populist, authoritarian government under Franjo Tudjman, one of Tito's former generals. When the

Serbian tanks, under the flag of the Yugoslav Federal Army, rolled across first Slovenia and then Croatia in response to their withdrawal from Yugoslavia, nationalism in the new republics became even more extreme than it had been. For more than a year there had been a ceasefire between the Croats and the Serbs, with the latter occupying a third of the country, separated from Croat forces only by a United Nations buffer contingent. Croatian cities had been bombed, some reduced to rubble, many people had been killed, but Zagreb had only been threatened with air raids, never hit. The war, in a more savage form, had moved south to Bosnia.

"So how is it here now?"

We had been joined by the visiting British political scientist.

"It's neither not-war, nor is it not-not-war," was the way Zoren formulated it, in a raspy voice that he soothed with Jim Beam bourbon.

The youthful Brit suggested to Zoren that the best way to understand the present situation was to study the period 1900 to 1914, just before the First World War exploded in the same area.

"Yes, we've always been in history." Zoren sighed on behalf of the Balkans, then added, "I wish we could have a five-minute break from history." He put back another Jim Beam.

Later, as I was leaving, I stepped into the kitchen to say goodnight. Slavenka, Vesna, and the woman from the foundation were engaged in a bitter argument. Their necks were stiff with barely contained rage, but they had slightly hunched over to lower their voices. Slavenka broke off for a minute to see me out. "It's a local thing," she murmured, "about who will control a radio station we applied for." Behind her, in the kitchen, Vesna and the other woman pursued the argument.

Slavenka appeared just after noon in the Gradska Kavana. It was crowded and noisy downstairs, so we went up the grand staircase and found a secluded table on the mezzanine. While waiting for her, I'd glanced at one of the local tabloid newspapers lying on a table. There was a photo of a United Nations truck convoy bogged down in the snow somewhere to the south, in the Bosnian mountains, where it was still winter.

When I asked Slavenka what had happened since I'd read her last words (the introduction to *Balkan Express* was dated some six or nine months before), she too referred to the bogged-down nearby war.

"The situation has continued to be almost the same," she said. "In Croatia, we live in some kind of limbo. At one moment it seems as if there is a war going on, at another it seems as if it's not going on."

A waiter came up to take our order. I asked for a cappuccino, and Slavenka wanted a glass of cherry juice. As she ordered, I again noticed her physical vigour, in contrast to the weariness with which she spoke of the war. She was wearing a black turtleneck sweater, a long skirt, and leather boots. Her hair, striated with several dark tints, fell onto the turtleneck.

"I mean, here in Zagreb you don't feel it. You can sit here in the café and see your friends as if nothing is happening.

But only fifty kilometres from here there is the front line, you know."

"Fifty kilometres?"

"Fifty kilometres," she repeated, "just about forty minutes' drive, nothing. So you are aware, constantly aware, that Zagreb could be hit at any moment. We learn to live with this kind of parallel reality. On one side feeling that you could practically die at any moment, and on the other side just pretending this is normality, keeping up with the normal kind of life as if nothing is going on. Because I think it's very important to live like this, to have music, to have flowers, to go visit friends, because it keeps the sanity of your mind."

We talked about the meaning of the war, which I had some idea of, having read her book. Its subject was how something unimaginable came upon you, closer and closer, until it was inside you. At one point "war was a distant rumour, something one managed to obscure or ignore—something happening to other people, to people on the outskirts of the republic, but never to us in the centre, in Zagreb," she wrote. "We were busy with our private lives, with love, careers, a new car. War was threatening us, but not directly, as if we were somehow protected by the flickering TV screen which gave us a feeling of detachment—we might just as well have been in Paris or Budapest. For a long time we have been able to fend off the ghost of war."

But even while you tried to live your own life, the war moved in, in the most intimate, poignant ways. "As my daughter"—the book was dedicated to Slavenka's daughter, Rujana—"pauses a little before packing her suitcase for a holiday in Canada, 'Shall I take only summer things? Perhaps, some light autumn clothes, too?' she asks me, as if not sure how long it will be before she comes back. In her question, I recognize war creeping in between us, because the real question behind her words is: am I coming back? . . . While she is packing, I notice at the bottom of her suitcase a little shabby grey dog, her favourite toy. I hold my breath for a moment, pretending not to see it. How does one recognize the beginning of it all, I wondered not long ago. Now I see the answer in a tiny stuffed dog packed away among my daughter's belongings; the war is here, now." Rujana had transferred to a university in Vienna.

Finally, the war arrived in Zagreb as Slavenka and a friend were sitting down to lunch. "I prepared *pasta al bianco*, opened a bottle of red cabernet and just as we were about to eat, we heard the strange, unnerving sound," Drakulic recounted in *Balkan Express*. "I remember looking at my fork half way down to the plate, holding it there for a long moment as if something, some unknown force, was stopping me from putting it down. Only then did we hear the air-raid alarm—a long howling sound that until that moment we only knew from TV reports. I knew what we were supposed to do—run to the nearest shelter and hide. Instead, both of us sat at the kitchen table listening to the roar of the MIGs flying low overhead. It was not fear that I felt, or panic. Nothing. There was no trace of emotion in me. Instead, I felt an empty space opening up like a hole in my chest, and with each passing moment my legs grew heavier and heavier, as if they were turning into stone. . . . The war was in my mind, in my legs, on the table, in the

plate of pasta getting cold." Fortunately, the bombs hadn't
fallen on Zagreb.

In Slavenka's conversation, as in the book, her daughter
remained a presence. When she referred to the future—
"We have lost the future twice," she said, meaning once
under Communism and again now—she seemed to be
thinking of Rujana. "I'm more or less old enough not to
have any illusions any longer, but you still have these young
people and when you talk to them you have this feeling that
they're not planning anything, they're not ... you know, it's
very difficult to live when the future has been taken away
from you."

Later, when we were talking about whether there was
any point in writing during a war—Slavenka had cited the
proverb "While there is a war, the Muses are silent"—she
again referred to her daughter. "I know that words are very
weak weapons, but I don't have any other. I'm too weak
physically to go and fight. I would never fight unless I was
absolutely forced to, in self-defence, because I think I would
be capable of killing in self-defence, or in defence of—I don't
know—the person I loved, or something, like my daughter. I
would be absolutely capable. So I am not one of those people who think they are saints and say, I can't. I would fight
for my life and the life of my daughter and my friends."

The great horror for her had been a terrible recognition
of the human capacity for war. "Part of us, as human beings,
is that we are capable of these kinds of things." She recalled
the Nuremberg trials, which had seemed to proclaim an end
to barbarity. "But when the first pictures appeared last year
of Bosnian concentration camps here on TV, everybody was

astonished. Did we learn anything from history? No, we didn't. Are we doing the same things? Yes, we are doing the same things." It was like a catechism. "Why are we doing the same things? Are we stupid? No, no, we are not stupid, we are just human beings, and human beings are really cursed in a way." The Enlightenment vision of human perfectibility had collapsed. "We are capable of everything. I think that I myself am capable of everything."

Her books had not been published in Croatia, though they had been translated into the languages of the world. One of her novels, *Marble Skin*—about a mother and daughter—was about to appear in English. "I am considered a *persona non grata* because I have criticized the government in the foreign press for not being democratic." The magazine for which she had written for several years, *Danas*, had been gutted by the regime, and the journalists dismissed. "In the media here there is some kind of picture of me as a dissident. They say I'm a traitor, that I'm not a good Croat, that I'm Yugo-nostalgic, and so on—"

"Yugo-nostalgic?" I asked. She explained that, in the mood of nationalist fervour, the Yugoslavian past had become unmentionable.

"What they mean is that nobody has the right to write the way our memories are, to reconstruct our past. Forty years of our past has been wrong and bad. That's not true, you know," she insisted. "I had a normal decent life for the last forty years, and I don't want to forget it. I want to keep the memory, I have a right to keep the memories of my past, and I have a right to speak about that. What I don't like is this erasing of the past."

The square outside the noisy coffee house offered an instance of history's zigzags. It had been named for a hero of the 1848 revolutions, but when Tito triumphed they redubbed it Republic Square, as it still was on the old street map I had. The new nationalist government had restored the old name, and had installed a replica of the equestrian statue of Duke Jelacic, which now gleamed in the windy afternoon.

But it was not only the historic noble who had reappeared in independent Croatia, Drakulic said. Names of figures from Fascist Croatia—the one previous era in the country's history when it had been independent—were now adorning renamed streets.

"Anti-fascism is something we should be proud of," said Drakulic, who was neither a Communist before nor a nationalist now. "I'm not saying Yugoslavia was good or bad, I'm saying this is part of my life and I have a right to remember it. So don't force me to forget it."

Slavenka went to a late lunch after our conversation, and I wandered the streets. The wind was down some, but the chill was still in the air as I traced the medieval streets of the upper town. The winding lane lined with cafés was spelled Tkalciceva; the fenced-in café patios were empty, the big shade umbrellas for the outdoor tables were folded. I retreated to the hotel, surprised by how quickly and sharply I was visited by loneliness. In the evening I went out again, and walked as far south as the railway station and the nearby Hotel Esplanade, aimlessly sauntering, admiring buildings and the darkness of parks. I passed through the Hard Rock

Café, the Zagreb branch of an international chain of bars, filled with people in their twenties chatting, colourful drinks set before them, enjoying an evening out in the "not-not-war". But I didn't stay. I was outside, or perhaps feeling left out, waiting for some encounter that didn't occur.

I phoned Drakulic again. "I thought I'd like to talk to someone from the university," I said. "Maybe from the philosophy department."

"I'll give you Vesna's number," she offered. "She teaches in sociology, but she'll know the philosophers." As we were about to hang up, she remembered that I had asked at one point if there were any gay bars in Zagreb. "Wait, Rujana's here, I'll ask." I overheard the mother and daughter talking in the background for a minute. It was a dead end; there had been a place a couple of years back, but it had closed.

"So, nothing now?"

"No, nothing," she said.

"Well, nothing tells me something," I said.

Vesna gave me the number of a philosopher she thought might be interesting. His name was Grozden Flego. He was at home.

"What hotel are you staying at?" he asked. I told him. "Then why don't I come by to get you tomorrow afternoon, about five?"

Flego was a lean, tall man, whose reserved manner I immediately liked. We crossed the square and went into the Gradska, where we found a free table near the windows that looked towards the duke, who brandished a scimitar above his head.

I sought the reassurance of shoptalk. "What's the mood of your students?"

"Well, I see them as withdrawn, apathetic; they're not very interested in discussing politics," Grozden told me.

Grozden had been a member of the renowned Praxis group, a circle of Yugoslavian neo-Marxist thinkers whose works were read in the West. The war had broken it up. The split between the groups in Zagreb and Belgrade had been bitter, exacerbated when the leading Serbian member of Praxis began spouting nationalist dogma with increasing vehemence.

Grozden didn't identify with the distasteful rhetoric. He was an admitted "cosmopolitan". Again the phrase "Yugo-nostalgia" cropped up, as an accusation of insufficient enthusiasm for nationalism. As Drakulic had written, "Before this war started, there was perhaps a chance for Croats to become persons and citizens first, then afterwards Croats . . . right now, in the new state of Croatia, no one is allowed *not* to be a Croat."

Increasingly, I was coming to think that perhaps "Yugo-nostalgia" was justified. The Yugoslav idea—flickering into life during the nineteenth century and then briefly realized between the first and second world wars—had been intended to solve the intractable geopolitical problem of the Slovene, Croat, and Serbian peoples—a linguistically and ethnically related population divided for centuries between the Ottoman and Hapsburg empires, then further divided by religious differences and bitter history. For all its faults, socialist Yugoslavia, with its emphasis on ethnic equality and federalism, its hope for the lessening of national ambitions through improved economic circumstances, struck me as both the most rational and the most intellectually advanced solution to the Balkan problem to date.

Furthermore, Yugoslavian socialism had been at least a partial success, notwithstanding the anti-democratic rule of a one-party state and the suppression of dissent. By the time Yugoslavia began to founder economically in the mid-1970s—partly through internal sclerosis, but also partly due to the developments of globalized capitalism—it had produced a relatively high standard of living for Eastern Europe, had spawned some interesting and lively alternatives to standard models of socialist production (thanks in part to the Praxis group), and had even won the allegiance of a significant proportion of a younger generation that saw itself as Yugoslavian rather than Croatian, Serbian, or whatever.

As Grozden verified for me, the standard of living, which had been at least three times that of most other East European states, had in the last three years collapsed to about one-eighth of pre-independence standards. "We're working for half a loaf of bread an hour, if that," he said.

The early evening was coming on. Our cups of coffee had been replaced with fresh brew, and the conversation had ranged from the details of everyday life to philosophy (Grozden was writing the preface to the Croatian edition of Richard Rorty's *Contingency, Irony, and Solidarity*). We had even, for a moment, found ourselves arguing about the twelfth-century craftsmen of Gradec, one of the two hillside villages that had been the precursors of Zagreb, which we could see from the windows of the Gradska.

Shortly before we left, there was an unforgettable anecdote.

I'd asked something about the period when Zagreb was under threat of air attack. Grozden remarked that he hadn't experienced any particular fear during the air-raid warnings, then added, almost as an afterthought, that he'd noticed that others were affected. "I was at home in my study, writing a paper that I was supposed to deliver at a conference in Strasbourg," he recalled. "My son—he's six and a half—was also there, playing or watching me." Then the air-raid warning sounded. "As usual, we went to the basement. When the all-clear was sounded, I immediately went back to my desk and continued writing. Then something strange happened."

The boy had just begun school. Although there had been air-raid warnings before, the child hadn't evidenced any reactions to the war situation that were noticeable to Grozden. "He came to my desk and said to me, 'Daddy, will you teach me to write?' I was surprised. I asked him why he wanted to learn to write." "If I was writing, I wouldn't be so afraid," the boy had said, learning prematurely the secret most of us come upon only much later.

The next day—my last in Zagreb before returning to Berlin—spring arrived, at least temporarily. The sun was out and the beach umbrellas blossomed along Tkalciceva—by now I'd learned that it was pronounced "T'kal-chee-chay-va"—as the café patios suddenly filled with customers, mostly young people. I sat outdoors and drank a pleasantly bitter coffee but, as before, I didn't manage to strike up an acquaintance. I walked back through the city, stopping at the Mimara museum, which I'd noticed recommended in a guidebook.

Until then, I'd come across none of the secondary effects of "not-not-war" other than in my conversations with Drakulic and the other people I'd met, or in the figure of an occasional soldier. I hadn't sought out the refugee camps where thousands of displaced persons from Bosnia were living, nor had I interviewed, as I habitually did in other places, politicians and newspaper editors.

The museum was open but almost empty. I walked across the deserted foyer, up marble staircases and through empty galleries, before I found an attendant who explained to me that the collection had been stored for the duration of the war. In a couple of the gallery rooms, there was an exhibition of children's drawings of Vukovar, a Croatian city that had been utterly destroyed by the Serb invasion. The war was crayoned bursts of fire and drifting black smoke.

I crossed a boulevard and in the afternoon sunshine walked through a park. At the end of it I found another, smaller museum, the Strosseman Gallery, named for a local bishop who had collected European masters and donated the paintings to the city in the 1880s. Again, everything was gone. As I was leaving, with a vague sense of being unable to penetrate to some interior aspect of Zagreb that I intuited was just beyond my reach, a woman came up to me.

"Everything's been put away, you know," she said.

"Yes, I can see."

"But I'm the librarian here. Why don't you come along and I'll show you a book with the paintings in the collection," she suggested. "At least you'll have an idea."

I followed her through a door off the foyer into a small library. She seated me at a long worktable and in a minute reappeared with the volume. I thumbed slowly through the colour-plate reproductions of the museum's holdings.

I turned a page and my gaze was suddenly arrested by a nineteenth-century painting by a Croatian artist. It was a portrayal of Abraham about to sacrifice his son Isaac as proof of his faith in God.

The knife-wielding old man—white-haired, hawk-nosed—was poised in an attitude of anguish as he testified to his belief. Isaac was sensuous, naked except for a ridiculous piece of gauze floating across his genitals. I was amused by the libidinous Isaac, which gave the painting its touch of nineteenth-century camp. It was obvious that the painter had wanted to paint a beautiful, nude young man, and that the biblical story had simply provided the opportunity to do so. I felt a similar surge of my own desire.

At the same time, I experienced the conventional meaning of the scene. In that test of faith, a god had intervened to stay the father's hand, satisfied by his piety. Here, the fathers had sacrificed everyone—children, spouses, themselves, and especially their sons—in a test of loyalty. Yet here also, I remembered, mothers had dedicated books to their daughters.

In the late evening light of springtime, I walked from the studio flat on Berlin's Akazienstrasse towards my current bar of choice, the appropriately named Pinocchio's. Beyond St. Paul the Apostle, across Grunewald Avenue, Akazien turns into Goltzstrasse, a narrow street lined with outdoor cafés and cheap Indian restaurants that sprawl haphazardly onto the sidewalks. The air was warm with spring; the bushes that fenced in a corner playground had turned green, the buds on the trees were ripe but had yet to pop into bloom.

Germany too had changed since my first springtime visit to East Berlin. As one newspaper report would recall on the fourth anniversary of the opening of the Berlin Wall, "exultant throngs from the East poured through the Wall to a boisterous welcome in the western half of the divided city, the long-suppressed dream of a united Germany flowered into possibility.... Today there is one Germany but it is a nation deeply divided, beset with problems and uncertain of the future." The newspaper story ticked off the litany of current woes. "The once powerful West German economy is mired in recession; unemployment is nearly forty per cent in the former East Germany; racist violence has resulted in dozens of deaths; right-wing parties with neo-Nazi undertones have made significant gains in local elections, and faith in the major parties that charted the West German economic miracle and the creation of its first stable democracy is at an all-time low."[4]

Perhaps the gloomy newspaper account, though accurate as to the facts, was a bit overdramatic in terms of mood. That year, I'd returned to Berlin in the middle of winter. Certainly there had been sporadic racist violence during the previous year, but that winter, in most of the major cities throughout the country, hundreds of thousands of Germans had turned out for candle-light marches and demonstrations against neo-Nazism.

The last of them was held a couple of weeks after I'd arrived in Berlin, on January 30, 1993, the sixtieth anniversary of Hitler's ascension to power—an occasion that had been marked in 1933 by an SS torchlight parade through the Brandenburg Gate. It was bitterly cold when I passed through that triumphal arch, which had been built during the height of nineteenth-century German imperialism. On the other side, I melded into the crowd (the press reported a hundred thousand people the next morning) as it milled about, its clumps of people illuminated by thousands of candles. It seemed to me that the Germany in which vast numbers of its citizens marched against half-century-old memories of Fascism was more exemplary of the current political climate than the more publicized outbursts of neo-Nazi aspirations.

Goltzstrasse gives way to the large paved space at Winterfeldtplatz, where twice-weekly open markets are held. Boys on bicycles were doing wheelies in the spring twilight, as if they were riding imaginary ponies. Along Maassenstrasse, just before it enters Nollendorfplatz, I turned into the street where Christopher Isherwood had lived. Pinocchio's is a block and a half away, on Fuggerstrasse, next door to the Tabasco bar.

Earlier that day, I'd gone with Michael and Vincent on an excursion to Treptow Park, at the eastern edge of the city, to see the monumental memorial to the Russian war dead. A huge sunken space was enclosed by a border of thin trees not yet in bloom. We entered between two giant chunks of marble, with kneeling bronze soldiers in greatcoats on either side. A series of stylized wreaths were placed down the centre of the sunken field, flanked by mausoleum-like concrete boxes bearing bas-reliefs of war scenes and Cyrillic quotations from Stalin in gold letters. All of it led, finally, to a towering statue of a soldier with a child in one arm and a sword in the other hand, his foot atop a crushed swastika. It was all kitsch, socialist-realist kitsch, and we laughed knowingly, but the scale of the thing almost made it a success.

The city government had changed the names of streets and squares in east Berlin in the last year, smearing away some of the Communist past. But what would they do with this? Would it be classified as ideology (and thus erasable) or as history (and therefore preservable)? If the changes of post-Communism were relatively visible in other places, in Berlin they seemed to be more various, available only in passing, seen from the corner of your eye. Here all the axes of history criss-crossed, both vertically and horizontally. Since I was living here part of the year, rather than simply visiting with an eye to assessing a post-Communist transformation, the changes appeared to me only tangentially, sometimes not at all. Indeed, "life" was as likely to present art or language or romance as the panorama of politics.

Pinocchio's was a tiny, smoke-filled shoebox of a bar—ten barstools around an L-shaped counter on one side; a half-dozen small tables, most of them along a wall-sized mirror; an overhead fan to stir the smoke; and a corridor lined with a few video games to entertain the boys who hung out and hustled there. In the evenings, the bar was invariably crammed with men, boys, drunks, dogs—a grotesque and/or stunningly beautiful sampling of the animal kingdom. At some moments it was a field of excruciating lassitude and boredom, at others it was an instant away from exploding into an orgy.

I squeezed into a space at a far table in the corner. I was hoping to run into Dominic, but Freddy, an ageing hustler in his early thirties who was my official bar crony, told me that he hadn't seen him. He flipped his hands open and rolled up his eyes at the unreliability of my favourite.

Dominic was a blond-haired, blue-eyed teenager from a small town in east Germany at the entrance to the Thuringian forest. When we first met he said the name of the town but I missed it, and he added, a bit self-deprecatingly, "I'm an *Ossi*." His particularity immediately appeared in the way he uttered that remark—humbly and mockingly—and in the political content of the sentence itself, whose slighting reference to East Germans existed only as a feature of reunified Germany.

Dominic was mercurial, secretive, playful. He reminded me of Woody Woodpecker. I amused him, too. The first time we undressed, he laughed at my hairy chest, so unlike his own smooth flesh. "Monkey," he laughed, "you're like a monkey." He showed up or didn't. "You know I like you," I said, after we'd been seeing each other for a few weeks. "I know," he replied, and I tried to gauge the seriousness of his tone of voice. I had no idea what he thought.

That night, Pinocchio's was an inferno of cheerful depravity. A bald-headed regular whose fringe of hair was tied in back in a tiny ponytail was groping various young men sitting by the wall-mounted slot-machine games; the boys were unresistant, compliant. An odd couple at the bar whom I'd intermittently seen over the months—one was in his forties with long unkempt hair and a beerbelly, and the other was a stocky, sad-eyed young man in his late twenties wearing work overalls—were drinking themselves into oblivion and slowly wrestling, jostling, poking each other, like drunken dancing bears. The man with the ponytail found Josef, a Czech boy with curly sand-coloured hair whom I slightly knew. The man reached out a hand towards Josef's crotch, then suddenly dropped to one knee. Josef's back was to me; all I could see was the reflection of what might be going on in the eyes and expressions of the men and boys along the far wall. Josef threw back his head with his eyes open, and groaned in apparent pleasure, a gesture I recognized. As suddenly as it had begun, the scene dissolved; an American rock song wafted through the smoke ineffectually stirred by the ceiling fans, as Pinocchio's sailed through space towards a far distant galaxy.

The next night, it was as if the previous evening had never happened. I took my usual route, summoned the shade of Isherwood to my cause as best I could, and entered a quiet Pinocchio's just before nine. At the corner table farthest from the bar, playing a game with dice and leather cups, were my pal Freddy, a pair of brothers, and Dominic, the youngest of the four. Freddy immediately spotted me, and when I came over with my drink he was avuncularly solicitous, rearranging the others so that there was an empty barstool I could squeeze onto next to Dominic.

"I was in Zagreb," I said to him.

"I know," Dominic said, "Freddy told me."

If I had felt in some way *outside* in Zagreb, even though

I'd met Drakulic and gotten closer to dismembered Yugoslavia, as I'd intended, in Pinocchio's there was a moment, as I leaned with my back against the wall, my thigh pressed against Dominic's, as the dice cup went around the table in a game I could only half follow, when I knew I was *inside*, completely inside, more than the bar, more than Berlin even, *inside the world*—which was, it occurred to me, my definition of paradise.

There was no hurry. I bought Dominic a cola, and a coffee for Freddy, but the latter discouraged the brothers from pestering me for drinks. Dominic won the dice game with his pals, who treated him as the favoured younger brother. Then we were out in the streets.

Later that night, after Dominic had gone, I walked down Akazienstrasse to the café I liked, the wonderfully named Forum of Unknown Authors. Irish whisky flowed through the flavours of coffee and whipped cream in the libation I drank to celebrate my return to Berlin.

One of my former students at the college where I taught in Vancouver was a Bulgarian named Plamen. Through one of those bizarre itineraries that were the lot of many enterprising East Europeans, he had managed to get out of Bulgaria in the late 1980s, and had zigzagged his way from Arab emirates through Europe until he finally landed one day in a Canadian classroom where I happened to be rambling on, under the rubric of environmental ethics, about the thoughts of dogs and the rights of trees.

Plamen was a dark-haired man in his late twenties, with a perpetual five o'clock shadow and a mouth that curved downward in what might be read as a frown or a smirk. He was eccentric, energetic, and intelligent, and quickly developed a passion for the fate of forests and aboriginal peoples. When he learned I would be in Berlin, he proposed that we meet in Sofia, since he was returning for a visit in spring 1993 for the first time since the political changes of the late eighties. We could meet Blaga Dimitrova there, he said. Dimitrova was a poet and novelist, some of whose essays I'd read in the *New York Review of Books*. In the first post-Communist elections, she'd become the country's vice-president on the opposition United Democratic Front ticket.

Though Plamen had promised to meet me at Sofia airport, I was nonetheless pleasantly surprised when I saw him waving from the other side of the passport control booth, since he was one of those people who always had a dozen things on his mind. He was with a large, reddish-blonde woman his own age named Diana, who was the daughter of the family where we were to stay. We'd barely piled into the car he'd somehow commandeered when Plamen began relating an adventure on the border between Bulgaria and Macedonia, from which he'd just returned.

"I've arranged for you to meet with the leader of the Macedonian opposition," he announced. "I just have to phone them tonight to confirm."

"Macedonia," I moaned. "Plamen, I've just gotten to Sofia."

He plunged into an account of the complexities of Macedonian, former Yugoslavian, and Bulgarian politics. I hardly had a chance to see the city we were weaving through, as I tried to conjure up a mental map on which to locate Macedonia. There was an onion-shaped church dome, a defaced Russian war memorial in a park, statues of two scholarly brothers eternally seated at either side of the entrance to the university they had founded, the white marble mausoleum that had displayed the remains of a famous Bulgarian Communist, Georgi Dimitrov, until "the mummy" was removed and cremated in the upheaval of 1989.

"Macedonia must be at least six hours away by car," I calculated, "and six hours back. Anyway, I don't have a visa."

"We can make it in four," he assured me. I snorted, imagining the kind of drive it might be. "And we'll get through the border without papers."

"What we'll get through is a Bulgarian jail. Anyway, I thought we were going to meet Dimitrova."

"We are, tomorrow afternoon."

Plamen had pulled up half onto the sidewalk and squeezed into a parking space in a narrow street in downtown Sofia. We were soon crammed into a small sitting room with a round table, armchairs, and a cabinet full of cut crystal and china, to meet Diana's parents. Her father was a pale, retired doctor with a grey brushcut who appeared from the next room, trailed by a small dog of indeterminate lineage. Her mother was a slim, energetic woman who was called Lilly Pepa. She put on a pot of coffee in a small kitchen that had a balcony outside where wash was drying.

The five of us, plus the dog, would be sleeping in their tiny apartment. The father and mother slept in the front

"The daughter of President Zhelev. Her name was Jordanka," Plamen said. The bookseller hadn't known any details.

We emerged from the underground into the large park. The night-time amble was beginning to feel like a forced march.

"It's time for a drink," I pleaded, and Plamen assured me that our next destination was a jazz café.

The next morning, everyone moved around the apartment with the gingerly solicitude of people in a crowded train compartment. Lilly Pepa and her husband trundled between the front room, the kitchen, and the bathroom. A radio was on in the next room with the news. Plamen was still asleep behind the frosted glass door. Diana brought me coffee at the sitting-room table, and received my thanks in halting French before heading off to her morning wash-up. I read some Dimitrova I'd brought along, and thumbed through a volume of Bulgarian politics. Successive scenes of horrible history—no worse than anywhere else, I suppose—tramped through the Thracian mountains in bloodstained boots. Byzantines, Ottomans, nineteenth-century Russians, twentieth-century Red Army liberators, a forty-year Communist regime.

We had to dash to make a ten a.m. meeting with Edwin Sugarov, the editor of *Democracy* newspaper, the opposition daily. Plamen's sense of timing was contrived to turn life into an imperative. He had appeared late, stretching from sleep, but as soon as he had a cup of coffee in hand he began working a recalcitrant phone, lining up a roster of appointments that quickly diminished the possibility of seeing the monastery at Rila, much less the Macedonian border. Diana came in carrying a jar of water in which a bright red comb was half-submerged. While he held the phone to his ear with a raised shoulder, meanwhile balancing a notebook stuffed with bits of paper and documents, all of which periodically spilled out onto the floor, she draped his shoulders in a towel and gave him a haircut. Lilly Pepa made us breakfast. The trip to Sugarov's—Plamen behind the wheel—was a last-minute scramble, and I reminded him that he'd always turned up for class fifteen minutes late. "We have plenty of time," he laughed, remembering that I duly noted his arrivals in the classroom with a loud announcement of "Now we can begin."

"How have you handled the coverage of the suicide of the president's daughter?" I asked Sugarov.

"Jordanka," he said pensively, handing me a copy of that morning's edition of *Democracy*. Sugarov was a tall, bald-headed man with a shaggy grey-tinged beard, wearing a grey suit and a striped tie. His fourth-floor office looked down onto red-tiled roofs of nearby buildings, which gleamed in the morning sun.

"We've been quite restrained in our comments. We've tried to avoid the wild speculations of some other newspapers." He paused to answer a phone. When he picked up the thread of his reply, it led not to the daughter but to her father. "Mr. Zhelev was nominated by the United Democratic Front, but afterward changed his course against the UDF. He did everything possible for the fall of the UDF government."

"Will the death of his daughter affect his political

course?" There had been talk that the suicide might have been something other than a personal matter, that perhaps it was partially a response to the political turmoil.

"Last night, on the TV, it said that there is an investigation," Sugarov replied, "so we've chosen restraint until we hear the results of the investigation." But then he added, "There was a very sharp reaction, a reaction from the people in the democratic forces who believed in Zhelev. The reaction is very passionate." Bitterness seeped from his sentences. "Our national history is full of betrayals," Sugarov said, "and our people don't have any respect for traitors."

Dimitrova was still at the funeral, Plamen and I were told by a lean, white-haired emissary who met us on the ground floor of the government building. He didn't know if she'd be able to keep her appointment with us but, if we wanted to, we could wait. We rode the elevator to the third floor and followed him down a length of red plush carpet to a pair of armchairs outside her office. He produced some coffee and orange juice, and then disappeared into an outer office from which we could hear a television blaring.

Time passed. I watched the red carpet narrow out to a horizon, and sank into one of those moments in a journey when you feel you'd be content never to move again, or to have to figure out how to put one disparate bit—landscape, history, human beings—next to the ragged jigsaw edge of another. Even the whirling dervish of Plamen's soul had subsided for a moment.

Dimitrova appeared at the far end of the corridor after about half an hour, a heavy-set, elegant woman with short blonde hair that curled down onto her forehead in bangs. She was wearing a dark dress and a plain coat, and approached us with the heavy tread of someone grieved. Two younger women flanked her. We stood up and shook hands through a round of introductions.

"I've just come back from the funeral," she explained, inviting us into her office. We sat down around a large oak conference table. The tall windows behind her were draped in brown velvet, with lace inner curtains that showed a view of the open square below. On a side table, in a glossy red vase, was a bouquet of brilliant orange marigolds.

The two young women, her assistants, both in suit jackets and with their hair similarly and severely drawn back, sat alongside Dimitrova. The poet and vice-president was, according to the biographical preface to a book of her poems, a woman of seventy, although she seemed much younger, closer to my own age.

"Mrs. Dimitrova is too upset," said the woman next to her, "for an interview today."

"Yes, I understand," I replied, glancing over at Plamen before he unpacked the vast amount of gear he'd loaded himself down with—cameras, books, documents, a camcorder with a tripod.

"Perhaps we could do it tomorrow afternoon," Dimitrova suggested.

"That would be fine," I agreed.

"But we can have coffee, yes?" she asked. One of her aides went to the outer office.

Plamen reached into one of his zippered carryalls and produced a coffee-table book of coloured photos of the

Amazon region that he'd brought as a gift; the rescue of the Brazilian rainforest was one of the environmental issues in which he'd become engaged. Dimitrova turned the pages of the book, gradually becoming absorbed in the lush green photos, as she and Plamen chatted in Bulgarian. The grey-haired attendant arrived with a trayful of coffee and mineral water.

We easily slipped into a conversation about writers and writing. I mentioned that I'd recently visited Slavenka Drakulic in Zagreb. Dimitrova knew her work. I commented on the difficulties of being a writer in Croatia.

It was not dissimilar in Bulgaria, Dimitrova remarked. "It's a very dangerous moment. We're all on our—how do you say?—on our toes."

"But are those the toes of a tiger?" I joked. I was thinking of a poem of hers I'd read that morning that asked, *How did you allow that tongue of yours—/ wild, unbroken, leaping/ over the toothed fence—/ to be tamed?* The poem said that the tongue *licks words/ like a tiger licks its wounds/ but in a locked cell.*

"A tiger?" asked Dimitrova. "No. Of a cat."

"This isn't the tiger who leaps through the bars of the teeth in your poem?"

"Ah," she laughed, remembering. "Perhaps. We have already jumped over the bars of the zoo. The first bars."

"Does that put you in the jungle?"

"In the jungle of the free market," she quickly replied. "It's a test period now, if our culture will survive, whether it will be created by officials, bureaucrats, or by true creators, men and women of art."

Dimitrova had published an essay that I'd read called "The New Newspeak". Like Vaclav Havel, she'd noted that "the reality is more surprising than anyone had at first thought. The euphoria of the early days when we first gained the freedom to say aloud what had been forbidden" had largely faded away. "The old totalitarian attitudes and stereotypes are being thrown away and are being replaced, by what? By the same attitudes and stereotypes, only now turned in the opposite direction. Newspeak, version two, one might say."[5]

The grotesque new vocabulary included: "Emotional exaggeration. Aggressiveness. Disdain for unconventional opinion. Black and white judgments, without nuance. Demagogy. Ceaseless repetition. Clichés." She hoped for "a sense of humour, even a coarse one."

I liked the detailed examples she provided. "The superlative 'most' is now conjoined with negative adjectives to describe yesterday's overpraised system: it was the 'most inhumane,' the 'most cruel,' the 'most criminal,' the 'most gloomy,' etc. In the city square you hear epithets that are not logically suited to superlatives: the 'most unparalleled tyranny in history,' the 'most pernicious methods,' the 'most unfathomable depths'...."

"The conditional mode is in any case out of fashion. Instead, there is the resort to the drastic imperative: 'No way back!', 'An end to communism!', 'Total dismantling!' While the old mechanisms of power still remain largely untouched, we have a new language for giving orders."

Was that the way to Europe? she asked. Or was there a danger of "creating a new totalitarian speech?... How can a different language, a human one, be created and cultivated, without lies, without fanaticism, without false promises of the future as a heavenly kingdom for the righteous, without hate?"

I wanted to know if the New Newspeak continued to drown out a more human language.

"We still haven't adapted ourselves to a new reality. All of us, we bear the traces, the scars of that period. It's the last wall, the most difficult one to destroy," she said. "Long ago, before the recent events and changes came, I had written about the Chinese Wall."

I recognised it at first sight, and it—me, she'd written, upon first seeing the Great Wall of China.

I patted the stones intimately
and spoke to it silently:
You were embedded in my cells
long before I was born.

"It was a foreboding of what was going to happen to us," she said. "This wall, especially in Balkan minds, lasts a long time."

Although we had put off the official interview, we had talked for an hour and a half. I apologized for our over-prolonged cup of coffee.

"No, it was good for me. It took my mind off it," she said, referring to the death of Zhelev's daughter, as she walked us to the doorway where the red carpet began.

Afterwards, I mixed up the order of events of those days. Had we met the film director Diana knew before or after the artist friend Plamen had to rescue from a local bureaucracy? Was it in the café around the corner from Lilly Pepa's? Or in the basement restaurant where we ate "real Bulgarian food", as Plamen declared with satisfaction? Could I remember— outside my jumble of notes—that sunny noonhour in a busy downtown square when Diana returned from a meandering tour of the local bookstalls to surprise me with the gift of an oversized volume of Bulgarian historical maps that traced the shifting shapes of her country? Or would I only recall that I had been moved by her generosity?

As we walked to an interview at the university one day, the morning sunlight filtered through the leaves of the springtime trees. Wooden scaffolding surrounded the plinth of the Red Army memorial, supporting the heroic sculpture on top. Some movable fencing had been put up to prevent further vandalism, and a police jeep was parked a discreet distance away. I moved closer to look at the bas-relief at the memorial's base. It portrayed a fearless platoon charging forward, flag waving, guns raised, and a small, wheeled howitzer being loaded. The monument's critics had carefully painted parts of the relief in fluorescent colours—the rifles were a glowing orange, the soldiers' boots were white and were labelled "Nike", a circle on a pike bore the international peace symbol in spray paint. The memorial had been not so much defaced as wittily desacralized. Perhaps that was a way to answer kitsch.

There was even a moment, amid our hectic schedule, of strange peacefulness, when Plamen and I went to a restaurant in the hills at the edge of Sofia. It was a roadside affair called The Barns, built around an open courtyard strung with lights which hadn't been turned on. The food was good and plentiful. The road outside led towards Mt. Vitosha, which we could see in the distance. Darkness descended over the courtyard. A candle smoked in the breeze, its light flickering across our plates.

"I guess we aren't going to get to the monastery at Rila," Plamen conceded.

"Not until we've talked to every person in Sofia," I teased.

"I have to figure out what I'm going to do with my life," he said, and we promptly dropped our usual banter. I glanced back outside the roadhouse restaurant, seeking a glimpse of the distant mountain in the night.

There was a phone call at Lilly Pepa's.

"I'd completely forgotten about her," Plamen said.

"Who?"

"It's an old friend of mine, Maya. She and her husband are artists, but I haven't seen them in five years. They're still very committed Communists. Would you like to meet them?"

"Yes, of course."

We arrived sometime after eight in the evening, at a tall concrete apartment building set back from a broad, dark boulevard. Inside, the building looked like an ordinary crowded set of flats, the rough concrete walls decaying, the smell of evening cooking trapped in the corridors. Bogomil and Maya had a two-storey studio flat on the top floors, where they worked at sculpture and painting; they apparently lived elsewhere.

When we entered the spacious atelier—I immediately recognized it as one of the perquisites of the status of officially approved state artist—a third person appeared, their sixteen-year-old son, Kalin. The boy had a puppy a few weeks old in his arms.

Maya—a woman in her thirties with straggly blond ringlets, wearing a subtly striped brown suit jacket with an enamel brooch on the lapel and a violet-coloured blouse—was the most politically vociferous member of what I could easily imagine as an official family portrait of the happy (but serious) ideal Communist Party household unit.

"The whole family have been and are members of the party. I have always been a member," Maya said, and then, her voice rising slightly in exasperation, added, "and for me it's unusual that in a difficult moment like now people are leaving the party. It's a betrayal of the principles of my father and grandfather, who devoted their lives to a great idea, unfortunately corrupted by other people."

It was a long conversation, lasting almost until midnight; they graciously insisted on their willingness to answer my questions. Bogomil was a slight, lean man, shaggily long-haired, bearded. His softer voice intermingled with Maya's quick emotions as they jointly fashioned answers, correcting each other, adding details to one another's accounts, all of which Plamen attempted to translate through the sniffles of an oncoming cold.

But it was difficult to locate exactly those people who had "unfortunately corrupted" a great idea. I couldn't pierce the soft armour of the ideology in whose vocabulary Maya and Bogomil had been raised. There had been "mistakes" in the past, of course, but the party had now adopted "two very important principles," Maya said. "That the party should function democratically, and that the market economy is the gradual way to solve the crisis, while maintaining social protection for everyone." Though one could hardly dismiss their evident sincerity, they were more intent on discussing the blatant shortcomings of the current opposition than those of the Communist Party's past.

"When we talked to Blaga Dimitrova . . . ," I began, and then glanced towards Plamen to check. "Was it yesterday or the day before?" When I looked back at Maya, I saw that the mention of the poet's name had had an effect.

"I don't want to talk about her, about Blaga," she said, using English for the first time.

"Because?"

"Because," she said, with a nervous laugh, and then switched back to her own language. Bogomil joined in. "She was one of those," Plamen translated, "who wrote poems for Zhivkov at one time, and later changed her colours."

I let the subject drop, but later, towards the end of the evening, I remembered Dimitrova's essay about the "New Newspeak". "Have you read it?" I asked Maya.

"No," she said, followed by a short, fiery outburst to which she again appended a bit of laughter, as if startled by her own anger. "And I have no intention to."

Normally I tried to avoid being intentionally provocative, especially if I had some sympathy, however distant, for people's views. But I was frustrated by the bland, if unintentional, evasiveness. I started to outline the argument in Dimitrova's essay.

Maya couldn't contain herself. "She was one of them," she broke in. "She was one of them who did this, and she has never been suppressed, or been in jail. She has been one of them!"

Diana brought me morning coffee. She was wrapped in a blue housecoat, slightly hunched over, looking worried. I couldn't tell if she'd slept badly or if her troubled look was simply a style of solicitous concern. Still, if even the most ordinary domestic moments contained a hint of ineffable mystery, what was I to make of larger ambiguities? The allegedly duplicitous Dimitrova that Maya had inveighed against late into the night didn't seem to bear any resemblance to the elderly woman whose sensuous poems I read in the little sitting room that morning.

> *More and more I confide*
> *in the dead, because the living won't discuss*
> *what's most important.*

She added,

> *And the dead are not afraid of death—*
> *they're its interpreters, their voices*
> *soothing as my father's used to be. . . .*

And who was it—her mother?—who died *without any cry, or moan, or shiver—*?

Carefully, your hand
grew cold in my hand
and imperceptibly led me
into that beyond to death
just to introduce me.

I felt at home with the dead who wandered through her texts, and with a "Self-portrait" that allowed

Loneliness when at the age of love,
*   love when at the age*
*   of loneliness.* [6]

Was Dimitrova the person she appeared to be in her poems—which whatever intuitions I'd had upon meeting her seemed to confirm—or was she was one of the "traitors"?

Plamen straggled into the sitting room, and Diana appeared with fresh coffee and a morning paper. I slowly disengaged myself from the poems.

"Zhelev Buries His Daughter," Plamen said, translating the headline for me. "Doctors claim that Jordanka Zhelev hanged herself in the government hospital, but no official source has confirmed this. Dr. Nicolae Alexandrov, head of the military medical academy, said unequivocally that the case is a suicide. 'The reasons are deeply personal,' said Dr. Alexandrov, without specifying his source."

There were the usual conflicting accounts. Jordanka, according to unconfirmed reports, had been undergoing treatment in the hospital where she committed suicide. There were rumours of unhappy love, but close friends who had seen her at a weekend party denied the story.

"The president learned about the tragedy at Sofia airport from the head of security and the doctor's team sent to meet him. . . ."

Dimitrova was in a blue dress with tiny white polka dots. Her hands rested in her lap as she leaned slightly forward to talk to me. A photograph that Plamen took of us showed that I too leaned forward, elbows on the oak table, a plump figure whose thinning hair unsuccessfully straggled across a mostly bald head. While the two women at Dimitrova's side translated, I had long moments to gaze at her face.

Plamen had hoped to get Dimitrova to sign a petition on behalf of the Bulgarian government protesting the destruction of the Amazonian rainforest. The sag of his disappointed shoulders told me he hadn't gotten everything he wanted—but then, I suspected he'd be satisfied with nothing less than the threat of a declaration of war. Dimitrova said that she might, for the moment, be able to add her name as a private individual. Getting a government declaration would take considerably longer.

We talked very little about politics. She'd been a young woman at the beginning of Communism in Bulgaria, never a member of the party, though she had gone to Moscow and what was then Leningrad to study and write a thesis about Mayakovsky. I tried to locate a point at which disillusionment had turned to opposition. Instead, she remembered the sources of her stories.

She recalled the time she'd gone to the Rhodope

Mountains in southern Bulgaria, in the late 1950s, to write a novel. There, she'd met a young engineer who had been assigned the job of building an extraction plant for a local mining operation.

"This engineer was given the task of finishing the construction," she said, "for some important holiday or anniversary—I think it was for the ninth of September, which was then the national holiday—and he argued that it was impossible because a container for the chemical tailings should be built. (At that time, the word 'ecology' didn't exist.) So he refused to undertake the project, but it was built anyway, by someone else."

The bureaucracy had its way. The requisite solemn ceremony was duly held, with the prime minister in attendance. "And all the contaminated waters went directly into the River Arta," Dimitrova said. "The river was famous for trout, and the next day all the trout were floating dead in the river with their bellies up, poisoned.

"And I witnessed an extraordinary scene. The women on both banks of the river were lamenting—long lamentations—on the hills along the riverbanks. There were groups of women who sang and the echoes from one group went to the next, and it just went along the banks of the river, the women mourning the fish."

I listened in silence to the story.

"I described that scene in a novel of mine, *A Journey to Oneself,* but the censorship wanted me to take out those scenes. Of course, I couldn't accept that because it was important, the culmination of my novelistic work. So the dilemma was in front of me, either to stop the novel, refusing to make the cuts, or to accept the cuts." She paused, with the second nature of a storyteller who knew where a moment of suspense was required, then added, "Chance helped me."

Chance took the form of the lawyer husband of a friend. It so happened that a similar incident of fish poisoning had occurred at the Bulgarian-Greek border, and the Greeks had formally protested. Dimitrova was telling her troubles about the book to her friend, also a writer, when the husband, whose specialty was international litigation, walked in and was caught up in both the story and the issue. "But this book must be published," he insisted, inspiring the novelist to fight for her book.

"So this is a story with a happy ending," I said.

"But the story doesn't stop there," Dimitrova replied.

Some twenty years later, when the book was due to be reprinted, it ran into another political storm. "This was in 1985, when the authorities were forcing the Turkish minority to add Slavic suffixes to their names," she explained. "They were very beautiful and colourful names, and those were the original names of the characters in my novel. Now the editors wanted me to change them. For example, I have a character named Raffina, and they wanted it to be Rafka. Of course I refused to change the names, and the second printing had to wait. So the adventures of just one of my books shows what we lived through."

Dimitrova had written another novel entitled *Face*. "It had an even more interesting fate, because it was imprisoned," she said. "Bulgaria is perhaps unique in the world because we had a book prison, a prison for books. Only for books."

"What do you mean?" I asked.

"What books were imprisoned there? The Bible, Dr. Zhelev's own book, *Fascism*, my novel." She named some other writers whose names I didn't recognize. "I'm proud that my novel was part of the group that was imprisoned, and stayed there for nine years."

"I don't understand," I said. "What do you mean, the novel was imprisoned?"

"The day the book was published, it was taken by trucks and distributed to bookstores, and whoever could bought the book," she said. "But the same day there was another truck, a black truck without windows—the trucks that took prisoners to jail—and it made the same tour around the bookshops, confiscating the books. At the time I didn't know what happened to the books, I thought maybe they were burned."

In fact, they hadn't been burned. Dimitrova paused to tell a story within the story. Once, when the regime had indeed ordered a book-burning, an updraft had swirled half-burnt pages through a chimney, scattering them through the surrounding neighbourhood. Her husband still had one of those singed pages in his possession. "Since then, less inflammatory measures have been adopted," she punned. "Instead, they established a special warehouse in the town of Slivan, a little way out of Sofia. That's where the books were taken."

It was a story with a little epilogue. "Afterwards, I wrote a poem on the imprisoned books. The books themselves—

the Bible, Dr. Zhelev's *Fascism*, some others, and my novel—have a conversation between themselves as they sit in their prison."

The plane from Sofia touched down at Shönefeld airport in the late afternoon sunshine. I made the long underground ride across Berlin to the subway stop at Akazienstrasse, emerging into the sunlight behind St. Paul the Apostle church. People sat on the benches that lined the path around the red-brick building. The sidewalk tables at the Forum of Unknown Authors café were crowded. Shoppers were making last-minute purchases before the May Day weekend. I climbed the winding staircase that led to my studio flat, dropped my bag inside the door, opened some windows to clear the musty air, and then sighed in that satisfied way you do when, after a journey, you get home.

For Berlin had become my second home. When I'd started out several years before, with the vague intention of obtaining an idea of the fall of Communism, I'd never expected—nor was I aware that I might desire—to find another city in which I was comfortable enough to want to live. That it was a city historically at the centre of the Holocaust—a fact inescapable for a visiting Jew—complicated my impulse with a chilling layer of irony.

Of course, Vancouver was still my home, or as much of a home as a Wandering Jew or "rootless cosmopolitan" could acquire, but from this distance it seemed like a peaceful encampment set in a great deer park, at the edge of Canada's vastness. Nonetheless, it had a life, a culture, people I valued—which, indeed, was what I had discovered in each place I'd been, each city in which I'd imagined my life going on, turning me into someone slightly different. If there was a banal but crucial lesson to be derived from the places where Communism had ruled for half a century, it was the recognition that what remained after a particular ideology had dissipated was human beings equal to ourselves, and cities equal to or greater than our own. In Berlin too I had a life, books on my desk to read, stories-in-progress, friends to see and talk to.

I checked in with Michael to let him know I'd safely made it back from Sofia.

"You know, the stores are closed tomorrow for May Day," he reminded me. "So get your shopping done today."

"Yes, I know."

As soon as I'd hung up, Karsten, a photographer who had sublet the studio to me, called to ask if he could come over to pick up one of his cameras; he was just down the street at a café. Even though he had a key to the flat, he was delicate about any intrusions.

"Sure, come on over, I'll go downstairs and open the door. I just got back from Sofia."

Karsten flipped through Dimitrova's poems, sitting on the soft black leather couch. He held a camera in the other hand, and occasionally took a picture of me as I sat behind a cluttered worktable.

A scowl of distaste crossed his face. "Too simple," he complained.

"Oh?" I said, getting up and taking the book from his hand. I found the poem I was looking for, "Refraction", and handed it back to him.

Before we can adjust
to our near-sightedness
already, still
(it doesn't matter)
we have moved so far apart
no matter how we close our eyes
we cannot see ourselves
the other or the same
(it doesn't matter)
till the final line
where one of us
the one more wounded
or the one more wounding
(it doesn't matter)
crosses over all alone
the line of sight is broken
then we'll gather
everything from yet
another angle
you or me
later or never
(what do you mean
it doesn't matter?)

"Nice," he murmured after reading it, his complicated German sensibility soothed. "*Schön.*"

"*What do you mean it doesn't matter?*" I quoted.

"*Schön*," he admitted. "Very nice."

Berlin had turned sultry. I walked down Goltzstrasse, past the Isherwood plaque on Nollendorf Strasse, and then crossed the wide corner that led to Pinocchio's, feeling slightly nauseated in the heat. The evening sky was still bright blue. One of the bartenders was crossing the corner playground at Fuggerstrasse and said hello to me as we passed.

In the bar, the manager, Hansie, was supervising the putting up of a sign reducing prices in honour of May Day; beer was fifty pfennigs cheaper. On my way over, I'd caught a newspaper headline reporting that the governing Christian Democrats and the opposition Social Democrats had agreed on a "Solidarity Pact" to diminish social services, and to reduce the German deficit, in the middle of the recession. They'd been acrimoniously debating it for weeks. The sign on the new price list was headed *Solidarpakt*.

The first person to appear from the corridor at the end of the bar, wearing ridiculously baggy shorts and a clashingly awful fluorescent orange T-shirt, was Dominic. His blue eyes brightened and he flashed me a quick smile as he plopped himself down on a stool. Hansie, who was still holding my hand from his greeting handshake, said, "Your *Liebling* is here," and led me over to where Dominic was sitting.

I ordered drinks for us, a Campari for me and a cola for him.

"You've been to Sofia," Dominic said.

"Yes, how did you know?"

He smiled with satisfaction. He knew everything about me, or everything he was interested in knowing; I knew almost nothing about him. It took me a few seconds to recognize his familiar grin, as I took in his fashionable new haircut, with the sides and back trimmed more closely than the hair on top. He'd also acquired some tan while I was away. His sun-darkened skin emphasized his blondness.

"You've been swimming," I said.

"Yo," he confirmed.

We took a cab from the bar to the flat at the end of Akazienstrasse. It was cooler within the thick walls, behind the closed blinds. He went into the kitchen with the familiarity of a frequent visitor, poured a glass of cola for himself, some mineral water for me, and then stuffed little wheat biscuits from a cereal box on the kitchen table into his mouth, turning to face me with his puffed-out cheeks.

"You look like a squirrel."

"A hamster," he laughed.

In the bedroom-studio, sprawled on the black leather couch, he peeled off his T-shirt and slid out of his baggy shorts. In the bar, he had looked like—or I'd imagined he looked like—just another kid who hung out there, attractive enough, but also rather invisible, except to me. But slouched down into the soft hide of the sofa, smooth thighs spread wide, wearing only white socks and gym shoes, he changed.

The details of where the legs went, how the genitals entered the cavities of the body, even the feel of the imperceptibly wiry blond hairs on the front of his thighs brushing back and forth against the smooth skin on the backs of my own suddenly seemed as little to the point as the word "beautiful" used in attempts to describe someone.

What I would remember about Dominic—and I knew this, or anticipated this thought, even as we were enjoined—was that he was distinguished from the other young men by the way he seemed to forget (or perhaps merely, and with great artfulness, gave the impression of forgetting) that our encounter was a transaction. Instead he treated it as a passion, and since he did so in the name of his own desire, he appeared to act innocently. So acute was his sexual intelligence that you never felt he had accorded you less than his full attention. Others might say, But how can you rhapsodize over a relationship so essentially impersonal? I suppose it was impersonal—since we almost never saw each other apart from those hours in the bar and in bed—yet it was Dominic's *personality* that I found so attractive.

I said we almost never saw each other elsewhere, but there was one time. Once during that spring, Dominic allowed me to take pictures of him. The day after he agreed to be photographed, I rushed over to Michael's to borrow a camera and receive a hasty photography lesson. Michael was amused that I would at last be making a contribution to the mythical Boyopolis archive.

"See, you just put the film in here, close the back, and press this button," he explained. "It loads automatically." It was idiot-proof. "You can't go wrong." I looked at the machine dubiously.

But it worked. When I couldn't get the second roll of film onto the spool, fumbling with it, all thumbs, Dominic patiently took the camera out of my hand, loaded it in a second, and then gave it back to me. I photographed an ordinary teenager in T-shirt and baggy shorts. Then a naked young man with a hard-on. Then Dominic sitting on a kitchen stool, crouching, standing against a wall with his taut butt to the camera, lying sprawled in bed. When it was over I was soaked in sweat.

Later, when I had the photos, I found myself arranging them into the story of Dominic. The photo I slipped into the first plastic page of the album was not one of Dominic, but a test shot I'd taken of the closed blind of my studio window and part of my cluttered desk. In the second page I put a picture of an open window looking into a courtyard, with a tiny sparrow perched on the window ledge. When I showed the album to friends, they said, "Oh, so this is where you live." In fact the window picture wasn't a photo at all, but a postcard of an 1865 painting called "View from a Window, Marienstrasse (Berlin)" by Adolph von Menzel, which I'd picked up at a museum. And then came the first photo of a grinning Dominic, slouched on the black leather sofa in a T-shirt, hands clasped behind his head.

When I showed the book of photos to Karsten, he offered a professional photographer's scowl as he carefully inspected them. "Just photos of a boy," he shrugged dismissively, "like in a pornography magazine."

But the time I'm thinking of was on the day I'd picked up the developed photos from the shop. I had them with me, in a plastic bag I was toting, when I met my friend Goertz for lunch. He enthusiastically told me about his new woman friend, an architect from Istanbul. We had agreed to go to an exhibit that afternoon of, coincidentally, photos of mostly young men, that was on display at a villa in the southern part of the city. We went down into the subway and a long string of pale orange subway cars pulled up to the platform. Goertz and I went into the end one.

Dominic was sitting on a green leather bench just inside the doorway. He was with two friends his own age, a girl dressed in a punk style and another boy, who was obnoxiously insisting on lighting a cigarette because he knew smoking wasn't permitted on the subway. The other boy was either drunk or stoned. Dominic grinned a familiar greeting.

"Goertz, this is Dominic," I said. A half-hour earlier, I had showed Goertz some of the photos of Dominic. My irrational sense of Dominic's nonexistence outside of the places I saw him was dispelled. The memory of that encounter stayed with me. Its accidental conjunction of friends from different circles, of representation and reality, of narrative itself, encapsulated some of the mysteries of my life.

The evening I returned from Sofia, the boy in the photographs had reappeared in person. "Don't move," Dominic urgently whispered in my ear, as he rode the crest of his orgasm. His gym shoes, which he'd worn to bed—a tiny, perverse touch—rubbed against my bare feet.

"Good?" I asked, after we'd disentangled, rolled over on our backs, subsided into two creatures breathing.

He turned his head to me, a centimetre away on the pillow.

"Yo," he grinned, a light sweat beading the skin above his upper lip.

We cleaned up the mess, dressed, prepared to go downstairs into the warm spring night.

I paid him, handing over a pale blue piece of paper with a picture of a grand piano on the back of it. We politely thanked each other for whatever had been traded in the transaction.

We parted at the corner of Akazien and Hauptstrasse, the busy main street whose traffic sounds I could hear through the open window of my apartment. They gradually faded away in the pre-dawn hours, leaving a silence between the end of the night and the early morning cooing of the pigeons.

———————

I went to Vilnius, Lithuania, because my father said he had been born there. Precisely when he had been born there, and when, as a baby, he had left Vilnius for Chicago, and the order and dates of the births of his three brothers and four sisters, were matters of endless and rollicking dispute whenever his side of the family gathered. Or I should say *our* side of the family, since I regarded most of my mother's family as unexplained strangers with whom my father and I had been accidentally and unfortunately linked by the fact of loving my mother.

In contrast, I loved the entire complement of our side of the family, starting with my grandmother Sarah, who made plum jam which I was allowed to taste from the pot. I loved all of my father's variegated sisters and brothers, beginning with his elder, crazy, sequestered sister Jane, who sat in a rocking-chair at Grandma Sarah's apartment, enigmatically muttering. Then there was Patty, an unmarried woman with a humpback who taught school, and Emma, who was surrounded by books—the first women with independent opinions I ever met. However, I hardly knew his youngest sister, Babe, who had divorced and remarried, moving to California. My father's brothers were Lew, who had become a passport photographer by marrying into a family in that trade (and thus took the only photo I ever saw of my grandfather, Jacob), Gob, who ran a clothing store on Division Street in the Polish district of Chicago, and the youngest and most brilliant, Harold, who was a biochemist in charge of his own laboratory. And just for the record, I liked all of the wives and husbands who had married into the family, and all of the cousins they had produced. But finally, in this bathos of affection, do I have to declare once more—but why not?—that, above all, I loved my father.

Theirs was one of the worlds that was gone for me. When they all gathered—my father's brothers and sisters, their spouses and offspring—the occasion was gregariously loud and laughter-filled as they told stories and lies and tall tales—each an unabashed, unselfconscious raconteur, good-hearted liar, myth-maker. And inevitably it devolved into an interminable argument over births and dates.

"Now, Morrie," Emma insisted, "you couldn't have been born in 1901 because . . ." and then would follow a set of genealogical details and circumstances that a choir of logic-chopping Jesuits couldn't harmonize.

"It was 1901," my father said, vainly attempting to hold his ground. "The old man"—Grandfather Jacob, that is—"was here two years before he sent for us."

"Morrie, Emma is right," my Aunt Patty broke in, "because I was born in—" and then there was another date in that history of fertility. Uncle Harold supplied the historical background of Grandfather Jacob's odyssey, Gob had his say, Lew offered his own fanciful version. And on and on it went.

Asta Markeviciute was a tomboyish woman in her early twenties who, through a number of phone calls between Berlin and Vilnius, had agreed to become my guide to the city of my father's birth. She was a student at Vilnius University—an English major writing a graduating essay on *My Antonia*, one of the novels of Willa Cather. She told me about school as a cab took us from the airport along the shore of the Neris River, which undulated through the city, into the Antakalnis Hills on the north-east edge of town. I had been booked into a hotel in that vicinity by a travel agent.

When we finally arrived at the hotel, I felt immediately uncomfortable. For one thing, it was too far from the city for my liking. Also, it wasn't so much a hotel as a sort of dormitory for visiting sports teams. As soon as I saw the room— a rough-hewn space with a bed and bad lighting, no toilet—I knew I had to get out of there. At that moment, two representatives from the local travel agency associated with my Berlin ticket agent showed up. I recognized that they were holdovers from the old regime, the days before Lithuania declared independence from the crumbling Soviet Union at the beginning of the 1990s. They were used to dealing with supervised tourist groups, but now in the privatized economy, where wandering loners brandished international credit cards, they were gamely attempting to become up to date. No problem, one of them told Asta, I could be relocated in a hotel downtown. At least I wasn't peremptorily informed that everything was full, as I would have been in the old days. He even attempted a friendly capitalist smile.

Asta and I took a long tram-ride back to Cathedral Square. As we stood between the white-columned neoclassical church and a baroque bell-tower, she gave me a choice of going down Gedimino Prospekt or into the winding streets of the Old Town. I chose Gedimino Prospekt, a long, wide boulevard that ran north-west from the cathedral all the way to the Parliament Buildings on the shore of the Neris. There was little vehicle traffic apart from the occasional lopsided, crowded bus, and people casually crossed the uneven black paving stones without fear of being struck.

The particular beauty of the street was derived from its linden trees, with their small, precisely serrated green leaves, which lined both sides all the way to the horizon. They were planted in the middle of the sidewalk, and each one had its roots guarded by a wrought-iron metal grille that formed a small black square around the base of the tree.

We sauntered along in the afternoon sunshine, partially protected from the heat by the intermittent shade of the trees. Asta occasionally pointed out a public building, café (the Literary Café at the beginning of the street), or theatre (a sculpture above its marquee presented three black-shrouded Fury-like women urgently pressing towards us). I knew, thanks to my curious assortment of guidebooks, that Gedimino was a street whose name, and even the languages in which it was named, had frequently changed. I'd brought with me three volumes of memoirs of Vilnius (or Wilno, Wilna, or Vilna, as it was variously called) by Tadeusz Konwicki, Lucy Dawidowicz, and Czeslaw Milosz, all of whom had either grown up or lived here. Actually there was a fourth, if you counted the fact that in Milosz's book there was a "Dialogue about Wilno with Tomas Venclova", a younger exiled poet with whom Milosz had exchanged letters about the city of their youth.[7]

The street was called Gedimino after the fourteenth-century nobleman who had allegedly founded Vilnius; the ruined ramparts of his castle towered above the city from a hill just behind Cathedral Square. According to Adam Mickiewicz, the nineteenth-century Polish poet who also lived in Vilnius, he had *"Built Vilna city like a wolf that broods / Mid bears and boars and bison in the woods.*

But Czeslaw Milosz, who had grown up here in the early decades of the twentieth century, recalled that "the street that was supposed to be the main street was definitely not cosmopolitan. It was officially named St. George Boulevard at first, then Mickiewicz Boulevard; less officially, it was known as St. George Street, and when I was a schoolboy it was still called 'Georgie' for short. This thoroughfare, laid out with a straight edge and bordered by rows of apartment houses from the second half of the nineteenth century, did not elevate Wilno any higher than a provincial town . . . a promenade where officers and students went to stroll. Later on, people gradually became accustomed to its new name, Mickiewicz Street."

Lucy Dawidowicz, who had studied Yiddish history in Vilna in 1938, said, "The most elegant street in Vilna and one of its longest (a little over a mile) was *ulica* Adam Mick-iewicz ... an east-west boulevard densely lined with trees." She remembered Sztral's café, with umbrella-covered tables on a large terrace, and across from Sztral's "a restaurant, Palais de Danse, which featured tea dances at five on Satur-days and Sundays.... A string trio played waltzes and tangos, while couples spun around the small dance floor. We feasted on tea and pastries—Polish pastries were rich and luscious. I imagined that Paris must be like this."

But Tomas Venclova, who knew Vilnius after the Second World War, reminded Milosz that "the history of that street's name deserves a separate description. The Lithuanian authorities changed it to Gediminas Street but left the name of Mickiewicz on its extension. In 1950 or thereabouts, it was announced that, in deference to the pleas of the working masses, the name of the street would be changed: it would become Comrade Stalin Boulevard. It bore that proud name until the Twentieth Party Congress [1956]. One of my ac-quaintances, a young graphic artist, wrote a petition to the authorities at that time proposing a return to the old name. He was immediately expelled from college.... In the end, of course, the street became Lenin Boulevard. My generation always called it Gediminke, however, and still does."

Asta and I passed a large park with red-gravel paths that made an "X" through its centre. "The statue of Lenin used to be there," she said, nodding towards the now empty space where the diagonals intersected.

The blocky, rough-hewn stone fortress facing the park had housed the local branch of the secret police. "The for-mer KGB headquarters," she noted.

Even walking the street that afternoon, I could feel the distinctive power of the place. Milosz had noted that one of his friends "asked me why I return so insistently in my memories to Wilno and to Lithuania, as my poems and prose writings reveal. I replied that, in my opinion, this has nothing to do with an émigré's sentimentality, for I would not want to go back. What is at work, no doubt, is a search for reality purified by the passage of time." Tadeusz Konwicki comically confessed "that all my books are stuffed full of Wilno, that I go round and round forever writing about Wilno, that actually I have been writing one and the same book all my life, a novel of identical content each time, identical plot, identical characters. I didn't even exert myself on descriptions of nature; I have been shoveling out the same old thing for twenty years."

When we reached the Parliament Buildings, a modernist affair with a large concrete plaza, Asta asked me if I wanted to go on across the river, where Gedimino became Mickiewicz. I simply put my hands up to indicate my sweat-dripping skull. She laughed. "We can get a drink in the Old Town," she assured me.

Returning down Gedimino, I remembered that Asta had unself-consciously referred to the implied lesbian aspects of Willa Cather's *My Antonia*.

"Is there a gay bar in Vilnius?" I asked her.

"It's right over there, the Akimirka," she said, pointing to a squat hotel across the street. There was a restaurant on one side of the entrance, and a bar on the other. "It's not really a gay bar, but it's where the gays go."

Later that afternoon, the search for my father, or my

Jewish heritage, if that's what I was looking for, was settled without an outward sign, but so swiftly—within the space of a single thought—that I was deeply surprised by the feeling of satisfied curiosity that followed it.

We had gone back to Cathedral Square, stopped along the way for a mineral water in a stuffy basement bar where men were slugging back shots of vodka, and then gone south along University into the Old Town until it turned into Gaona Street. Asta paused to give me a quick glimpse of the network of courtyards and buildings that made up Vilnius University, founded in 1579. "There are nine or perhaps thirteen courtyards," Tomas Venclova said. "We used to say that there were places in that labyrinth where no human had ever set foot." In one of the courtyards, a group of students was standing in a circle and rehearsing a song—in preparation for some religious festival, Asta told me.

Beyond that, where Gaono Street began, was the old Jewish quarter. Napoleon, hastily passing through Vilnius on his retreat from Russia in 1812, had dubbed the city "the Jerusalem of Lithuania". The Gaon of Vilna (1720–1797) was a Jewish scholar. "He was not only a master of the Torah. He also studied Hebrew grammar, astronomy, geography, algebra and geometry, and encouraged others to do the same . . . for he believed that this knowledge would enhance one's understanding of the Talmud," Lucy Dawidowicz recorded. By the time she arrived in Vilnius in 1938, Jews had been living there for five hundred years. The city's population had been thirty to fifty per cent Jewish from the seventeenth century to the middle of the twentieth. Jewish or Zydu Street dated from 1600, the Great Synagogue—its gates a gift of the Society of Psalm Reciters—had been built in 1633. The Jews had multiplied in Vilnius, even through a hideous history of recurrent pogroms. The oppression under the Russian czar Alexander III had "set in motion a mass migration between 1881 and 1914 when Jews in unprecedented numbers left Russia, among them Jews from Vilna as well," wrote Dawidowicz. Among the émigrés had been my grandparents and their young children.

Asta led me through narrow lanes until we emerged onto what had been German Street, or Niemiecka—the Polish for "German"—and was now Vokieciu Street, lately widened into a grass-divided parkway with a contemporary art centre and the national art museum at its far end. "Niemiecka was primarily a shopping street, the center of Jewish retail trade, with stores for everything from sweets to pianos, from notions and trimmings to ironmongers," Dawidowicz remembered. Milosz said that, entering it, one "penetrated into a region of sudden density. Sidewalks, gates, doors, windows all sprouted multitudes of faces and seemed to bulge from the crowds. It seemed that on German Street every house concealed an infinite number of inhabitants who engaged in every possible trade. . . . Loaded carts, pulled by straining horses, thundered past. Touts circulated among the passersby; their job was to spot potential customers, praise their goods, and conduct those people they had managed to corral to a shop that was located somewhere in a distant inner courtyard. . . . German Street was exclusively Jewish . . . it acted as the representative of a whole labyrinth of twisting, astonishingly narrow medieval alleys, the houses connected by arcades, the uneven pavements two or three metres wide."

An old photo in my pocket guide showed three-storey storefront buildings narrowing towards church belfries on the horizon. A horse and wagon moved towards the viewer, and there were pedestrians, women in long skirts, on the sidewalks. "A significant part of the Jewish ghetto was sacrificed for the widening of Vokieciu Street," my city guide reported. "Stalinist architecture replaced the splendid façades." As we stood in an open space looking across Vokieciu, Asta pointed out where the Great Synagogue had stood. "It's completely gone," she said.

I was dazed with the heat, and Asta promised me that there was a nice shady bar in the art centre. As we turned in that direction, I found myself looking at a bit of grass, or a cobblestone on the path, asking myself if I had felt anything while walking through the Jewish quarter. My grandfather had walked on these streets. He had come here from Russia at the beginning of the twentieth century, and he had gone on after a time to the New World, leaving his wife and baby daughter and son in Vilnius while he established himself. Eventually he had arrived in Chicago and got a job driving a horse and wagon for the owner of a junkyard, a man named Wexler. It was said that my grandfather made Wexler's fortune for him, by virtue of his knowledge of the value of metal in demolished buildings and his sheer brute strength (my father boasted that his father could lift a cast-iron water heater by himself). Perhaps it was Jacob I was seeking, rather than my father, I thought to myself.

Somehow, the thought of my grandfather crossing German Street had sated my desire for sources. The real story of the Jewish quarter was to be found on a small plaque on

Zydu Street, which Asta translated for me. It said that eleven
thousand Jews had been rounded up from this ghetto during
the Second World War and shipped to nearby Paneriai Forest, where they had been killed.

My new hotel was on Gedimino Prospekt, No. 12. I had a
beautiful room in back, overlooking an untended grassy
garden in which a statue of Hermes presided over puffy-
headed dandelions beneath a maple tree. There was a wonderful writing desk, a perfect lamp, a round table and chairs,
a comfortable box bed, and a bathroom. Downstairs was a
coffee shop where I could get mineral water to rehydrate
myself from the fluid-draining heat, as well as early morning
coffee.

Asta and I had dinner at the Literary Café on Gedimino,
an old-fashioned, formal room that included a pianist playing romantic arrangements of popular tunes. She'd collect
me in the morning and we'd interview some politicians.

Though almost nine, it was still light out when I walked
beneath the lindens on Gedimino to the Akimirka Hotel.
Inside the foyer, I glanced at the restaurant on the right. The
city guide had awarded it a little cameo portrait of Lenin in
its listings, as a sardonic sign that apart from "fast service, it
remains true to the past."

I turned left and entered the gloom of the Akimirka bar.
Along the far wall there was a set of wooden booths occupied mostly by mixed couples, several of whom seemed well
advanced towards a state of vodka blankness. Immediately
off the entrance there was a long bar that ran all the way to
the back of the room. Various men sat on stools along its

length. White muslin curtains shaded the window that faced onto Gedimino, and contorted plastic extrusion lamps from the 1950s gave off a faint glow down the bar. Once my eyes adjusted to the dark, I saw that the men sitting on the barstools were the ones for whom I was looking.

I'd been sitting at the bar for a minute, waiting for the woman serving at the far end to notice me, when a man on my right, who had been talking to a friend, leaned over and said something to me. He was in his late twenties and had curly, slightly thinning hair.

"What did you say?" I asked.

"You have to go down there and order," he said in English.

When I came back with a coffee and brandy that I'd acquired mostly through pointing at things, he introduced himself as Igor. His friend was named Vytas.

"Where are you from?" he asked.

"I've come from Berlin, where I'm staying, but I'm a Canadian. Are you from here?"

"Yes, I live in Vilnius. He's from Minsk," Igor said, nodding toward Vytas. Minsk was the nearest major city, across the border in what was now independent Belarus, formerly the Belorussian Republic of the Soviet Union.

"Your English is excellent," I said.

"Well, it's one of the subjects I teach at a grammar school here," Igor explained.

That led to a discussion of work and living standards.

"About six thousand *talonas* a month," Igor said, in answer to my question about the average monthly wage. *Talonas*, or monetary coupons, were the local currency; the government was having banknotes printed abroad, but there had been a screw-up of some sort. The going rate of exchange was three hundred and some *talonas* to a U.S. dollar.

"But that's less than twenty dollars a month," I said, doing a quick, shocking calculation. Igor nodded unhappy confirmation.

"What does coffee cost?" I asked.

"Mmm, about eight hundred *talonas* for a small tin," he said.

"Then it's impossible."

"Very difficult," he amended.

"What's it like here for gays?"

"Well, you can see," Igor said, indicating the Akimirka. The repression of homosexuals, he claimed, had hardly been improved by the demise of Communism, the rise of nationalism, the fall of the incompetent conservative government, or the re-empowerment of the reformed Communists. But since the Akimirka was tolerated, it seemed that economic misery was higher on the list of difficulties than legal harassment.

Then we just gossiped, as men do in a bar anywhere. I bought Igor and Vytas drinks, eager to do something sociable with my sudden incongruous wealth. Vytas had to go off to his night watchman's job at a local restaurant, so Igor walked me back towards my hotel, down the dark, dusky Gedimino Prospekt.

"Is it possible for us to do an interview sometime?" I asked, when we stopped to shake hands goodnight at the door of the hotel.

"Sure," he agreed. "I'll bring Vytas. When?" We made a date for a couple of evenings hence. In my room, I stepped out on the balcony for a minute to check that the wing-footed, helmeted Hermes was still there. A spotlight from an adjoining building fell on his naked, greenish body. Through the leafy maple, the full moon rose.

The next day, the politicians were charming but strangely elusive. At a reasonable mid-morning hour, Asta and I walked the length of Gedimino to the modernist Parliament Buildings with their windows of copper-tinted glass.

We spoke to Laima Andrikiene, an agricultural economist and a member of Parliament from the newly proclaimed centre-right National Union Party, the organization that had developed from the Lithuanian independence movement, Sajudis. She wore a beautifully patterned black and brown dress, and had a vase of yellow tulips on her desk.

Her mother's family had been deported to Siberia during the Stalinist terror after the Second World War; her father had been sentenced to ten years. "They came back after Stalin's death in 1953, and sometime in 1964, 1965, my father was invited to KGB headquarters and they said, Forget everything, you were not guilty. And he said, I will never forget, because I lost my best years in Siberia, working in the labour camps."

She had been present at the founding of Sajudis in 1988. The Lithuanian Communist Party declared itself independent from the Communist Party of the Soviet Union, of which it had been a segment, but Sajudis nonetheless won the election of 1990. Though Soviet tanks rolled through Vilnius at the beginning of the following year, and unarmed civilians were killed by Soviet troops in their assault on the

local television station, Lithuanian independence was declared through an eighty per cent referendum majority in
February 1991. But the Sajudis government ran into problems, and the standard of living precipitously declined.

A few years before, the economy had been part of the
Soviet rouble system. The average wage had been about 250
roubles then, Andrikiene said. "It was enough to buy coffee,
to pay rent, to buy gasoline, but it was not enough to buy a
house." At the next election, in autumn 1992, the former
Communists, reconfigured as the Lithuanian Democratic
Labour Party, won a landslide victory over the bumbling
Sajudis government.

I wanted to know what the former Communists believed.

"I don't think that they are Communists, that they have
a vision of Communism," Andrikiene said. "Probably they
joined the Communist Party for other reasons. They were
thinking about their careers, their lives."

Three months before my arrival in Vilnius, the Labour
Party had confirmed its dominant position by handily win-
ning the country's presidential election.

"What brought that about? Why did they win?" I asked
her.

"I don't have an answer to this question," the charming
MP replied, and then she laughed in helplessness. "You
know, I can understand our people because they have a lot
of problems, but I can't understand how the Labour Party
was able to persuade them that they would solve all their
problems, to give cheap milk, cheap meat, cheap everything, and do it all this year."

The man reputed to be the brains of the Democratic Labour Party, Gediminas Kirkilas, was proud to be a professional politician. He was the eldest of three brothers and four sisters, and though his parents had never been members of the Communist Party, while Kirkilas was doing his military service in the Soviet navy an opportunity had arisen to join the party. He had joined in 1972, "because Lithuanians needed to be party members to occupy positions in Lithuania." He had a taste for literature and wrote some journalism, rising rapidly to be cultural commissar for Lithuania and a member of the Lithuanian Party's central committee.

"You make it sound like joining the party was necessary to one's life, but there must have been an ideological commitment too," I remarked.

"I have to admit that my reasons for joining the party were career-oriented," Kirkilas confessed easily. "I think most Lithuanian Communists didn't deeply consider Communist ideology, or Leninist theory, or even Marxism. The question was simply whether to accept the rules of this game."

"Are you saying that you were a Communist without being a Marxist?"

"I read Marx," he allowed. "But I wouldn't consider myself a Marxist."

Rather, he was a practical politician. Kirkilas had masterminded the party's successful campaign during the recent elections. He was more comfortable talking about political technique.

"There are articles in the press saying that on television I'm the master of spontaneity," Kirkilas said. "But this is not true, because I never say anything on the spot. I'm always carefully prepared, because the camera is ruthless."

The former Communist lamented the state of the economy, as had Andrikiene earlier in the day, and pondered whether the intrusion of the Mafia into the Lithuanian economy should be regarded as normal in the initial stages of capital accumulation. He didn't think it ironic that former Communists had turned out to be the most adept at commanding capitalist enterprises. It was actually the right who had turned out to be more collectivist, and not the former Communists. He described Andrikiene's National Union Party as "state socialist and national fundamentalist", whereas the left represented "social liberal" thought. Asta and I laughed at his cleverly turned definitions.

When I trotted out my by-now-standard question about the price of coffee, Kirkilas agreed. "Of course this price for coffee is much too much, it's overpriced." But once there was a stable currency, matters would improve. The new currency would arrive in a couple of months, but couldn't yet be officially announced. "That's a state secret," he laughed.

Looking over my shoulder as we left, I saw that there was a vase of yellow tulips on his desk, as there had been on Andrikiene's. They seemed perhaps the most substantial reality in a bewildering tableau in which conservatives were baffled by their ouster and former Communists had never been Marxists.

Between the morning and afternoon meetings with the parliamentarians, I had met Richard Gavelis at the Writers' Union building. He had published a rather shocking bestseller a few years earlier entitled *Vilnius' Poker*. Asta explained that the title referred to cardrooms around town where poker players had gathered in the old days.

We entered through a narrow, unprepossessing wooden door on a hilly sidestreet. But inside was a grand black marble stairway whose metal grillework was trimmed in gilt, as were the flanking lampstands and the details of the wooden ceiling. Gavelis, a slim man in faded jeans, a black T-shirt and tinted glasses, led us up the staircase to a noisy antechamber where our conversation was punctuated by passers-by, the creaking of frequently opened doors, and the clicking of secretaries' heels on the parquet. But I immediately felt more comfortable with him than I had with the politicians.

Gavelis understood English but preferred to speak Lithuanian, so Asta only had to translate his replies to my questions. *Vilnius' Poker*, he said, was shocking not so much for its frank sexual scenes but for its "not really benevolent attitude towards what we call the Lithuanian national character." It had been a success—"As many copies of *Vilnius' Poker* sold as the Bible," he said—"but all the money was eaten up by inflation, so again I'm a free artist without a cent in my pocket."

As for the book itself, "it's an attempt to describe the world in which we lived for many, many years. It's difficult to sort out where it's reality, where it's a vision, where it's a dream, a fantasy."

He had begun as a physics student, but when it was time to write a doctoral thesis, he decided he wanted to write literature instead. He had gone from Joyce and other modernists to read the Latin American magic realists, "literary monsters" like Jean Genet, and post-modern writing. He'd worked on *Vilnius' Poker* semi-secretly through the 1980s. "Even my wife didn't know about the existence of the manuscript," Gavelis said. "I was afraid she might speak out about it unintentionally." Since then he had published another novel and a volume of short stories; a new, related book, *Vilnius' Jazz*, was due to appear shortly.

We talked briefly about politics and the economy. The successful new businessmen, he noted, were not only "the old Communist *nomenklatura*, but young flexible guys with an orientation towards crime and the Mafia."

One thing I wanted to know was whether any of his writing was available in English.

"About thirty pages of the beginning of *Vilnius' Poker* are translated, but I don't have it with me now," he said.

"That's what I want to read."

"Well, it's possible to borrow it," he offered.

We arranged to meet Gavelis again later, after my interview with Kirkilas, and photocopy the translated pages. Asta and I had lunch—cold borscht and traditional "zeppelins", potato-meal dumplings stuffed with ground meat—at the Leander Jazz Club, and then we stopped at a local newspaper office where the young journalists mainly talked about the Mafia. After the politician, we again walked along Gedimino into Old Town, where Gavelis, as promised, was waiting for us with his pages.

That night, instead of going to the Akimirka—I'd be meeting Igor and Vytas the next evening anyway—I stayed in my room and read. I left the door to my balcony open;

the Hermes was below, spotlighted. I noticed that in my absence someone had cut the grass and dandelions around the statue.

The opening of *Vilnius' Poker* took place sometime in the 1970s. It began with a dream: "a strange entry into another world—on the other side, children and dogs scampering, but on this side—only an empty street and billowing dust fanned by the wind. An oval face, turned toward me: thin lips, sunken cheeks and peaceful eyes (probably brown)—a woman's face, milk and blood, questioning and suffering, divinity and dissipation. . . ." It was, as Gavelis had said, a shifting, dark mixture of dreams, memories, horror, interspersed with the briefest moments of mundane reality: "you open your eyes, and once again see your room, books on the shelves, clothes flung on a chair."

There was a woman, a ghost-woman or vision-woman, memories of KGB torture, the city of Vilnius.

A man is laid out on a table. The torturer's "mournful fish-eyes gape at me: maybe he does not like me lying there naked and contorted." There's a portrait of Stalin on the wall. "'Fry his dick,' says the snarler. The portrait on the wall snorts uncontrollably through its fat moustache." There are other portraits, other women. "Bit by bit, I revert back to my exterior 'I,' soon he will be quietly sipping coffee. Brezhnev's portrait is hanging at the end of the hall, Stefa's hips are waving in front of my eyes. It is almost a scene from my childhood: little Robertas is sitting under a portrait of Vytautas the Great, and Mrs. Gedraitiene, even in front of me, an adolescent, is erotically undulating her hips. Unfortunately, the portraits are too unalike. Brezhnev is puffed up, with prominent air-brushed cheekbones. Even his brain is air-brushed."

Tomas Venclova also remembered that time. "Ultimately, people grew accustomed to everything," he said in the letter to Milosz, in a book that lay on my desk next to Gavelis's photocopied pages; ". . . to obligatory parades, mandated friendships, a special language that was diametrically opposed to what they really meant to say. Later, there was conformity and relative peace. People, the educated stratum in particular, feel that daily lying is the tribute one must render unto Caesar in order to have a more or less bearable life, and they do not see a moral problem in this. Perhaps that is precisely what the authorities want."

But in Gavelis' pages, mostly there was the woman, and Vilnius, and a dead friend named Gediminas. "He is standing on the streetcorner even now (*that evening* he stood there). Around us festers a doubtful Vilnius autumn, the air smells of damp dust. . . .

"It seemed Vilnius stopped sighing, pulled itself together and became quiet, waiting alertly. Waiting, too, greyish monuments and grimy, smoke-eaten Vilnius limes. Something had to happen, both of us sensed it, standing lost in the gloom of the old town, drenched by the fine city rain . . . Gediminas saw the woman first. She materialized as if she came out of the earth, or maybe she was newborn in the autumn damp . . . She looked around as if she found herself here on this earth for the first time. Such a thing can only be encountered in dream and in Vilnius at night: the street had been empty as far as the eye could see, but suddenly standing beside you is a dark-haired woman. . . ."

It was midnight when I finished, turned out the wonderful light of the desklamp, closed the balcony door (the spotlight on the Hermes had been extinguished), and settled into bed, haunted by the ghostly dimension of Vilnius that seeped through Gavelis's pages.

The Lithuanian State Jewish Museum was located on a hillside street a couple of blocks above Gedimino, in a faded green wooden building resembling a barracks. Its rooms were bright in noon sunlight that not only entered the windows, but crept under doorways and seemed to penetrate the worn walls, causing our eyes to squint. A white-haired man in his sixties was our guide. He spoke only Russian, but it was another of the languages that Asta could translate.

Those rooms were the archive of the slaughtered Jews of Vilnius. During the Second World War, ninety-four per cent of Lithuania's Jews had been exterminated. What was left was some maps, photocopied documents, a few objects, photographs. It was an impoverished but straightforward display.

I stared at the faces of those long dead, as if I might recognize someone I knew. A Polish journalist, the Russian-speaking guide recounted, had lived in the vicinity of the forest. He had seen those who were to be executed marched past his cottage, and had recorded what he'd observed in his diary, a proof of the slaughter, if one was needed (and alas, it would be). Fearing for his own fate, he had put the diary pages in sealed bottles, and buried them in his garden. The journalist was shot by the Nazis in 1944, but the evidence was eventually dug up from the garden. Photocopies of his journal pages were affixed to the museum wall. I was transfixed by his handwriting, as Asta recited translated passages that I only half heard.

There were maps of the Vilnius ghetto, a few copies of letters, photographs of the dead that appeared to have been taken in the forest (by the Nazis?) at the time of the shootings. Had someone actually photographed the victims as they were toppling into the pit?

There was also a display of the resistance conducted by Vilnian Jews. Not all of them had gone to the slaughter "like sheep", as it was sometimes put. Later I saw a videotape of the resisters—old men who had been in the ghetto and in the woods, who had survived and lived to tell the tale, years after, mostly in Israel.

But it was not the resisters who haunted us a half-century later. We understood them, or thought we did. "You always find a hero willing to fight against everybody," remarked the Polish writer Ryszard Kapuscinski, in a magazine interview I had recently read.[8] Nor was it the few who were rescued by some miraculous stratagem, as Thomas Keneally recorded in *Schindler's List*, or even the survivors of the Nazi concentration camps to whose experience Primo Levi's books testified. Their lives raised other issues. No, it was those who had died without crying out, whose silence echoed in these rooms.

"You know," Kapuscinski said, "Hannah Arendt in her book *Eichmann in Jerusalem*, she was unable to understand why the Jews were going so passively to their deaths—why the Holocaust was possible, why there was no resistance. But I understand it, because I was there and I saw the thing. And I have an answer that I would say to Hannah Arendt."

His answer was this: "There was nothing strange in the behaviour of those people. It was natural. Because if you don't see any hope, you are very passive. . . . Lack of hope paralyzes their will, paralyzes their brain, their movement."

Kapuscinski had interviewed people who had witnessed the liquidation of the Jewish ghetto in Pinsk, the town where he'd grown up. "When the moment of the Final Solution came, they were sent through the town, in columns. Rabbis marched at the head of each column. And in columns—one huge, huge column—they walked to the place which is about ten kilometres outside of town, in a small forest. There were mass graves dug there, long graves, and on the opposite side of every grave was a Nazi soldier with a machine gun. And the Jewish people of Pinsk were taken to the verge of the grave and were shot. One row fell in the grave, and the next row came, was shot, fell down, and the next row. . . . All in silence." Kapuscinski added, "So Hannah Arendt couldn't understand it, but it is understandable. If you are in Pinsk, and you are already so desperately run-down—no food, sick, hopeless, no way to escape—you will just follow the orders of your religious leaders. You will march in columns. You will wait while [the Nazi soldiers] smoke. You will go to your death."

Here too, in Vilnius, they had gone to their deaths. Here too there was a forest, mass graves, and these few scraps of testimony by which a visitor might remember.

Before we left, I mentioned to the Russian-speaking guide—he had enquired, out of politeness, if this was my first time in Vilnius—that I thought my father had been born there. He asked me my name. When I told him, he said, "Oh yes, that's a quite common name here, mostly of Jews from Belorussia. I've seen it in the city archives."

On the hillside below the museum, Asta and I sat in a bucolic tree-protected space that seemed far from the city streets. As tiny as the museum had been—a few rooms, financially poor—it was impossible not to have some sense of the horror. We sat on a bench, smoking cigarettes, under a flowering maple tree whose blossoms drifted onto our hair. There was a paving-stone rectangle at our feet, and at one end a sculpture of an abstracted human figure with his arms half raised, bearing on his head a watermelon-shaped wedge of pale red stone.

In a city that spawned ghosts, the least threatening of them resided on top of Castle Hill. Asta and I walked through the spacious park behind Cathedral Square, following the slippery scree path up through a leafy forest to the remnants of Gedimino's tower at the top. The fourteenth-century founder was but a pale, beneficent presence as we climbed the twisting wooden staircase of a combination museum and viewing tower. Emerging high above the city, we could see the winding path of the Neris making its way through the landscape. When we came down, we headed directly to the café in the arts centre for the cold orange juice that seemed to be waiting especially for us.

Asta told me she'd had a dream the previous night in which she was supposed to catch a plane to America at seven-thirty in the morning—she was thinking of doing her graduate work in the U.S.—but only woke up at seven-thirty in the evening, and rushed to the airport to find that someone had used her place on the flight. That morning she'd received her new Lithuanian passport. She extracted it from her purse to show me.

I stopped at the Akimirka in the late afternoon after Asta had taken the tram home. Since we had nothing more to do that day, we had decided to skip dinner so she could go and work on her essay. Igor and Vytas weren't due to show up at my hotel for a couple of hours, so I ducked out of the heat into the cavelike coolness of the bar. It was mostly deserted, except for a handsome but drunk young man who soon staggered off with a woman. The gays probably came in later, I figured. Daylight from the street filtered through the muslin curtains to give the Akimirka its only relief from darkness. Though I never could have anticipated it, I felt strangely at home in this forsaken spot. A friend of mine had once pointed out that any place, however apparently remote, could, properly viewed, be understood as the centre of the universe. But it was also true that the Akimirka bar conveyed, as much as any place I'd ever been, the sense of being at the very end of the world.

Igor and Vytas were standing outside my hotel door when I came down around eight o'clock.

"I'm not sure we can go in," Igor said. Apparently, in the past, there had been restrictions on locals entering hotels that had been reserved for foreign tourists.

"Don't worry, I'll explain it to the desk clerk if he asks," I said, brushing aside their fears, but I too was caught for an instant—like a jerky hitch in a film—in a history of repression I could only distantly understand. The night clerk, as it happened, was watching television in a room off the lobby, apparently indifferent to foreigners and their local guests.

"Since childhood," Igor said, "I noticed that I was interested in males. Especially when I saw the beautiful bodies of boys, I was attracted to them."

The three of us sat around the small table in the centre of my room, the balcony door open onto the warm night. Igor had been born in Vilnius but was of Russian descent. After high school he had served in the army, then gotten a teaching degree in Minsk. He had a soft, hesitant voice.

"My first contact was in the army. Because in the army it's possible to meet gay people—sometimes, not very often, but possible. I served in Germany, in East Germany, at Halle. Do you know where that is?"

"Yes. And so you met Germans?"

"No, I met soldiers."

"Ah," I said. "When I was in the military, I had the same experience."

Igor had been working as a typist when another soldier came up to him and said he had a magazine in English and needed some help in translating it.

"I came to his room and he began to try to kiss me," Igor said, laughing softly. "I can't say it was love; maybe he was attracted by me." Again he laughed, remembering.

"So that was your first experience?"

"I was attracted to him, but in this situation I was very afraid. He only kissed me, he didn't insist to have sex with me," Igor said. "I was eighteen. He was just finishing his service, and I saw him off, and as he was leaving he told me, You will understand who you are, and you will meet such people."

Then Vytas told his story. "It happened in 1983. I was fifteen years old," he said, with Igor translating from the

Russian. Vytas was travelling in East Germany and was staying in a youth hostel, since he didn't have enough money for a hotel. "I lived with one German, older, eighteen years, and it was a very hot summer. I decided to take a shower." The older boy had gone with him, and in the shower, or afterwards, when they were back in their room, the German boy had initiated sex. He may have taken Vytas "by force"; I lost that detail in the filters of Vytas's Russian and Igor's translated English. But Vytas didn't seem, retrospectively, to object.

There were other stories, of friends, schoolmates, parents, and some of it was lost in translation, no doubt, but I liked their shy yet innocently straightforward accounts. These were "coming out" stories, no different from the tales of first sex, first love, that homosexual men told each other in cities everywhere.

Vytas's parents had found out about him when someone who had taken photos of him and his friends having sex on a beach threatened him with blackmail.

"Were you frightened?"

"*Nyet.*"

"Because?"

"Because I knew this photographer was also gay, and I thought he wouldn't send them to my parents. But he did."

"Then what happened?"

"When I came home, my father showed me these photos and asked, What does it mean?" Vytas continued. "I explained to my parents that I liked men, and my mother cried for a long time, but my father still doesn't understand me."

I returned to Igor. "You were about to tell me what happened after you got out of the army."

"Yes. So I entered the institute in Minsk." There, a friend gave him the number of another person in Vilnius, whom he later met. "We had a walk about the streets—"

"Here in Vilnius?"

"Yes, in Vilnius. Then we went home and we slept together. But it was nothing because, as he told me later, he was not sure that I was gay. He was afraid to touch me." Nor had Igor known if the man with whom he shared a bed was gay. It was only on a later occasion, at a friend's flat, that they had sex.

"So that was really the first time? How old were you?"

"I was twenty-one. He was older than me, maybe twenty-five, twenty-six. We are only friends now, only friends," Igor said. He had a boyfriend now, a law student at the university, but they were able to meet only infrequently. I imagined another Vilnius, a Vilnius of young men who lived with their parents, who met each other uncertainly, shyly, their hearts in their mouths.

We walked down Gedimino under the lindens, occasional streetlamps shining on their serrated leaves. The Akimirka was crowded on a Friday night. I was introduced to Gerard, a self-confidently flamboyant Frenchman in his twenties who had come to Vilnius via Finland, and was now running an AIDS information office which also served as a gay organizing centre. We were joined by Valeri, a friend of theirs from Minsk, who made them laugh. There were drinks, conversations in various languages, gossip, music. For a few hours the natural gloom of the Akimirka dissipated; companionship made us forget the world.

The bar closed at eleven. Outside, there were police

waiting to collect drunks. The five of us strolled under the dusty trees along the warm, silent boulevard, our voices the only sounds in the night. Igor was off to the countryside for the weekend to plant potatoes with his mother. Vytas had to work. Valeri complained that his boyfriend wouldn't do this or that, and we laughed over his complaints.

In the morning sunshine, I took my cup of coffee and walked into the back garden of the hotel where the Hermes statue was. The day's heat had yet to descend. I drifted in thought, walking around the wing-footed figure whose body had mildewed into a striated aquamarine colour.

Asta arrived at noon. We took a series of buses southwest, through an industrial zone, to a place about ten kilometres outside the city. At the end of the bus line, we walked from the edge of a suburban neighbourhood to the railroad yards. A high walkway was built across the tracks. Down below there was a train station. Dandelions spotted the grass between the rail lines. At the bottom of the stairway on the other side of the tracks, we turned right and went along a road that ran parallel to the tracks, passing small farmhouses. A few brown hens wandered in and out of picket fences.

The road ended in a paved parking area, but there were no cars. A large memorial stone, roughly hewn, carried a Hebrew inscription for the seventy thousand killed and entombed in unmarked pits in these Paneriai woods.

When I had asked Asta if she would take me to Paneriai (or Ponary, as the Jews of Vilnius had called it), she had pleased me by not questioning my proposal, but only remarking, "I've never been there."

The small cottage that housed a museum was closed for renovations, and a couple of workmen were the only people we saw. In the forest, winding footpaths led to two or three unobtrusive monuments. Behind one of them there was a broad swath of burned pine trees, an abandoned rusted-out bus. I wandered through the charred remains of the trees. But what had happened in these woods had occurred long before the fire. There was, in a sense, nothing to be seen here. There was only the quiet, sunlit forest.

We walked back along the road by which we had come. It was possible that some of the older people still living in the farmhouses had seen the Jews marching along this road on the way to their deaths. Had one of these gardens, where hens now roamed, contained the bottles in which the Polish journalist had buried his diaries?

Back in the city, as we were on our way to catch a bus at Cathedral Square—we had an appointment with a Jewish writer—we passed the theatre on Gedimino where the sculpture of the three shrouded woman presided above the entrance. Outside there was a small handwritten placard on a tripod. It was only after we had passed it that Asta mentioned that the inconspicuous sign announced a tulip show in the lobby.

When I paused, she asked, "Are you interested?"

"Will we have time to get to Kanowitsch?" He was the writer we were about to visit.

"Yes, I think so."

In every story, I had discovered, there were inevitably other stories, often no more than digressions that seemingly had little connection to the story you thought you were following. "Sure," I said.

The theatre lobby was spacious, constructed of marble-like slabs of tan stone. In vases around the sunken central area, there were nearly a hundred different varieties of tulips, as the sign had promised.

We wandered slowly around the display, stopping to admire particular tulips that caught our eye, pointing out ones we liked to each other, reading the labels alongside the vases. I stopped before a flower called the Abu Hassan, with deep brown petals fringed in brilliant yellow. Though I had seen tulips on the desks of the politicians, and there would also be some at Kanowitsch's house, I felt as if I had never really looked at, really seen one before.

"What did Vilnius look like in 1945?" I asked Grigory Kanowitsch. He was a Jewish novelist in his mid-sixties. His parents had somehow escaped Lithuania and made their way to Kazakhstan, in the Soviet Union. Kanowitsch had returned to Vilnius at the end of the Second World War as a sixteen-year-old.

"It's in Kafka's novels," he replied, sitting across from us on a sofa in the large living room of the apartment where he and his wife lived. He was wearing a short-sleeved shirt and a tie slightly askew. "Everyone, not just Jews—soldiers, Lithuanians, Polish—seemed uprooted, flying between the heavens and earth. That's why I remembered Kafka."

"When you returned, was the extent of the Holocaust apparent to you then?"

"It was shouting. It was shouting," he said, and repeated that phrase a third time. "From every window, from every basement, from every hole."

"When we were at Paneriai today, my colleague here," I said, nodding towards Asta, "she asked me why they hated the Jews so much."

"Well," he began, sighing, "this is not a simple thing...."

After we left the novelist's, Asta showed me the tram that would take me back to the city; she was going home in the opposite direction. Standing towards the back of the street-car, catching an occasional glimpse of the sun on the river, I experienced an instant in which I felt both the comfort of being alive—just to see the powdery substance of falling maple and linden blossoms clogging the cracks between the black bricks—and the melancholy of our losses. Nothing returned the dead to us.

I was walking up Gedimino in the early evening when I ran into Vytas. Since we had no mutually understandable language, we made do with signs and gestures until we reached the Akimirka. Gerard was sitting at the bar so we joined him for a drink and translation services. It grew dark on Gedimino Street, and the blinking neon light outside the Akimirka filtered back into the smoky bar. For a moment, considering the arbitrariness of our lives, I could imagine my own continuing here.

For an even longer moment, I thought of the various places I had been to ponder the end of Communism. In its last years, Soviet Communism had not been as brutally tyrannical as in its early phases. It had fallen because of economic stagnation, its inability to compete with the West, doctrinal bankruptcy and the loss of legitimacy, corruption and patronage, and the fortuitous appearance of Mikhail

Gorbachev, whose belated attempts to reform it only hastened its demise.

What succeeded the tyranny was still indeterminate, and the spectrum of possibilities was broad, ranging from the integration of some societies into the system of democratic capitalism to out-and-out savageries. Capitalist democracy was momentarily triumphant, but the notion in the West that what followed would be as simple as "Then we take Berlin"—as a phrase in a song by Leonard Cohen satirically put it—had proven illusory.

We could leave it to the theorists to argue whether the end of history was nigh. But it was the savageries that suggested otherwise. Enough time had passed since the fall of the Berlin Wall to dispel the idea that democracy, like nature, abhorred a vacuum. Democracy did not necessarily rush in to fill the gap. What rushed in after Communism was largely dependent upon the particular conditions, traditions, loves, and hatreds of a given country. In the former Yugoslavia, a nearly impossible country had splintered into nations baring their teeth. Here in Lithuania, a nation that had barely become a country, the economy hardly provided subsistence. Yet in both places, and elsewhere that I'd been, there were citizenly people, if not yet citizens; streets and buildings and landscapes whose magic required only imagination and memory. Democracy would require as much.

During the night, I remembered what I had imagined that afternoon in the Paneriai forest. Some of the dead were sitting on chairs, others were standing around in the charred woods, coffee cups and saucers in hand, wearing their death

clothes—dark jackets and trousers, white shirts with slightly
frayed collars, black hats on their heads; the women were in
plain black dresses like the one I'd seen my grandmother
wear, one or two of them absently smoothing wrinkles in
the cloth. The dead children were farther off, among the
trees.

They were not all Jews, though Jews were prominent
among them. Their ranks included contemporary combat-
ants from places in Yugoslavia, Armenia, Afghanistan, and
elsewhere whose unfamiliar names we had forgotten as soon
as the nightly news pronounced the unfamiliar names of
new cities under siege. Perhaps I even imagined an ancient,
sightless Bulgarian.

They gazed at us, oddly but patiently, from the other side
of a piece of time. They didn't speak among themselves, nor
did we, the living. But I felt that both the living and the
dead, separated by that piece of time, wanted to speak to
each other. It seemed that there was everything to say.

Afterword: Berlin 1995

U NLIKE THE CHARACTERS IN A NOVEL, whose existence, in a sense, ceases when the book ends (although their "unforgettability" may confer a certain immortality upon them), the people and places who appear in a non-fiction narrative not only continue to exist in life, but often make surprising reappearances in the life of their narrator. As a reader of such stories, I'm invariably delighted to find—"beyond the end"—an epilogue in which I might discover what became of some of them.

In May 1995, when I returned to Berlin—where I had spent part of each year since the beginning of the decade—I'd come to the end of the particular series of "stories from the other side of Europe" whose origins were in the once-walled-in city. The pages I'd written over the course of several years had been published that spring as *Then We Take Berlin*—I'd already done the obligatory author's book tour—and upon arriving at Tegel Airport bearing some gift copies of the book in my luggage, I was met by Manuel, the young man who appears on the very first page of my narrative.

I mention him because of a curious, recurrent response to the book that I'd already encountered during interviews and in reviews. Indeed, the first question I was asked by the first journalist interviewing me (for a "profile" piece in a Vancouver newspaper) was, "Explain exactly what your sex life has to do with the fall of Communism in Eastern Europe." That set the tone for much of what was to follow, although the degree of vulgarity varied. Of course, I'd expected a certain amount of curiosity about what were admittedly unconventional sexual tastes and experiences, which I had consciously, even insistently, made explicit in the course of "discovering" the stories I was writing. Still, I wasn't altogether prepared for what would be, at times, an almost prurient interest in homosexual desire to the exclusion of any real attention to the book's primary subject matter, the historical transition initiated by the "fall of Communism". What troubled me about the apparent "interest" was not only its disproportionality, but that in most cases it wasn't an interest at all; instead, it was merely a journalistic convenience, a salacious ploy upon which to hang a story.

I don't mean to be disingenuous. I was certainly responsible for introducing the details of my personal life, and it's possible that I failed to make plausible the connections between an epistemology of desire and the problem of understanding the complex political events I was investigating, however circuitously. It's even possible that my private revelations were a sort of perverse vanity, although I hoped they would provide a contrast to the conventional political or travel tales in which the narrator maintains a resolutely discreet presence, seldom taking the risk of being more than

the victim of mildly amusing misadventures. Still, such dis-
closures were intended, both in terms of the space they
occupied and their importance, to be subsidiary—mainly
there as an exposition of the character of the narrator—
to the main themes of the narrative. So, sighing—and
knowing that the sinking feeling in the pit of my stomach
was probably an accurate premonition of what I'd be in for
during the next couple of weeks—I dutifully "explained
exactly" to a series of interviewers just what my sex life had
to do with history, knowing perfectly well that the real
answer to that question was, "Gee, probably very little." At
most, my adventures in Boyopolis, apart from their intrinsic
pleasures, had something to do with how I understood political reality.

Anticipating some of this, I'd written, at the urging of
my friend Brian Fawcett, a passage entitled "DeCoda",
about the sociology of "Boyopolis", that was intended to
forestall exactly such questions. But during the process of
book editing, I persuaded myself to cut the passage on the
grounds that readers and reviewers would be sophisticated
enough to get along without it. (It's now, suitably revised,
reinstated in this edition.) In its absence, there was nothing
left but to gamely reiterate that the "boys" were all of age.
At least, I might be absolved of kiddie-porn suspicions.

Even in the better-written, intelligent reviews—where
there was a more carefully balanced attention to the histories
and prospects of Eastern and Central Europe than in interviews—once the critic inevitably got around to the trouble-
some objects of my desire, an ill-informed, almost panicky,
distortion set in. Perfectly fair-minded assessments, otherwise

generously praising the book's engagement with history and philosophy, appropriately critical of its shortcomings, had only to encounter an exotic hustler or two to set off a threnody of indirect moral opprobrium.

One review, which stays in mind, ended by deciding there were "two books. The one, the greater part, is of the mind—at times considered, thoughtful, sophisticated and compassionate. The other is of the body—self-absorbed, self-indulgent, and blindly, wildly, romantic (the same 'rent-boy' twice robs the author and is twice forgiven)."

Two cheers for forgiveness, then. For there, at the airport gate in Berlin, was Manuel, the young man whom I'd met some four years before. Far from the almost offhand assumption on the part of various critics that such encounters were of necessity short-lived and casual (as in "casual sex"), in fact, Manuel and I had managed to stay in touch by telephone or letters and to spend a week or ten days together each of the years I'd returned to Berlin. And while passion had cooled, each time together had been memorably different, dependent on seasons, our mutual or differing preoccupations, our divergent senses of amusement or boredom. My almost instinctive refusal to take his initial monetary transgressions too seriously had resulted in, among other things, an enduring friendship of sorts. He was now in his mid-twenties, still blond, slim, solarium-tanned, but his boyishness, which he studiously attempted to preserve, struck me as something of an effect, rather than possessing the artlessness that made such a quality attractive. He had recently acquired a slightly older boyfriend who was in housing management, and Manuel was thinking about becoming a trainee in the business. We agreed that the time had come for a career change.

There was a charming literary addenda to our latest encounter. Manuel knew that I'd written about him and had made me promise to bring him a copy of the book once it was published, which of course I did, though not without some trepidation about his reaction to what might be read as a not entirely flattering portrait. A few nights later, over dinner, he delivered, to my relief, a succinct verdict: "Very realistic, not too much, not too little." I was thus afforded one of the secret pleasures of writing, namely, the judgment of one of the characters in the story—the equivalent of the reader's reward of an epilogue. Manuel assured me that he wasn't distressed by the detailed accounts of our intimacies. "It's what happened," he said with characteristic German earnestness and what I recognized as a typical Berlin shrug that accepted the facts of our lives.

As with Manuel, one by one the people and places who had appeared in my writing returned, each with the news of what had since befallen them. I ran into Michael Morris a few days after my arrival, while wandering in the crowded open market around the church in Karl-August-Platz where he shopped on Saturday mornings. He had gamely put up with being portrayed as a docent of Boyopolis, quipping that it would be "career suicide" for both of us. The economics of remaining an independent artist were as complicated as they had been when he first introduced me to the city five years ago, but he'd had a recent bit of personal luck. Michael had struck up a friendship with Nikolai, a former

Russian tank corps soldier whom he'd met the previous year and who had preferred to stay on in Berlin rather than return to the uncertainties of his homeland. The end of Communism had thus produced, amid all else and for the time being, an unlikely couple.

When the three of us met for lunch a couple of days later, Michael had a surprise for me. He had gone to Tirana, Albania in the spring, for a short stint as a visiting artist, and somehow had managed to find Ilir, the boy I'd met there in 1991. Michael produced a packet of photos.

I'd had messages from Zef and Pavli, the translators who had been my hosts in Tirana. They had both been invited into the diplomatic service, and were now living in Geneva and London. Ilir, Michael had learned, was still with a dance company, and had toured in Europe and America. I hardly recognized the person in the snapshots. The boy was gone; in his place was a handsome, dark-haired young man in his twenties with a sharp jawline and a two-day growth of stubble, seated at an outdoor table in a hotel courtyard. Well, of course the desired one becomes someone else, I noted him, rather than my enamoured fantasies of him. (A few months later, back in Vancouver, there was a call from Ilir. If I no longer recognized the image in the photographs, at least his voice was familiar. He was calling from, of all places, a small town in Tennessee where he was attempting to be admitted to an American college. He was thinking of applying for citizenship; there was a silent, helpless shrug about his Albanian homeland.)

As well, in this catalogue of notables, there was Dominic, and with him, the timeless, but ever-changing scene at

Pinocchio's. We'd met there in 1993, and I'd also seen a good deal of him the following year. Once more, I made my way to the tiny bar near Nollendorfplatz, which had become my strange sanctuary of desire and meditation. I'd become friends with another of the regulars there, a computer technician in his thirties named Mark, and through him became attached to the various circles of camaraderie that existed among the bar's regular customers, and that spilled out beyond its boundaries into dinners and visits and even some holiday-sharing (Mark and I planned a brief trip to Prague for later in the summer).

It was one of those informal obligations of friendship that put me back on the trail of the ever-elusive Dominic. One of our drinking companions, a man known as Rosa, was in the hospital for minor surgery and naturally, it was our duty to relieve his boredom by visiting him. What I liked about all this—as we sat in the hospital cafeteria, drinking a beer, gossiping, and playing a card game—was its sheer ordinariness. I was simply here, doing whatever I was doing—thinking about a next book, reading philosophy (my steady consolation), walking familiar routes, having leisurely, late dinners with my upstairs friends and neighbours, Thomas and Ilonka, at whose wedding the year before I had served as an official witness. When I walked down the street where we lived, Kaiser-Friedrich-Strasse, a busy, broad, north-south avenue, with a median of straggly grass, and lined with five-storey apartment buildings, I had the idea that if only I could really see it—but see what? its mixture of linden and maple trees that lined the sidewalk? the new bicycle shop that had opened in mid-block?—that I would understand everything.

Rosa was up-to-date on Dominic's whereabouts. Of course, there were the usual complications, people to phone, and messages to be scattered, since Dominic was more or less currently off the "scene". In the end, between Rosa's ready laughter and Mark's mock-sternness—they sometimes seemed to me like the classic masked figures of Greek theatre—the sprite who alternately bemused, inflamed, and puzzled me made his appearance. I can forego the subsequent episodes; it's enough to note that, somehow, we still fitted into each other's lives, another unlikely pairing.

What is it that so impels me to trace, keep up with, record bits of these otherwise unremarkable lives? Simply this: that if I didn't, they might be lost to memory. Who would know of the unique man who was my father—the person who taught me to read, who fostered my freedom—if I hadn't thought to write about him in these stories? Thus I resist our eventual disappearance.

There was a man named Florian Gohla—he doesn't appear elsewhere in this book—who I'd come to know through another acquaintance, Karsten, with whom I occasionally attended the Berlin symphony. It was a season when the orchestra was performing the works of Mahler. Florian, who went with us, seemed particularly knowledgeable about the music, and when the three of us had a drink afterwards, he offered authoritative judgments on the quality of the performance, and instructive comments about Mahler's symphonies, whose haunting sounds struck me as the bridge between the romanticism of the last century and the modernism of this one.

Florian was in his mid-thirties, and had belatedly returned

to university, to resume studies in the biology department, I think. Once, when we were at lunch together, he'd casually referred to having AIDS. Startled, I was about to make some intendedly sympathetic remark, which he forestalled by a slight gesture, and said something like, "No, don't be alarmed, it's been many years now. I'm quite used to it."

One day in summer 1995—it was raining, and unseasonably chill—I visited him. He was living at Dennewitz Platz, the next stop on the U-bahn line beyond Nollendorfplatz, where I usually got off to go to Pinocchio's. Florian was spectrally thin now. The simplest movements, even sitting on the sofa, were painful for him. I knew that this would likely be the last time we'd see each other. The rain beat against the windows of his apartment, which overlooked one of the typical red-brick Gothic churches located in the centre of the square, and Florian and I talked about the prospect of having a drink together in Pinocchio's, should his health temporarily improve, and with equal casualness about the possibility of suicide, which he was inclined to refrain from only on the grounds of some lingering religious reservations. The horror of it all was utterly mundane; when I departed, after a couple of hours of conversation, he would again turn on the television. (A few months later, a memorial card arrived, sent by our mutual friend, announcing Florian's death.)

My arrival in Berlin in 1995 coincided with the concluding events of the commemoration of the fiftieth anniversary of the Second World War. Film footage of the war had flooded North American television screens just before my

departure—even interrupting the ubiquitous televised murder trial of a former athlete (whenever one passed a TV
screen, one seemed to invariably see, out of the corner of
one's eye, the brooding figure of the accused, O.J. Simpson),
and more ominously, the terrorist bombing of a government building in Oklahoma that killed scores of people (the
terrorists were not the familiar stereotypes, but crazed
Americans, connected to shadowy paramilitary forces scattered throughout the country). In the wake of military
marches, formal ceremonies, and inevitable media satura-
tion (German television, Thomas and Ilonka told me, had
shown grim film from Auschwitz, which was all the more
shocking for being in colour), I nonetheless had the sense
that this was not simply an historical occasion, but curiously
enough, the end of the Second World War itself. It was only
now, in 1995, a half-century after the fact, that the war was
finally over as a matter of living memory.

Increasingly, it belonged solely to history. The aging participants in the war who commemorated the fiftieth anniversary of its end wouldn't be present when (or if) it was
formally recalled twenty-five or fifty years hence. Conversely, the Germans I knew, especially those in their twenties, had been born to parents who themselves were born
after 1945. When I thought of Thomas and Ilonka, my current bar-pal Mark, or Goertz (my musician friend was now
selling guitars in a big music shop), or of Manuel, Dominic
and all the others I'd met since the fall of Communism, it
was no longer possible to think of Germany in terms of half-
century-old stereotypes.

If there was a Berlin whose life belonged firmly to history

as well as to an incessant political future, there was also a great city in which our lives took their own little idiosyncratic courses, far from the grand scale of things. It was the latter that I was most aware of that summer. In the winters, Berlin made no pretense of being other than a rough, unglamorous, indifferent metropolis. But in the summer, there was a remarkable transformation. A city of waterways and foliage-thick green spaces blossomed everywhere, the undistinguished plaster faces of apartment complexes built after the bombings of the Second World War gave way to the ornate loggia-like balconies and art-nouveau adornments of older, solidly-rooted turn-of-the-century buildings, cafés sprawled out onto the sidewalks. Michael took me walking in the vast Tiergarten across the lawns where nude gay sunbathers lolled in the hot afternoon. I went with Ilonka to the university to hear visiting lecturers whom we mercilessly criticized on the underground ride home. On Sunday afternoons, Mark and I ate a mid-day meal at the back of a restaurant called the Ali Baba; the windows opened to provide a circulating breeze in the otherwise still heat of summer. Late at night, Thomas and I walked his aging golden retriever along the dark parkway-divided avenue that led up to Charlottenburg Castle, glowing under spotlights. The sidewalks were sticky with the droppings of linden blossoms; at our backs the full summer moon rose.

There was one event that summer that served as a sort of hinge between the pleasures of a private Berlin and its public role in the world of cities. The artist known as Christo, whose specialty involved large-scale spectacular art events, had persuaded the German parliament to permit him to wrap the Berlin Reichstag building in a cloth covering. For weeks, this absurdist project had been relentlessly hyped; not only were images of the about-to-be-wrapped historic building hawked everywhere, but the idea had been taken up by advertisers, so that pictures of wrapped commodities—especially giant beer glasses—peered out from every billboard. To make matters worse, the local government had decided to tie the spectacle to its own architectural plans for the city, which were already being realized at dozens of construction sites (whole neighbourhoods of east Berlin seemed to be behind fences and under giant building cranes). A series of tented rotundas were strategically placed near the Reichstag, each containing photos, models, and three-storey painted panoramas of "Berlin 2000" (Mark dragged me along one Saturday morning to join the burgerlich crowds lined up to dutifully view the future).

The "fall of Communism" and its aftermath—briefly a matter of interest for North Americans, especially when it had provided television visuals of celebrating youths atop the Berlin Wall or crowds in Prague looking into an unknown future—had long since subsided into an ahistorical past, even for Europeans. Ironically, the end of Communism, at first hailed as the epochal triumph of capitalist democracy, had yielded, some five years later, a series of governments headed by, of all people, former Communists, in Poland, Hungary, Russia and elsewhere. The alternative to this unexpected return of ex-Communists-but-without-Communism was a series of bloody nationalisms, ablaze throughout various former Soviet Republics, but more immediately present in war-ravaged former Yugoslavia.

Christo's wrapped Reichstag seemed a whimsically accurate, if enigmatic, comment on all that had happened.

The oversold prospect of the event had left me bored, convinced that we were being subjected to one more instance of kitsch in the name of art. When Mark came back to Pinocchio's from an early viewing of the wrapped Reichstag, improbably enthused by this artistic phenomenon, I put it down to ignorant populism (after all, I could barely get Mark into a museum to look at a masterpiece). But then, there was a call from Michael or Vincent, I can't remember which, who reported that it was like standing next to a glacier. Goertz told me it was as if a cloud had been tied down to the earth. Thomas and Ilonka biked there one morning; when they returned, Thomas said, referring to the long history of the Reichstag, "They've used it, burned it, abandoned it, renovated it, and none of it worked. Wrapping it *works*."

So, one morning, I walked up the vast lawn before the Reichstag, along with thousands of others, gazing at the shrouded outlines of the old building, wrapped in a thick, silvery, shimmering industrial material, held in place by pale blue cording, the whole thing slightly fluttering in a late June breeze. The preceding weeks of earnest TV and newspaper pondering over such fabricated questions as, "Is it Art or . . . ?" instantly dissolved. The secret of its success, I saw (and one could only know by seeing it), was its actual size, its huge objectness revealed by wrapping it, and its size was not reproduceable in any representation (in pictures it simply looked like a piece of household furniture with a sheet thrown over it). But its scale, commensurate to the size of the city, was crucial to its magic; for a moment, this Berlin fantasia relieved us of the burden of being in history. In the morning sunshine, it proclaimed that beauty was both comic and autonomous, that the future was waiting to be unwrapped.

Notes

The Translators' Tale

1 Paul Koring, "Awakening from the Nightmare", *The Globe and Mail* (Toronto), April 10, 1991.

Borkowicz's Death

1 Adam Michnik, "Notes on the Revolution", *New York Times Magazine*, March 11, 1990.
2 Tadeusz Konwicki, *A Minor Apocalypse*, trans. Richard Lourie (1979; New York: Farrar, Straus, Giroux, 1983).

Berlin/Boyopolis

1 Herbert List, *Söhne des Lichts* (Hamburg: Hoffman und Campe, 1988).
2 Christopher Isherwood, *Goodbye to Berlin* (London: Hogarth Press, 1969); the quotations on pages 147-149 are from *Christopher and His Kind, 1929-1939* (London: Methuen, 1985).
3 Herbert Tobias, *Herbert Tobias Photographien* (Berlin: Frölich & Kaufmann, 1985).

4 Ray Monk, *Ludwig Wittgenstein: The Duty of Genius* (London: Jonathan Cape, 1990); Ludwig Wittgenstein, *On Certainty*, trans. Denis Paul and Gem Anscombe (New York: Harper & Row, 1969).

Meditation In A Moonstone

1 George Konrad, *Antipolitics*, trans. Richard E. Allen (London: Quartet, 1984).
2 Gaspar Tamas, "The Legacy of Dissent", *Times Literary Supplement*, May 14, 1993.
3 Miklos Haraszti, *The Velvet Prison: Artists under State Socialism*, trans. Katalin and Stephen Landesmann (New York: Basic Books, 1987).

The Springtime of Nations

1 Timothy Garton Ash, *We the People* (London: Granta, 1990).
2 Vaclav Havel, *Summer Meditations*, trans. Paul Wilson (Toronto: Knopf Canada, 1992).
3 Slavenka Drakulic, *Balkan Express* (London: Hutchinson, 1993).
4 Paul Koring, "Hopes wither in divided Germany", *The Globe and Mail* (Toronto), Nov. 9, 1993.
5 Blaga Dimitrova, "The New Newspeak", *New York Review of Books*, March 5, 1992.
6 Blaga Dimitrova, *Because the Sea Is Black*, trans. Niko Boris and Heather McHugh (Middletown, Connecticut: Wesleyan, 1989); *The Last Rock Eagle*, trans. Brenda

Walker, Belin Tonchev and Vladimir Levchev (London: Forest, 1992).

7 Tadeusz Konwicki, *New World Avenue and Vicinity*, trans. Walter Arndt (New York: Farrar, Straus and Giroux, 1991); Lucy S. Dawidowicz, *From That Place and Time: A Memoir 1938–1947* (New York: Norton, 1989); Czeslaw Milosz, *Beginning with My Streets*, trans. Madeline G. Levine (New York: Farrar, Straus and Giroux, 1991)

8 Stephen Schiff, "The Years of Living Dangerously", *Vanity Fair*, March, 1991.

Acknowledgements

ABOUT FIVE YEARS AGO my friend Tom Sandborn and I were travelling by train from Bucharest to Budapest. In the compartment we were riding in was an elderly Hungarian-speaking woman on her way home to the Romanian border town of Arad. She immediately took us under her wing, pointing out the important passing sights, conducting a conversation that we seemed to understand despite the lack of a mutually intelligible language, and sharing the food she had brought along for the journey. That wonderfully generous woman from Arad seems to me emblematic of the hospitality I've received in the course of researching, writing, and living this book, and it is the virtue I wish to honour here.

In Berlin, Thomas Marquard and Ilonka Opitz provided not only hospitality but intellectual companionship and affection during countless discussions, meals, and walks. I'm deeply grateful to them, as I am to Michael Morris and Vincent Trasov, who introduced me to Berlin and shared their knowledge both of the city and of the visual arts. Others who offered me their friendship and guidance there include

Herman Verpalen, Alexander Götz, Karsten Hintz, Ulf Heinsohn, Arno Schmitt, Sylvie Krankemann, and Mark Johnson.

My debts to Zef Simoni and Pavli Qesku of Tirana, Albania, are evident, I believe, in the story in which they appear, although it is a pleasure to acknowledge them once again. Janos Bak, Vera Szelenyi, and Gaspar Tamas were particularly kind and helpful to me in the course of my visits to Budapest, as were Asta Markeviciute in Vilnius, Olga Titkov in Warsaw, Plamen Gantchev in Sofia, and Slavenka Drakulic in Zagreb. I'm also grateful to the dozens of people who graciously permitted me to subject them to a stranger's questions.

Numerous friends and colleagues helped me to write this book. Alberto Manguel, Brian Fawcett, Thomas Marquard, Scott Watson, Gena Gorrell, and Louise Dennys read the manuscript in its entirety and offered extensive and perceptive comments. Others who were kind enough to read and discuss portions of the manuscript with me include Tom Sandborn, Rolf Maurer, Leo Cooper, Dubravka Ugresic, Myrna Kostash, my longtime colleague Margaret Randall, and members of the Sodomite Invasion writers' group, especially Daniel Collins, Don Larventz, and the late Fred Gilbertson.

As well, I'm grateful for a Maclean-Hunter Arts Journalism Award at the Banff Centre for the Arts (Banff, Canada), and to Alberto Manguel, Barbara Moon, Rosemary Sullivan, Morris Wolfe, Stefan Richter, and Tomas Eloy Martinez, who were, respectively, director, editor, and participants in the Arts Journalism Program. Dan Gawthrop helped me prepare transcriptions of tape recorded interviews. The Toronto *Globe and Mail*, and my editors there—Katherine Ashenburg, Elizabeth Renzetti, and Cheryl Cohen—were sympathetic to, and encouraged my interest in, the subject matter of these stories. The same is true of the administrators, colleagues, and students at Capilano College. I'm grateful to them all for their sustained support.

Versions of portions of this book have appeared in the following publications: Alberto Manguel and Craig Stephenson, *Meanwhile, in Another Part of the Forest* (Toronto: Knopf Canada, 1994), *The Globe and Mail* (Katherine Ashenburg, arts editor), *The Vancouver Sun* (Max Wyman, arts editor), *Vancouver Review* (Bruce Serafin, editor), *Sodomite Invasion Review* (Don Larventz, editor), *Paginas 12* of Buenos Aires (Tomas Eloy Martinez, editor), and Karen Mulhallen, *Voices in Descant* (Toronto: HarperCollins, forthcoming). Last, and most obviously, my thanks to publisher Louise Dennys and her talented colleagues at Knopf Canada.

Of course, none of the aforementioned is to be held accountable for whatever errors and infelicities of expression are to be found in this book; they are wholly the responsibility of the author.

S.P.
Vancouver, B.C.
February 1996